MONASTICISM IN SU

Monasticism in Suffolk

A history of religious
communities in Suffolk from
Anglo-Saxon times
to the present day

Francis Young

Lasse Press

First published 2020
by the Lasse Press
2 St Giles Terrace, Bethel Street, Norwich NR2 1NS, UK
www.lassepress.com
lassepress@gmail.com

ISBN 978-1-9997752-9-2

Typeset in Garamond by
Curran Publishing Services Ltd, Norwich, UK

Manufactured in the UK by Short Run Press, Exeter.

Contents

Maps, illustrations and tables

Maps

Illustrations

Illustrations (continued)

Tables

Abbreviations

Publications and databases

Bede, HE	Bede (trans. L. Sherley-Price), *Ecclesiastical History of the English People*, 4th edn (London: Penguin, 1990)
MIM	'Monks in Motion' project database, community.dur.ac.uk/monksinmotion
ODNB	*Oxford Dictionary of National Biography*, online edition
PSIA(H)	*Proceedings of the Suffolk Institute of Archaeology (and History)*
SRS	Suffolk Records Society
VCH Suffolk	J. C. Cox, 'Ecclesiastical history' in W. Page (ed.), *The Victoria History of the County of Suffolk, Vol. 2* (London: Archibald Constable & Co., 1907), pp. 1–156
WWTN	'Who were the nuns?' project database, wwtn.history.qmul.ac.uk

Religious orders

CJ	Companions of Jesus (Mary Ward Sisters)
CRSS	Sepulchrines (Canonesses Regular of the Holy Sepulchre)
O.Carm.	Carmelite friars and nuns (calced)
OCD	Carmelite nuns (discalced)
O.Cist.	Cistercian monks and nuns
OESA	Augustinian friars
OFM Cap.	Capuchin friars
OFM Conv.	Franciscan friars conventual (Greyfriars)
OIC	Conceptionist nuns
OP	Dominican friars (Blackfriars)
O.Praem.	Premonstratensian canons
OSA	Augustinian canons and canonesses
OSB	Benedictine monks and nuns
OSC	Poor Clare nuns
OSsS	Bridgettine monks and nuns
OSU	Ursuline religious sisters
RA	Assumptionist religious sisters
RJM	Religious of Jesus and Mary
RSM	Sisters of Mercy
SSL	St Louis Sisters

For Joseph

Foreword

Although I have been acquainted with the priory for over 30 years, I took up residence in Clare Priory as the Prior Provincial of the Augustinians in Britain in 2018. Living in the priory, founded in 1248, is a remarkable experience, as every corner of our home is simply bursting with historical facts. When Francis Young asked me to write this foreword in my capacity as prior provincial of the sole medieval religious house in Suffolk still functioning I felt I could not refuse. Dr Young's research on monasticism and religious life in Suffolk has produced a book that will be of great interest to those who wish to grasp an understanding of the complexities and challenges of conventual religious life in this part of East Anglia from the earliest foundations of the seventh century, through the confusion and turmoil of the Reformation, to the revival of religious life in this present time.

The Augustinians (Austin Friars) of Clare Priory became part of that living history and present-day reality when we willingly rose to the challenge and returned to our original priory after an interval of just over 400 years. For those of us who are religious, monks, friars and sisters and indeed everyone who has a keen interest or might like to develop an interest in the contribution of monasticism to the culture, architecture and landscape of Suffolk, Francis Young's book will be invaluable. He writes from a wealth of experience, having already presented detailed research on monastic history, folklore, hagiography and the history of East Anglia. He exhibits in this latest work a painstakingly comprehensive and thoroughly enjoyable account of monasticism in Suffolk, which will benefit all those who wish to understand this remarkable way of life in its past and present forms and its continued contribution to our wider society.

Fr Robert Marsh OSA
Prior Provincial of the Augustinian Friars in England and Scotland
Clare Priory, Suffolk
July 2019

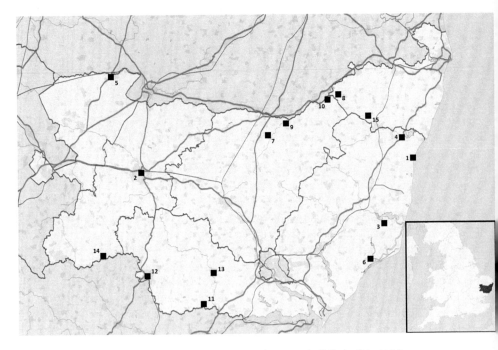

Map 1 Known and probable minster churches in Anglo-Saxon Suffolk, c. 630–1066
Numbered in approximate order of foundation:

1   Dommoc (traditionally identified as Dunwich), c. 630
2   Beodericsworth/Bury St Edmunds, c. 633
3   Icanho/Iken, c. 653
4   Blythburgh, c. 654
5   Brandon (foundation date unknown)
6   Burrow Hill, Butley (foundation date unknown)
7   Eye (foundation date unknown)
8   Elmham, c. 803
9   Hoxne, fl. 942
10 Mendham, fl. 942
11 Stoke-by-Nayland, fl. 946
12 Sudbury, fl. 961
13 Hadleigh, fl. 962
14 Clare, c. 1045
15 Rumburgh, c. 1047

Preface

The year 2020 marks Suffolk's most significant monastic anniversary: the traditional foundation date of the Abbey of Bury St Edmunds by King Cnut. Yet while St Edmunds Abbey was undoubtedly the largest and most historically significant monastery in medieval Suffolk, it was not the only one. Medieval Suffolk was home to over 50 monastic houses of varying size, yet the complete history of monasticism in Suffolk has not been told until now. This book is a history of all Suffolk's monastic communities, from the earliest beginnings of monasticism in the seventh century to the present day. It is the first book to examine the monastic history of any English region over such a broad chronological range; Suffolk, with its especially plentiful supply of monastic houses, makes an excellent case study for trends that were often replicated in other parts of England. Rather than presenting new research on monasticism in Suffolk, the present book offers a narrative synthesis of research on Suffolk's monasteries that has hitherto been inaccessible to most readers.

Ever since I completed my book about St Edmunds Abbey, *The Abbey of Bury St Edmunds: History, Legacy and Discovery* (2016), I have felt that a history of all Suffolk's monastic communities was needed; a great deal of research has taken place since J. C. Cox compiled his account of Suffolk's monastic houses for the *Victoria County History* in 1907. In spite of the apparent timelessness of monastic life, monasticism is not a historically fixed phenomenon and has evolved a great deal over the centuries: from the informal organisation of Anglo-Saxon minster churches to the highly regulated conventual life of the twelfth and thirteenth centuries and the more informal religious life of mixed clerical and lay religious communities today, monasticism has a tendency to mirror the wider world outside the monastery. Monastic communities are a source of endless fascination to the historian not only because they were much preoccupied with producing documentation of their rights and possessions, but also because these institutions developed a communal identity that survived across centuries and which it is difficult to compare with any other kind of organisation. Monastic houses are thus arks of history and memory which, despite their dissolution and the scattering of their records and treasures, continue to fascinate many people.

At the millennium of Suffolk's greatest Benedictine abbey, the aim of this book is to draw attention to the rich monastic heritage of the county as a whole, not only in the Anglo-Saxon and medieval periods but also today. Religious communities continue to exist in Suffolk, and their story is one in which I have played my own small part, having been briefly part of the Community of Reconciliation at Hengrave Hall in 1998–99. The ideal of the monastic life – of prayerful co-existence and communal unity of purpose – is a compelling one, albeit an ideal that is hard to realise (as the evidence of history amply testifies). However, the history of several of Suffolk's monastic houses remains under-researched, with the only literature on them dating from the nineteenth century; I should be delighted if this book stimulates new research and fresh interest in the county's monasteries.

I am very grateful to Fr Robert Marsh, Prior Provincial of the Augustinian Friars in

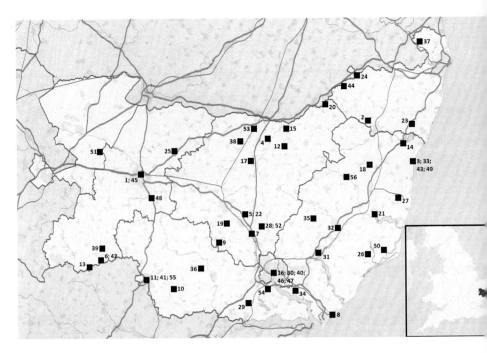

Map 2 Monastic houses in medieval Suffolk (active at any time between 1066 and 1540). Numbered in approximate order of foundation.

England and Scotland at Clare Priory, for writing a foreword to this book. Many people have kindly offered their advice and expertise during the course of the writing of this book, all of whom deserve to be thanked. I am especially grateful to Dr Richard Hoggett for guiding me towards excellent sources on Anglo-Saxon monasticism in East Anglia and the archaeology of monastic sites; to Nicky Moxey for offering her insights on the history and locations of Dodnash Priory; to Dr Harriet Lyon for sharing her PhD thesis on the legacy of the dissolution; and to Dr Laura Wood for advising me on houses of recluses. Dr Simon Johnson likewise provided insights on the post-Reformation Benedictines in Suffolk. I thank Simon Knott for giving permission to reproduce the photograph on the front cover of this book, and I acknowledge the kind permission of the Trustees of the British Museum to reproduce Figure 3, of the Portable Antiquities Scheme to reproduce Figure 6, and of Dr Roberta Anderson and Downside Abbey to reproduce Figure 39. I am very grateful to Dr Margaret Hilditch and Stephen Hilditch for providing numerous photographs of monastic sites. As always, my wife Rachel and daughters Abigail and Talitha have borne patiently with my research and writing, and they have my thanks.

1   St Edmunds Abbey (Bury St Edmunds),
    c. 1020
2   Rumburgh Priory, c. 1047
3   Dunwich Priory, c. 1080
4   Eye Priory, c. 1080
5   Creeting St Olave Priory, c. 1087
6   Clare, Priory of St John the Baptist, 1090
7   Blakenham Priory, 1092
8   Walton Priory (Felixstowe), c. 1105
9   Bricett Priory, c. 1114
10 Edwardstone Priory, c. 1114
11 Sudbury, St Bartholomew's Priory, c. 1115
12 Redlingfield Priory, 1120
13 Stoke Priory, 1124
14 Blythburgh Priory, c. 1130
15 Hoxne Priory, 1130
16 Ipswich, Holy Trinity Priory, c. 1133
17 Wickham Skeith Priory, c. 1135
18 Sibton Abbey, 1150
19 Battisford Preceptory, c. 1154
20 Mendham Priory, c. 1155
21 Snape Priory, 1155
22 Creeting St Mary Priory, c. 1156
23 Wangford Priory, c. 1159
24 Bungay Priory, c. 1160
25 Ixworth Priory, 1170
26 Butley Priory, 1171
27 Leiston Abbey, 1183
28 Coddenham Priory, c. 1184

29 Dodnash Priory (Bentley), c. 1188
30 Ipswich, Priory of St Peter and St Paul,
    c. 1189
31 Woodbridge Priory, c. 1193
32 Campsey Priory, c. 1195
33 Dunwich Preceptory, c. 1199
34 Alnesbourne Priory (Nacton), c. 1200
35 Letheringham Priory, c. 1200
36 Kersey Priory, c. 1213
37 Herringfleet Priory (St Olave's), c. 1216
38 Gislingham Preceptory, c. 1222
39 Chipley Priory (Poslingford), c. 1235
40 Ipswich Greyfriars, c. 1236
41 Sudbury Blackfriars, c. 1248
42 Clare Austin Friars, 1248–9
43 Dunwich Blackfriars, 1256
44 Flixton Priory, 1258
45 Babwell Greyfriars, c. 1263
46 Ipswich Greyfriars, 1263
47 Ipswich Whitefriars, c. 1271
48 Whelnetham Priory, c. 1274
49 Dunwich Greyfriars, c. 1277
50 Orford Austin Friars, 1299
51 Cavenham Preceptory, 13th century
52 Coddenham Preceptory, 13th century
53 Mellis Preceptory, 13th century
54 Wherstead Priory, 13th century
55 Sudbury Preceptory, 13th century
56 Bruisyard Abbey, c. 1364–7

Finally, I am deeply grateful to Susan Curran, my publisher, for supporting this book and several of my other research projects over the last few years. If any errors remain in the text they are mine alone.

Francis Young
Peterborough
August 2019

The publishers thank Chris Carr for his assistance with the preparation of this volume.

Introduction

Suffolk is famous for its churches, the county's landscape defined by their towers and reputedly gaining its epithet 'silly Suffolk' from the piety of those who filled Suffolk with seely (holy) buildings to the glory of God. Yet many visitors to Suffolk may be quite unaware of another religious legacy which once defined the county as much as its proliferation of parish churches. Suffolk was once home to an astonishing number and variety of religious communities, each living together under a common rule of life. Those communities ranged from one of the mightiest abbeys in Europe (at Bury St Edmunds) to modest monastic cells, yet all the men and women who comprised them had in common that they strove (albeit not always successfully) to grow in likeness to Christ through obedience to a monastic rule. This book is the story of how these institutions dominated and informed the religious and secular life of one county, from the earliest experiments in English monasticism to the height of medieval monastic power and the cataclysm that was the dissolution of the monasteries. However, this book also looks beyond the watershed of the dissolution to attempts to re-establish religious life in Suffolk after the Reformation. The great monasteries are long since gone, but religious life quietly continues in Suffolk to this day.

Religious life in England, and in Suffolk, met an ignominious end in the 1530s when monastics were officially written off as worthless, superstitious idlers – a popular stereotype of monks and nuns that endured for many centuries after the Reformation. In earlier histories of monasticism, the development of monasteries was sometimes told as a story of ever-greater material acquisition and enrichment, followed by an inevitable (and perhaps deserved) fall in the form of the dissolution. Yet Suffolk's monasteries were far more than just a mechanism for acquiring and retaining ecclesiastical wealth and patronage; they were living communities of men and women where, at their best, people sought to realise their full spiritual and intellectual potential free from the worries and cares of the secular world.

While parish churches may have been patronised by successive local families and monumentalised their local communities in wood and stone, monasteries were institutions with a continuous corporate identity whose communal memory and written archives often reached into the distant past. Depending on their size and significance, monasteries became repositories of local, national and even European cultural memory. St Botolph, the founder of one of the first monasteries in Suffolk, came to be venerated throughout northern Europe as a great monastic saint, while anyone with a slight knowledge of medieval history and literature will know of Abbot Samson and John Lydgate, both monks of the great Benedictine abbey at Bury St Edmunds. Yet the intellectual ferment of monasteries also produced dangerous and iconoclastic figures such as the Reformation controversialist John Bale, once a Carmelite friar in Ipswich.

The history of monasticism is not the history of a remote, forgotten world of otherworldly prayer and ritual, but rather the history of dedicated communities which played a central role in the transmission of European and global culture. While monasteries were, in theory, retreats from the world, on another level they were remarkable windows on the wider world at a time when most ordinary people led very parochial lives. Even

1

small priories often belonged to vast international monastic networks, linking Suffolk and England with the rest of Europe. While this book does not ignore the material remains of monasteries in Suffolk, it is not primarily an architectural history of these buildings; nor is it, first and foremost, a history of the institutional power and influence wielded by monasteries through their wealth, ownership of land or ecclesiastical patronage. The focus of this book is the monastic communities themselves: how these communities came to be, how they functioned, what they achieved both collectively and as individuals, and how they met their end.

What is monasticism?

The word 'monasticism' usually conjures up images of monks and nuns, but it can also have a much broader meaning. Any community of men or women devoted to communal prayer and spiritual growth guided by a rule of life may be called a monastery, and monks and nuns are just one kind of monastic. In this book, I include within the definition of monasticism any group of religious believers who live and pray communally, following a rule of life of some kind. Technically, the terms 'monk' and 'nun' should be applied only to monastics who have solemnly vowed poverty, chastity, obedience and stability – the latter being a promise to live in the monastery for the rest of their lives. Clearly, there are many other kinds of monastic: canons and canonesses regular, who follow a rule of life but may engage in a greater range of activities than monks and nuns; mendicant friars, who live a communal life but are tied to no single place; and religious sisters, who are often mistakenly called 'nuns' but who make temporary vows and often work outside their community.

Non-monastic religious orders also exist, such as the Jesuits (members of the Society of Jesus), who follow a rule and make vows, but who do not routinely live together in a community and do not practise communal prayer. On the other hand, some religious communities are non-monastic, such as colleges of secular priests and secular cathedral chapters who practise communal prayer but do not observe a rule of life. While the secular colleges, chantries and Jesuit missions of Suffolk are fascinating subjects in their own right, on account of the definition of monasticism adopted here they do not form part of the subject of this book. Also excluded from this study are the so-called 'monastic' hospitals of Bury St Edmunds and Sibton; although these institutions were 'monastic' in the sense that they were under the direct control of their respective abbeys, their personnel were not monks but rather a warden and secular chaplains.[1] Since the hospitals were not religious communities living under vows and a rule of life they do not fall within the scope of this book.

Although it is not necessary for people pursuing the monastic life to be members of a religious order (and, as we shall see, it is problematic to attach such labels to monastics in

---

1	On the monastic hospitals of Bury St Edmunds see J. Rowe 'The medieval hospitals of Bury St. Edmunds', *Medical History* 2:4 (1958), pp. 253–63; C. Harper-Bill, (ed.), *Charters of the Medieval Hospitals of Bury St Edmunds,* SRS 14C (Ipswich: Boydell Press for the Suffolk Records Society, 1994); J. B. Milner, *Six Hospitals and a Chapel: The Story of the Medieval Hospitals of Bury St Edmunds, Suffolk* (Bury St Edmunds: St Nicholas Hospice/Suffolk Institute of Archaeology and History, 2013).

Suffolk before the twelfth century), the religious orders are often considered synonymous with monasticism in discussions of religious life. In theory, and at its most basic level, a religious order includes all those men and women who follow a particular rule of life in their monastic practice. In reality, however, religious orders are more complicated than that, because different groups of monastics may follow the same rule. For example, the Cistercians follow the Rule of St Benedict, but are not usually considered to be Benedictines, while the Rule of St Augustine is followed by a number of different religious orders such as the Augustinian Canons Regular, the Augustinian Friars, the Premonstratensians and the Dominicans. The second component that makes a religious order distinctive, therefore, apart from its adherence to a particular rule, is its mode of organisation.

Until the tenth century in Europe, and the eleventh century in England, every monastery was a law unto itself and independent of other jurisdictions (except perhaps that of the local bishop). While monastic networks existed (such as the numerous early monasteries in Britain founded by Irish missionaries), monasteries were self-governing. However, concern about the potential deterioration of the quality of religious life and a desire to return to ancient observances led some large and successful abbeys to found daughter houses which continued to be governed by the motherhouse. Cluny, the motherhouse of the Cluniacs and Cîteaux, the motherhouse of the Cistercians, are perhaps the most famous examples, but large Augustinian abbeys also did the same thing. In England, most English heads of monastic houses were replaced after the Norman Conquest with Norman appointees, but Norman religious houses also acquired property in England and founded new dependent daughter houses. Traditionally known as 'alien priories' (monasteries governed by a motherhouse in a foreign jurisdiction), these dependent cells would later face significant political problems as a result of England's wars with France.

Medieval monasteries ranged in size from enormous royal abbeys like Bury St Edmunds to tiny monastic cells such as St Bartholomew's Priory in Sudbury. Late medieval St Edmunds Abbey, staffed by around 80 choir monks, along with numerous lay brothers, chaplains and abbey servants, was almost a town in and of itself, while houses like St Bartholomew's sometimes had as few as three members. Dependent cells were sometimes so small that they did not have any distinct corporate existence; rather than having a prior of their own, they were sometimes administered from a larger daughter house of the parent monastery, and were not always the object of specific land grants and other acts of patronage. Instead, in some cases, these dependencies were essentially monastic granges whose purpose was to administer lands held by the motherhouse.[2]

An abbey was any religious house headed by an abbot or abbess, which usually meant that the house was independent of any other religious house (although Cistercian houses, governed by abbots but dependent on Cîteaux, are an exception). Few abbots enjoyed the right to wear a mitre, sit in Parliament and exercise both royal and episcopal authority in their territory like the abbot of St Edmunds. A priory was any monastery headed by a prior or prioress, which could range in size from quite large houses like the Augustinian priory at Butley to small houses like Dodnash Priory. The term 'priory' is not a very illuminating one, however, as some priories were completely independent, electing their own prior or

---

2   T. Pestell, *Landscapes of Monastic Foundation: The Establishment of Religious Houses in East Anglia c. 650–1200* (Woodbridge: Boydell & Brewer, 2004), pp. 173–4.

prioress, while others were dependent priories governed entirely by a motherhouse which appointed the prior or prioress. Although the term 'cell' is usually used to refer to very small dependent priories, all dependent priories were technically cells regardless of their size.

The thirteenth century brought a religious revolution to western Christendom in the form of the mendicant friars, who pioneered a radically new model of monastic life that was outward rather than inward-facing. The mendicants focused not so much on escaping the world through the development of the monastery's spiritual life as on preaching and pastoral ministry to the laity. The two most famous founders of mendicant orders, St Francis of Assisi and St Dominic, were concerned respectively with ministering to the poor and preaching against heresy. The spiritual revolution was accompanied by a financial one; the mendicants would support themselves not from grants of land by wealthy patrons but by begging alms, and they would lead a wandering life, founding friaries and living in community but not committed to remaining in one place. The Franciscans and Dominicans were not the only mendicants, who also included the Carmelite, Augustinian and 'Crutched' friars (the latter so-called because they wore a cross on their habit), among others. There were also mendicant nuns (although, unlike the friars, they remained within their monasteries), such as the Poor Clares (sometimes called Minoresses) founded by St Francis's collaborator St Clare of Assisi.

Because they were committed to gaining the largest possible audience for their preaching, the friars gravitated towards urban areas. In Suffolk, they founded their friaries in towns such as Ipswich, Dunwich, Sudbury and Bury St Edmunds (the latter producing significant tension with the protective Benedictines of St Edmunds Abbey). In popular usage, the different religious orders were often identified simply by what they wore: black monks (Benedictines), white monks (Cistercians), black canons (Augustinian canons), white canons (Premonstratensians), greyfriars (Franciscans), blackfriars (Dominicans) and whitefriars (Carmelites). An exception were the Augustinian friars, usually known as Austin friars rather than named after the colour of their habits.

One final group of religious who differed markedly from the rest but were nevertheless monastics were the members of the military orders, such as the Knights Templar and the Knights Hospitaller of St John of Jerusalem. The military orders were founded during the Crusades and served as a standing army protecting the kingdom of Jerusalem; these knights took vows of poverty, chastity and obedience and followed a monastic rule, living together in community when they were not on campaign.[3] The houses of the military orders, known as preceptories or commanderies, received endowments of land just like other monasteries, and the Knights Templar became renowned for the wealth they accumulated. The Templars were dissolved by the papacy in 1312 and eventually suppressed by the English crown, which seized their assets and transferred most of them to the Knights Hospitaller of St John of Jerusalem, another military order.

---

3   On the monastic life of the military orders see J. W. Brodman, 'Rule and identity: the case of the military orders', *Catholic Historical Review* 88:3 (2001), pp. 383–400.

The monastery

The official purpose of any monastery was to perform the *opus Dei*, the 'work of God', which involved the choral singing of the divine office, the celebration of mass, and prayer for the souls of the founders. In many cases, founders of monasteries were indeed motivated by the prospect of a monastic community praying for their souls until the end of the world; by supporting religious persons, founders were also brought into confraternity with them and therefore gained some of the spiritual benefits of the religious life themselves.[4] Yet monasteries served many other purposes, from the perspectives of both the founders and the religious. For founders, monasteries were a mark of prestige; being a monastic founder marked someone out as a true member of the aristocratic elite. For some religious, gaining office within a monastery (and especially becoming the head of the house) was clearly a path of career advancement, and the enrichment of the house with additional lands and benefices was a path to personal and institutional enrichment. On a less worldly note, other religious found in their monastery a place to pursue learning and devotion; some religious, especially those in monasteries with an attached school, a pilgrimage shrine or attached chapels and parishes found themselves teaching, preaching and engaged in pastoral work. For the friars, teaching and preaching were their *raison d'être*.

The architecture, structure and organisation of monasteries differed slightly depending on their size and affiliation, but not usually in a significant way. Anglo-Saxon monasteries followed no set architectural pattern, but the Norman Conquest introduced the claustral plan. After the Conquest most monasteries followed the classic pattern of a cruciform church with a cloister (square covered walk) usually attached to the south side of the nave, with a dormitory, infirmary, chapter house and other buildings attached to the other three sides of the cloister. The generally predictable ground plan of a monastery aids in the archaeological interpretation of those sites in Suffolk (such as Sibton Abbey) where little of the monastery remains visible above ground.

In addition to this basic plan, most monastic houses also had an outer precinct which delineated the monastery from the surrounding town or countryside. The impressive gateways to these precincts, which contained buildings ancillary to the monastery such as guesthouse, brewhouse and bakehouse, are among the most common survivors of monastic buildings. The monastic precinct was a fluid boundary between sacred and secular where the monastic community interacted with the outside world, and larger monasteries such as Bury St Edmunds were divided into different zones focused on their sacred and secular functions. At Bury, the abbot's palace at the north end of the abbey was the focus of the abbot's temporal power, while farther to the south the abbey church was the centre of worship and pilgrimage.

Some monasteries were so small that the local parish church doubled as the monastic church. In other places, such as Great Bricett, a church built as a monastic church doubled up as a parish church because parishioners claimed the right to use it. Although it remains unclear in many cases why this situation developed, parochial use of monastic churches may have been an ancient customary right going back to an earlier phase of Anglo-Saxon minsters before the delineation of parochial and monastic churches in the later Middle

---

4   Pestell (2004), p. 156.

Ages. Alternatively, parish churches may have ended up as monastic because founders wanted monasteries close to their halls and therefore made use of an existing church.[5] Such arrangements ensured that monastics were frequently bound closely into the lives of local communities. However, monastic and parish use did not necessarily sit together comfortably, and religious generally preferred to have their own independent church. The abbey church of St Edmund was so huge that one of the parish churches, St Denis, was gobbled up inside the abbey church's vast west front and replaced with a new church, St James (later to become St Edmundsbury Cathedral).[6]

The principal source of income for any monastery was its endowment of land and clerical patronage. As a landowner, a monastery would receive rent from its tenants like any secular lord. Ecclesiastical income could take more than one form, however. A monastery might 'impropriate' the endowments of parish churches, meaning that the monastery's head of house became the rector of the parish and was entitled to the 'greater tithes' due to that church. A monastery could either appoint a vicar to serve impropriated parishes, who received the 'lesser tithes' for his upkeep, or appoint chaplains who simply received a stipend from the monastery itself. Monasteries could also acquire the patronage of ecclesiastical livings without impropriating them, meaning the monastery was entitled to 'present' (appoint) the incumbent. In this case, clergy might purchase livings from the monastery, which as patron could also draw on the income of the parish for pensions and portions. Monastic houses followed different policies in this regard: St Edmunds Abbey built up a vast endowment of land, making the abbey the single largest landowner in west Suffolk (by a long way) throughout the Middle Ages, but St Edmunds preferred to exercise patronage over local livings without impropriating them. By contrast, parishes in north-east Suffolk were heavily impropriated as a result of the concentration of smaller monasteries including the priories of Eye, Hoxne, Sibton and Leiston.[7] Although the mendicant orders, by contrast, were not supposed to gain an income from endowments, in practice the friars usually accepted what they were offered.

The most important source of information on medieval monastic finances is the *Taxatio Ecclesiastica* of 1291, a survey of the incomes of all religious houses in England as part of an ecclesiastical tax levied by Pope Nicholas IV in order to support a Crusade.[8] In some cases, the value given in the *Taxatio* is the sole source of information we have on the smaller religious houses, and other information – such as the number of religious supported by the monastery – has to be inferred from the size of the endowment. Founded by charter by wealthy patrons, monasteries performed 'an alternative form of feudal duty', bestowing spiritual benefits on the patrons and their descendants, who retained a 'tenurial bond' with the monastery. While founding a monastery was ostensibly an act of charity, it was also an act of conspicuous consumption that demonstrated a patron's control over the

---

5   Pestell (2004), pp. 200–1.
6   F. Young, *The Abbey of Bury St Edmunds: History, Legacy and Discovery* (Norwich: Lasse Press, 2016a), p. 50.
7   D. Dymond, 'Vicarages and appropriated church livings' in D. Dymond and P. Northeast (eds), *An Historical Atlas of Suffolk* (Ipswich: Suffolk County Council/Suffolk Institute of Archaeology and History, 1988), pp. 56–7.
8   Pestell (2004), p. 167 n.41.

land he or she could afford to grant to a monastic community. Perhaps more importantly still, a monastery provided a permanent reminder of the local significance of the patron family, and a reminder of genealogical continuity if patronage passed by inheritance to a different family.[9]

Pilgrimage was another potential source of monastic income. The shrine of St Edmund was one of the top three relic-shrines visited by foreign visitors to England, along with St Thomas Becket at Canterbury and St Cuthbert at Durham,[10] as well as being a routine site of pilgrimage for English kings. No other Suffolk monastery could boast relics as impressive as the incorrupt body of the martyred St Edmund, and St Edmunds even expropriated the bodies of saints from other Suffolk houses for its relic collection – the abbey claimed to be in possession of the bodies of the martyred Anglo-Saxon kings Sigebert and Anna, as well as the arm of St Botolph, all obtained from Blythburgh.[11] Nevertheless, Blythburgh still possessed the empty tomb of King Anna, which continued to be venerated by pilgrims into the twelfth century.[12] Similarly, from around 1100 Hoxne Priory (a dependent daughter house of Norwich Cathedral Priory) claimed to be built on the original burial site of St Edmund (and even to be the real possessor of the saint's body). Both Hoxne Priory and nearby Newark Chapel, which claimed to be built on the site of the discovery of St Edmund's head, were developed by Norwich into focuses of pilgrimage as part of the cathedral's ongoing feud with St Edmunds Abbey.[13] Suffolk's most important pilgrimage sites besides Bury – the miraculous images of Our Lady of Grace in Ipswich and Our Lady of Woolpit – were not located in monasteries, although St Edmunds controlled the Woolpit shrine.[14]

A final source of income, peculiar to priories of nuns and canonesses, was the payment of dowries. Just as a father was expected to provide a dowry for his daughter in the event of her marriage, so if his daughter entered a monastery he was usually expected to pay the dowry to the house. In addition to being a source of income to religious houses of women, this requirement also ensured that choir nuns (the nuns who sang the office in choir, as opposed to the lay sisters who kept the monastery running) largely remained a socially elite group drawn primarily from the local gentry and sometimes from the higher echelons of the nobility.

Canonical obedience to a religious superior was and is the mainstay of religious life, and even those houses dependent on a motherhouse still had their own superior in the form of a prior or prioress. Canonically speaking, a monastery consisted of two parts: the superior and the convent. The superior was the head of the house, to whom its members owed obedience, while the convent was the collective body of religious apart from the superior. The legal distinction between the superior and the convent mattered because

---

9   Pestell (2004), pp. 156–7.

10   F. Young, *Edmund: In Search of England's Lost King* (London: I. B. Tauris, 2018), p. 94.

11   Young (2016a), p. 32.

12   Wessex Archaeology, *Blythburgh Priory, Blythburgh, Suffolk: Archaeological Evaluation and Assessment of Results*, unpublished report, September 2009, p. iv.

13   M. Carey Evans, 'The contribution of Hoxne to the cult of St Edmund king and martyr in the Middle Ages and later', *PSIAH* 36:3 (1987), pp. 182–95.

14   C. Paine, 'The Chapel of Our Lady at Woolpit', *PSIAH* 38:1 (1996), pp. 8–12.]

the lands of a monastery were sometimes held by the superior alone, sometimes by the superior and convent together, or (much more rarely) by the convent alone. Thus it was the abbot of St Edmunds who received most of the abbey's income from its endowments, and not the monks; in the late eleventh century, when Bury's monks complained that the convent was without possessions, Abbot Baldwin granted the monks two manors and a fishery.[15] However, the fact that most of Bury's possessions belonged to the abbot was a disadvantage, because it meant the king was able to confiscate them during any inter-regnum between abbots.

St Edmunds was so large that, in addition to the abbot, the abbey had a prior, a sub-prior and even a 'third prior' who assisted the sub-prior. The prior led the convent while the abbots of St Edmunds often busied themselves with matters of state. The abbot was supposed to receive the advice of the monks in chapter, and the seals of most monastic houses were the seals of the abbot (or prior) and chapter – implying that abbots were not meant to make decisions in isolation.[16] Nevertheless, many heads of religious houses had

their own personal seals in addition to the common seal of the superior and convent.

While the head of a religious community was in theory elected by the chapter, it was not always this simple, and the wishes of patrons mattered a great deal. Patronage of religious houses was often heredi-tary, with the descendants of the original patron continuing to act as patrons and sometimes making use of the monastic church as a family mausoleum. In the 'sacred economy' of medieval England, a

Figure 1 A modern carving of the common seal of the abbot and convent of Leiston Abbey

---

15   A. Gransden, 'Baldwin, Abbot of Bury St Edmunds, 1065–1097', *Proceedings of the Battle Conference on Anglo-Norman Studies* 4 (1981), pp. 65–76, at p. 69.

16   For an analysis of East Anglian monastic seals see J. L. W. V. Mattich, 'Friars and society in late medieval East Anglia: mendicants and their material culture in Suffolk, Norfolk and Cambridgeshire, c. 1225–1538', PhD thesis, University of Cambridge, 1995, pp. 417–20.

guarantee that monks or nuns were praying for the souls of your ancestors was a significant asset and mark of prestige.

The independence of religious houses from local ecclesiastical jurisdictions varied greatly. The local bishop (who, in Suffolk, was the bishop of Norwich from 1094) generally exercised visitatorial jurisdiction over smaller monasteries, meaning that he had the right to periodically inspect them for the quality of their observance of religious life. Some large monasteries, such as Bury St Edmunds, were exempt from any visitatorial jurisdiction other than that of a papal *legate a latere* (a cleric empowered with full papal authority in a specific locality). The links between dependent priories and their foreign motherhouses often weakened over the course of the Middle Ages, owing to English laws against foreign ecclesiastical jurisdiction and the ability and willingness of the motherhouses to control their dependent priories.

The term 'alien priories', which has often been used to describe cells dependent on motherhouses in a foreign jurisdiction, is of limited usefulness when categorising different kinds of monasteries. In the twelfth century, there was little or no difference between dependency on an abbey in France or Normandy and dependency on distant English monasteries such as Westminster or Rochester. In the later Middle Ages, few houses that had begun life as dependencies of foreign abbeys remained under their jurisdiction, and most became independent houses or dependencies of local English abbeys. The labelling of houses founded by foreign abbeys as 'alien priories' has meant that some historians have been tempted to ignore them and exclude them from study,[17] and the term's origins as a pejorative should make us wary of categorising monasteries in this way. There is no evidence to suggest that these monasteries were any less integrated into local society, landscape and economy than independent houses. Furthermore, since no stable idea of nation states existed in medieval Europe and Norman French was the *lingua franca* of many English monasteries as late as the fourteenth century,[18] even the concept of 'foreignness' is scarcely meaningful in a medieval monastic context.

At the heart of monastic life is the liturgy of the hours, times of prayer punctuating the day when monastics gather in choir to sing or recite the psalms together. Traditionally, there are eight monastic offices: Matins (or Vigils), Lauds, Prime, Terce, Sext, None, Vespers and Compline. However, beyond the unifying liturgy of the hours monastic life differed significantly between religious orders. Some orders, such as the Cluniacs, placed a heavy emphasis on liturgy, so much so that Cluniac monks spent most of their lives in choir. The Cistercian reform, by contrast, attempted to return to an ideal of simplicity and manual labour. The mendicants prioritised preaching, teaching and pastoral work, while Augustinian canons were sometimes involved in parish ministry. The administration of the monastery and its possessions also absorbed a great deal of time, especially in larger monasteries; St Edmunds had at least 20 major officeholders and dozens of

---

17 R. Midmer (ed.), *English Medieval Monasteries 1066–1540* (London: Heinemann, 1979), p. 16; Pestell (2004), pp. 171–5.

18 On the persistence of Norman French in monasteries see C. Canon, 'Monastic productions' in D. Wallace (ed.), *The Cambridge History of Medieval English Literature* (Cambridge: Cambridge University Press, 1999), pp. 316–48, at p. 327.

subordinates,[19] meaning that most, if not all, of the Bury monks were effectively professional administrators.

Copying and illuminating manuscripts were frequent activities for monks and nuns, while female religious sometimes became skilled in embroidering ecclesiastical vestments. Monastic scriptoria did not just copy texts, however, but also produced new literature; chronicles, scriptural commentaries, and treatises on theology, philosophy and every other discipline, poured from medieval monasteries, not to mention poetry and prose literature. In the eleventh century Bury St Edmunds was a renowned centre of medical research.[20] By the late Middle Ages, it was common for novices in religious houses to study at Oxford or Cambridge, while Franciscan and Dominican friars frequently held doctorates in divinity. At the dissolution, the library of St Edmunds was the largest in England after that of the University of Oxford;[21] ironically, it served as a resource for early English Lutherans in the 1520s.[22] While St Edmunds was clearly exceptional, learning was immensely important within monastic communities right up to the dissolution.

Monasticism in Suffolk

Between the Norman Conquest and the final dissolution of the monasteries in 1539–40 Suffolk was home to nearly 60 religious houses, most of them small, of which some have left substantial remains while others have vanished altogether. Most of the religious orders present in medieval England were represented in Suffolk, apart from the Carthusians and a few fairly minor orders such as the Gilbertines, the Friars of the Sack, the Pied Friars and the Bridgettines. Putting an exact number on Suffolk's medieval religious houses is not altogether straightforward, because it is not always clear what counted as a monastic house. The Suffolk landscape is littered with houses called 'priory' or even 'abbey', some of which are on or near the site of a former religious house, but many of which are simply on land once owned by a monastic house. 'Lavenham Priory' is a case in point – a property that was given to Colne Priory but did not, as far as we know, actually house a community of Benedictine monks. Another example is 'The Priory' in Little Waldingfield, identified as a priory by local tradition and boasting a fourteenth-century crypt (which, in reality, is probably part of a medieval chapel).[23] Similarly, religious houses often held the advowson (the right to present the vicar) of numerous parish churches, but this did not make those churches 'monastic', nor were those churches served by monastic clergy. Even when chapels and hospitals were run by monasteries, they were rarely served by monastics. The historical and archaeological remains left behind by some houses are significant; but in a few cases there is uncertainty about the most basic facts, or even whether an alleged religious house really existed. Furthermore, the number of religious houses in Suffolk was constantly changing as new foundations were endowed, existing religious

19 R. Yates, *History and Antiquities of the Abbey of St. Edmund's Bury*, 2nd edn (London: J. B. Nichols & Son, 1843), pp. 18–206.
20 D. Banham, 'Medicine at Bury in the time of Abbot Baldwin' in T. Licence (ed.), *Bury St Edmunds and the Norman Conquest* (Woodbridge: Boydell Press, 2014), pp. 226–46.
21 D. MacCulloch, *Suffolk and the Tudors: Politics and Religion in an English County 1500–1600* (Oxford: Clarendon Press, 1986), p. 136.
22 Young (2016a), p. 120.
23 M. Birch, *Suffolk's Ancient Sites – Historic Places* (Mendlesham: Castell, 2004), p. 253.

houses changed in purpose, and numerous religious houses were suppressed from the early fifteenth century onwards. Although the dissolution of 1536–40 is the best known, the experience of dissolution was hardly unknown to the religious men and women of Suffolk; the difference was the comprehensiveness of the final dissolution.

Although the very idea of religious life was an object of hatred and ridicule for the godly reformers of the sixteenth century, and a major target of anti-Catholic propaganda, historical interest in Suffolk's monasteries nevertheless began at the very moment they were dissolved. While monastic history was, in the eyes of many, distasteful, there was a practical reason for many landowners to take an interest. When the crown sold former monastic lands to the local nobility and gentry, it became incumbent on the new owners to prove that the original monastic owner had a legitimate right and title to the land in the first place. The litigious tendencies of the early modern East Anglian landowning class thus facilitated the preservation of monastic records, as the new owners were keen to own charters and other documents demonstrating a succession of ownership. However, antiquarian interest in the monasteries soon began to expand beyond matters of legal title. Some owners of former monastic property became troubled in conscience by the fact that they were in possession of land that rightly belonged to the church, a concern encouraged by high churchmen such as the Norfolk antiquary Henry Spelman (*c.* 1562–1641), who meticulously recorded the deaths and misfortunes which occurred to the occupiers of monastic land in East Anglia.[24]

The religious polarisation of the English Civil War produced a more sympathetic attitude towards the relics of monasticism on the part of Royalist high churchmen, keen to preserve the medieval past in the face of iconoclastic Puritanism. The Royalist herald and antiquary Sir William Dugdale (1605–86) produced the first complete historical survey of all the English monastic houses, the Latin *Monasticon Anglicanum* (1655–73), a work so thorough that it remains valuable to this day. An English translation of Dugdale's *Monasticon* appeared in 1693.[25] Thomas Tanner (1674–1735), bishop of St Asaph, also made a crucial contribution in his *Notitia Monastica* (1693), where the monastic houses of Suffolk were listed together for the first time (Dugdale had listed monastic houses by religious order rather than by county).[26] Antiquarian studies focusing specifically on Suffolk monasteries remained sparse, however. John Batteley (1646–1708) left a Latin history of St Edmunds Abbey incomplete in the early 1690s, and it remained unpublished until 1745.[27] At a time when the word 'monkish' remained synonymous with ignorance and barbaric superstition, there was little incentive even for antiquaries to devote significant time and attention to monastic history.

While popular travel guides often gave brief notices of monastic remains throughout the eighteenth century, the first book dedicated to the monastic history of East Anglia was Richard Cowling Taylor's *Index Monasticus* (1821).[28] Taylor (1789–1851) was a geological

---

24 Young (2016a), p. 156.
25 W. Dugdale, *Monasticon Anglicanum* (London, 1693), 3 vols.
26 T. Tanner, *Notitia Monastica* (London, 1693), pp. 209–17.
27 F. Young, 'John Batteley's *Antiquitates S. Edmundi Burgi* and its editors', *PSIAH* 41 (2008a), pp. 467–79.
28 R. C. Taylor, *Index Monasticus* (London: Richard and Arthur Taylor, 1821).

surveyor by profession with an interest in antiquarianism. He emigrated to America in 1830, where he worked as a surveyor for various mining companies.[29] Taylor's *Index* was funded by subscribers who were mainly the owners of former monastic lands in Norfolk and Suffolk (the diocese of Norwich). As Taylor made clear in his preface, the book's purpose was not just to complement the earlier work of Dugdale and Tanner, but also 'to trace [the monasteries] to their present possessors', the original and ongoing pragmatic justification for all antiquarian research into monastic history.

In my earlier book *The Abbey of Bury St Edmunds: History, Legacy and Discovery* I chronicled the development of antiquarian, archaeological and historical interest in St Edmunds Abbey, while Richard Hoggett has collected and summarised all archaeological information to date on the abbey precincts in a recent report for the Abbey of St Edmund Heritage Partnership.[30] A vast antiquarian, archaeological and historical literature exists on St Edmunds Abbey which is unparalleled for any other religious house in Suffolk – understandably, given the relative size and importance of St Edmunds compared with other monasteries in the county. However, in the mid-nineteenth century the journals *Proceedings of the Suffolk Institute of Archaeology*, founded in 1848, and *East Anglian Notes and Queries,* founded in 1858, created an opportunity for local antiquaries to contribute shorter papers on smaller religious houses; one of the earliest meetings of the Suffolk Institute of Archaeology, on 14 June 1849, included a visit to Ixworth Priory.[31]

M. R. James focused his attention on St Edmunds Abbey in the late nineteenth and early twentieth centuries, but also included a brief yet useful regional 'Monasticon' in his *Suffolk and Norfolk* (1930).[32] The *Victoria County History of Suffolk* included detailed coverage of the histories of some (though by no means all) of Suffolk's religious houses by J. C. Cox.[33] In the interwar years the archaeologist F. H. Fairweather investigated several of Suffolk's lesser monastic houses. Fairweather excavated Eye Priory and Great Bricett Priory in 1926, followed by Orford in 1933.[34] The dissolution of the monasteries in Suffolk has been treated as some length by scholars including Diarmaid MacCulloch and Gordon Blackwood.[35] It remains the case, however, that many of Suffolk's monastic houses are still in need of a modern scholarly treatment, since little has been written about them since the work of Victorian antiquaries published in the pages of the *Proceedings of the Suffolk Institute of Archaeology and History.*

---

29   G. C. Boase (rev. E. Baigent), 'Taylor, Richard Cowling (1789–1851)', *ODNB*, doi. org/10.1093/ref:odnb/27075, accessed 29 April 2019.

30   Young (2016a), pp. 151–71; R. Hoggett, *The Abbey of St Edmund: Heritage Assessment,* unpublished report, June 2018, pp. 69–256.

31   'Quarterly meetings: Ixworth, 14 June 1849', *PSIA* 7 (1853), pp. 84–8.

32   M. R. James, *Suffolk and Norfolk* (London: J. M. Dent & Sons, 1930), pp. 23–31.

33   *VCH Suffolk*, pp. 1–156.

34   F. H. Fairweather, 'Excavations on the site of the priory church and monastery of St Peter, Eye, Suffolk', *Antiquaries Journal* 7:3 (1927a), pp. 299–312; F. H. Fairweather, 'Excavations on the site of the Augustinian alien priory of Great Bricett, Suffolk', *PSIAH* 19:2 (1927b), pp. 99–109; F. H. Fairweather, 'Excavations in the ruined choir of the Church of St. Bartholomew, Orford, Suffolk', *Antiquaries Journal* 14:2 (1934), pp. 170–6.

35   MacCulloch (1986), pp. 150–4; B. G. Blackwood, *Tudor and Stuart Suffolk* (Lancaster: Carnegie, 2001), pp. 72–89.

Figure 2 A medieval tomb on the site of Ixworth Priory, one of the earliest sites visited by the newly formed Suffolk Institute of Archaeology and History in 1849

In 1934 Claude John Wilson Messent, who is better known for his work on the churches of Norfolk, produced a short illustrated survey of the monasteries of Norfolk and Suffolk.[36] However, it was not until 1940 that David Knowles truly kick-started modern scholarship on medieval English monasticism with *The Monastic Order in England*.[37] Like a latter-day Dugdale, Knowles collaborated with R. Neville Hadcock to produce what is still the definitive reference work on English monasteries, complemented by the slightly later work of Roy Midmer.[38] J. W. Wilton's *Monastic Life in Norfolk and Suffolk* (1980), a short book of only 71 pages, likewise followed the 'Monasticon' model, providing a monastery-by-monastery gazetteer (albeit an incomplete one) of the houses of Norfolk and Suffolk.[39] Frank Meeres's *Not of This World* (2001) is the most recent survey of Norfolk's monasteries.[40] The first book to go beyond this approach was Tim Pestell's *Landscapes of Monastic Foundation* (2004), a study of monasticism in East Anglia between 650 and 1200 (based on an earlier PhD thesis) which sought to set monastic houses within their context in the landscape.[41]

36   C. J. W. Messent, *The Monastic Remains of Norfolk and Suffolk* (Norwich: H. W. Hunt, 1934).

37   D. Knowles, *The Monastic Order in England: A History of its Development from the Times of St Dunstan to the Fourth Lateran Council, 940–1216* (Cambridge: Cambridge University Press, 1940).

38   D. Knowles and R. N. Hadcock (eds), *Medieval Religious Houses: England and Wales,* 2nd edn (London: Longman, 1971); Midmer (1979).

39   J. W. Wilton, *Monastic Life in Norfolk and Suffolk* (Fakenham: Acorn Editions, 1980).

40   F. Meeres, *Not of This World: Norfolk's Monastic Houses* (Norwich: privately published, 2001).

41   T. Pestell, *An Analysis of Monastic Foundation in East Anglia, c. 650–1200*, PhD thesis, University of East Anglia, 1999; Pestell (2004).

In this study, Pestell noted the reluctance of historians to question the self-construction of monastic foundations by the monks themselves. For example, chroniclers' presentation of monasteries as retreats from the world are not always borne out by archaeological evidence which reveals early monasteries as focuses of trade and urban development. Most studies focus narrowly on the monastic buildings and fail to consider the wider context of a monastery's setting: 'monastic studies have tended to remain innately conservative, frequently following a research agenda derived from the earliest, antiquarian, investigation of monasteries'.[42] The fact that we only know of the existence of some monastic houses from archaeology is a salutary reminder that the material remains of monasticism cannot be interpreted solely in the light of the surviving historical sources; both archaeological and historical evidence must be integrated in order to produce a rounded account of monasticism.[43]

Dedicated historical and antiquarian studies of individual monastic houses in Suffolk were confined, for a long time, to the great St Edmunds Abbey. The first modern edition of documents from St Edmunds, by Thomas Arnold, was published in three volumes between 1890 and 1896.[44] It was not until 1951 that the distinguished historian Geoffrey Dickens edited the register of Butley Priory,[45] and it was not until the foundation of the Suffolk Records Society in 1957 that a vehicle existed for the systematic publication of Suffolk's monastic records. In 1960 Anthony Howe Denney edited a selection of estate documents belonging to Sibton Abbey;[46] then, in 1976, R. Allen Brown announced a new Charters Series for the Suffolk Records Society, with the first volume published in 1979. This series has proved an invaluable resource for the study of the county's monastic history, and so far covers ten houses: Leiston Abbey and Butley Priory;[47] Blythburgh Priory;[48] Stoke-by-Clare Priory;[49] Sibton Abbey;[50] Clare Priory;[51] Eye Priory;[52] St Bartholomew's

42 Pestell (2004), p. 1.

43 Pestell (2004), p. 17.

44 T. Arnold (ed.), *Memorials of St Edmund's Abbey* (London: Her Majesty's Stationery Office, 1890–96), 3 vols.

45 A. G. Dickens, *The Register or Chronicle of Butley Priory, Suffolk, 1510–1535* (Winchester: Warren, 1951).

46 A. H. Denney (ed.), *The Sibton Abbey Estates: Select Documents, 1325–1509*, SRS 2 (Ipswich: Suffolk Records Society, 1960).

47 R. Mortimer (ed.), *Leiston Abbey Cartulary and Butley Priory Charters*, SRS 1C (Ipswich: Boydell Press for the Suffolk Records Society, 1979).

48 C. Harper-Bill (ed.), *Blythburgh Priory Cartulary: Part One*, SRS 2C (Ipswich: Boydell Press for the Suffolk Records Society, 1980); C Harper-Bill (ed.), *Blythburgh Priory Cartulary: Part Two*, SRS 3C (Ipswich: Boydell Press for the Suffolk Records Society, 1981).

49 C. Harper-Bill and R. Mortimer (eds), *Stoke by Clare Cartulary, BL Cotton Appx. xxi: Part One*, SRS 4C (Ipswich: Boydell Press for the Suffolk Records Society, 1982); C. Harper-Bill and R. Mortimer (eds), *Stoke by Clare Cartulary, BL Cotton Appx. xxi: Part Two*, SRS 5C (Ipswich: Boydell Press for the Suffolk Records Society, 1983); C. Harper-Bill and R. Mortimer (eds), *Stoke by Clare Cartulary, BL Cotton Appx. xxi: Part Three*, SRS 6C (Ipswich: Boydell Press for Suffolk Records Society, 1984).

50 P. Brown (ed.), *Sibton Abbey Cartularies and Charters: Part One*, SRS 7C (Ipswich: Boydell Press for the Suffolk Records Society, 1985); P. Brown (ed.), *Sibton Abbey Cartularies and Charters:*

Priory, Sudbury;[53] Dodnash Priory;[54] and the Priory of St Peter and St Paul, Ipswich.[55] At the time of writing, further volumes are currently in preparation on Great Bricett Priory and Rumburgh Priory.[56]

Peter Northeast provided a helpful cartographic overview of the medieval monastic houses of Suffolk in the *Historical Atlas of Suffolk* (1988), which remains a good starting point for research.[57] The most in-depth modern history of any individual monastic house in Suffolk is undoubtedly Antonia Gransden's two-volume history of St Edmunds Abbey between 1182 and 1301.[58] No other Suffolk house has so far attracted an extended book-length treatment of this kind, although shorter books exist on St Olave's Priory, Herringfleet, Clare Priory and Butley Priory.[59] One obstacle to a more detailed and systematic study of male religious in Norfolk and Suffolk is the absence of any surviving medieval ordination registers for the diocese of Norwich.[60]

Suffolk monasticism after the Reformation has received little attention from many scholars. Edward Crouzet's book *Slender Thread* (2007) ably chronicles the Benedictine

---

Part Two, SRS 8C (Ipswich: Boydell Press for Suffolk Records Society, 1986); P. Brown (ed.), *Sibton Abbey Cartularies and Charters: Part Three,* SRS 9C (Ipswich: Boydell Press for Suffolk Records Society, 1987); P. Brown (ed.), *Sibton Abbey Cartularies and Charters: Part Four,* SRS 10C (Ipswich: Boydell Press for Suffolk Records Society, 1988).

51   C. Harper-Bill (ed.), *The Cartulary of the Augustinian Friars of Clare,* SRS 11C (Ipswich: Boydell Press for Suffolk Records Society, 1991).

52   V. Brown (ed.), *Eye Priory Cartulary and Charters: Part One,* SRS 12C (Ipswich: Boydell Press for the Suffolk Records Society, 1992); V. Brown (ed.), *Eye Priory Cartulary and Charters: Part Two,* SRS 13C (Ipswich: Boydell Press for Suffolk Records Society, 1994).

53   R. Mortimer (ed.), *Charters of St Bartholomew's Priory, Sudbury,* SRS 15C (Ipswich: Boydell Press for Suffolk Records Society, 1996).

54   C. Harper-Bill (ed.), *Dodnash Priory Charters,* SRS 16C (Ipswich: Boydell Press for Suffolk Records Society, 1998).

55   D. Allen (ed.), *The Cartulary and Charters of the Priory of Saints Peter and Paul, Ipswich: Part I: The Cartulary,* SRS 20C (Woodbridge: Suffolk Records Society, 2018); D. Allen (ed.), *The Cartulary and Charters of the Priory of Saints Peter and Paul, Ipswich: Part II: Charters,* SRS 21C (Woodbridge: Suffolk Records Society, 2019).

56   *The Suffolk Records Society: Celebrating Sixty Years and Sixty Volumes, 1957 to 2017* (Ipswich: Suffolk Records Society, 2017), p. 13.

57   P. Northeast, 'Religious houses' in D. Dymond and P. Northeast (eds), *An Historical Atlas of Suffolk* (Ipswich: Suffolk County Council/Suffolk Institute of Archaeology and History, 1988), pp. 54–5.

58   A. Gransden, *A History of the Abbey of Bury St Edmunds 1182–1256* (Woodbridge: Boydell, 2009); A. Gransden, *A History of the Abbey of Bury St Edmunds 1257–1301* (Woodbridge: Boydell, 2015).

59   W. A. S. Smith, *St Olave's Priory and Bridge, Herringfleet, Suffolk* (Norwich: Goose, 1914); K. W. Barnardiston, *Clare Priory: Seven Centuries of a Suffolk House,* ed. N. Scarfe (Cambridge: Heffer, 1962); S. M. Harrison, *Butley Priory 1171–1538: An East Anglian Monastery* (Woodbridge: B. J. and S. M. Harrison, 2000).

60   A. B. Emden (ed.), *A Survey of Dominicans in England based on the Ordination Lists in Episcopal Registers, 1268–1538* (Rome: S. Sabina, 1967), p. 168.

mission in north-east Suffolk originally established at Flixton by the Tasburgh family,[61] and my book *The Gages of Hengrave and Suffolk Catholicism* (2015) examined in detail the eighteenth-century Benedictine mission at Bury St Edmunds and Hengrave Hall.[62] Two recent prosopographical online database projects, 'Who were the nuns?' and 'Monks in motion', are essential resources for studying individuals from Suffolk who sought to enter the religious life after the Reformation. Roy Tricker has also provided a valuable – and so far unique – survey of Anglican monastic communities in Suffolk in his book *Anglicans on High*.[63]

The majority of books about the history of monasticism have a national scope, or focus on the national or international development of a single religious order. As Pestell has observed, few studies examine monasticism as a regional phenomenon.[64] One early example was Christopher Haigh's 1969 book on the monasteries of Lancashire on the eve of the Pilgrimage of Grace.[65] Another is Janet Burton's *The Monastic Order in Yorkshire* (1999), although its chronological scope is restricted to the years 1069–1215.[66] Both Burton and Cassandra Potts, in a slightly earlier study of monasticism in Normandy,[67] made the argument that monasticism contributed to regional identity. Pestell's study of East Anglian monasteries has already been mentioned. In her unpublished 1995 PhD thesis, Lucy Vinten Mattich also focused specifically on the mendicant friars in late medieval East Anglia. The religious women of the region have received attention in book-length studies by Roberta Gilchrist and Marilyn Oliva,[68] testament to the particular richness of monastic life (and the abundance of evidence for it) in the diocese of Norwich. However, no regional study of monasticism has hitherto taken in the complete chronological range of monasticism in one area.

By focusing on monasticism within a smaller, county-sized region (rather than the much larger area of the medieval diocese of Norwich) it is possible to pay more detailed attention to the full range of monastic houses in the county, including the smaller ones. One intriguing question of English monastic history is how so many of these smaller

---

61   E. Crouzet, *Slender Thread: Origins and History of the Benedictine Mission in Bungay, 1657–2007* (Downside: Downside Abbey Books, 2007).

62   F. Young, *The Gages of Hengrave and Suffolk Catholicism, 1640–1767* (Woodbridge: Boydell & Brewer for Catholic Record Society, 2015).

63   R. Tricker, *Anglicans on High: The Anglo-Catholic Revival in Suffolk and the Surrounding Area* (Snetterton: Fitzwalter Press, 2014), pp. 145–50.

64   Pestell (2004), p. 152.

65   C. Haigh, *The Last Days of the Lancashire Monasteries and the Pilgrimage of Grace* (Manchester: Manchester University Press for Chetham Society, 1969).

66   J. Burton, *The Monastic Order in Yorkshire, 1069–1215* (Cambridge: Cambridge University Press, 1999).

67   C. Potts, *Monastic Revival and Regional Identity in Early Normandy* (Woodbridge: Boydell Press, 1997).

68   R. Gilchrist and M. Oliva, *Religious Women in Medieval East Anglia: History and Archaeology c. 1100–1540* (Norwich: Centre of East Anglian Studies, 1993); M. Oliva, *The Convent and the Community in Late Medieval England: Female Monasteries in the Diocese of Norwich, 1350–1540* (Woodbridge: Boydell Press, 1998).

houses, some of them very tiny indeed, survived right down to the dissolution. By studying monasticism in one county it is possible to examine a 'monastic ecosystem' in which houses competed for resources, yet occupied and survived within specialist niches in the spiritual economy of medieval England. This book is the history of one monastic ecosystem, shedding light on an aspect of Suffolk's past which is often forgotten, frequently invisible, yet shaped the modern county in important ways.

Scope of this book

For the purposes of this book the boundaries of Suffolk are taken to be those of the modern county rather than the slightly larger ancient county of Suffolk. Thus, St Mary's Priory in Thetford and Gorleston Priory, both now in Norfolk but anciently located in Suffolk, are not covered. Between 1094 and 1837 the entirety of Suffolk was located in the diocese of Norwich; the archdeaconry of Sudbury (covering western Suffolk) was then transferred to the diocese of Ely during Queen Victoria's reign, until it was finally reunited with the archdeaconry of Suffolk (covering eastern Suffolk) on the erection of the new diocese of St Edmundsbury and Ipswich in 1914.

The first chapter traces the earliest beginnings of monasticism in the Anglo-Saxon kingdom of East Anglia, whose King Rædwald was one of the first English kings to embrace the Christian faith, at least publicly. Rædwald's Christian successor Sigebert was responsible for inviting St Felix, a missionary from Burgundy, to establish a monastic site and episcopal see at a place called *Dommoc* (traditionally yet contentiously identified as Dunwich). Sigebert founded his own monastery, perhaps at what later became Bury St Edmunds, while the Irish missionary St Fursey founded another monastic site at *Cnoberesburh* (possibly Burgh Castle) and St Botolph established a community at *Icanho* (probably Iken). However, the early monastic landscape of Suffolk was shattered by the Viking invasions of 865–9 which ended with the death of the last East Anglian king, Edmund, and the establishment of a Danish kingdom in the region. A monastic revival from the tenth century onwards led to the foundation of numerous minster churches around the county, only some of which proved successful in the long term.

The second chapter covers a period of rapid and feverish monastic growth and change between the Norman Conquest and the end of the thirteenth century, an era which saw the introduction of dependent cells under Norman patronage, the arrival of reformed orders such as the Cistercians, and the appearance of the mendicant friars in the first half of the thirteenth century. The subject of Chapter 3 is the consolidation of monastic life, power and patronage in the late Middle Ages between 1307 and 1525, a period in which monastic life faced considerable challenges including the Black Death, the Peasants' Revolt, war with France resulting in the dissolution or reassignment of priories dependent on foreign houses, and economic change.

Chapter 4 focuses entirely on the period of the dissolution of the monasteries, which in Suffolk began as early as 1525 as Cardinal Thomas Wolsey sought to dissolve lesser religious houses in the county whose income he sought to appropriate in order to fund his Cardinal's College in Ipswich. Dissolution of the remaining monasteries by royal commissioners followed between 1536 and 1538, leaving only the great St Edmunds Abbey to be dissolved in the final wave of surrenders in 1539. Religious men and women have often been viewed as passive victims of the Dissolution, but members of monastic houses in

Suffolk were also active participants in the Reformation, such as the Bury monk Richard Bayfield and the former prior of the Ipswich Carmelites, John Bale. The dissolution was a complex process, and the chapter seeks to unravel some of its consequences for Suffolk.

The book's fifth chapter goes beyond the dissolution to tell the little-known story of monasticism in Suffolk and Suffolk monastics after the Reformation. Dozens of men and women from Suffolk went abroad to fulfil their monastic vocations in the seventeenth and eighteenth centuries. The chapter examines the missionary activities of Benedictine monks and Franciscan and Dominican friars in post-Reformation Suffolk, who established clandestine chapels in various locations around the county. One clandestine seventeenth-century mission, which evolved into the Roman Catholic parishes of Bungay and Beccles staffed by monks from Downside Abbey, remains to this day. However, it was not until 1794 that a regular monastic community was openly established in Suffolk for the first time since the dissolution, when the Augustinian canonesses of the English Convent, Bruges, settled at Hengrave Hall. The canonesses returned home in 1802 but this brief experiment inaugurated a century of monastic experimentation which saw the establishment of a major abbey of Benedictine nuns at East Bergholt in 1857, while in 1862 the village of Claydon hosted the world's first Anglican Benedictine monastery, founded by pioneer of Anglican monasticism, Joseph Leycester Lyne ('Father Ignatius'). A variety of active orders of women religious, such as the St Louis Sisters and the Religious of the Assumption, were active in education and other fields in nineteenth and twentieth-century Suffolk. The book includes two appendices, the first a complete gazetteer of Suffolk's monastic houses, of all eras, and the second a list of all those Suffolk-born men and women who entered religious life after the Reformation.

Chapter 1

Monasticism in Anglo-Saxon Suffolk, c. 629–1066

The first monks ever to set foot in the land of the South Folk may have been chaplains sent to accompany King Rædwald of the East Angles on his return to his kingdom after baptism by Augustine at Canterbury in around 604.[1] We know that Rædwald maintained a chapel at his royal estate of Rendlesham, albeit next to a shrine to Woden,[2] so he presumably required a priest to say mass. Over the next century, against all odds, the kingdom of the East Angles became a bulwark of Christianity against those Anglo-Saxon kingdoms – particularly Mercia – that clung to their ancestral paganism. Communal religious life, if not monasticism in its later sense, was central to early Anglo-Saxon Christianity. This chapter considers the development of the minster system in Suffolk, examining what can be known about these early communities and their ministry. It then assesses the impact of the Viking invasion on 865–9 on Suffolk's religious houses, arguing that the destruction of minster sites may not have been as total as some have presumed. The chapter then moves on to look at the post-Viking reconstruction of religious life in late Anglo-Saxon Suffolk and the state of monasticism in the county prior to the Norman Conquest.

Anglo-Saxon monasticism in East Anglia can be divided into five phases. The first phase, which we might call the 'missionary station' phase, began in the 630s with the arrival of missionaries such as Felix, Fursey and Botolph. This first phase can be said to end with the nominal conversion of East Anglia to the Christian faith, something that had probably been accomplished by the death of Botolph of Iken in 680. The second phase, between around 680 and the Viking invasion of 865, saw the spread of early minsters across the landscape. The First Viking Age (865–917 in East Anglia) is the third phase, when some monastic communities may have survived in some form, but underwent considerable transformation. The fourth phase is the age of reconstruction, when traditional minsters were revived between 917 and the reign of Cnut. In the fifth and final phase reformed Benedictine monasticism was introduced to Suffolk in the eleventh century.

Minsters

By the 630s East Anglia had a bishop, and along with ecclesiastical organisation came minsters: ecclesiastical settlements led by an abbot, abbess or priest, and united by liturgy and devotions which provided pastoral care to the surrounding community and sometimes acted as the seat of a bishop.[3] Anglo-Saxon minsters should not be confused with the later

---

1   R. Hoggett, *The Archaeology of the East Anglian Conversion* (Woodbridge: Boydell & Brewer, 2010), p. 28.

2   Bede, HE II.15, pp. 132–3.

Figure 3 A plaque, possibly from a Gospel cover, depicting St John the Evangelist, discovered at the minster site at Brandon. Reproduced by kind permission of the Trustees of the British Museum.

meaning of the term, which referred to a cathedral with a priory of monks attached to it (as at Norwich). The minsters housed Suffolk's first religious communities, and it is from them that the evolution of monasticism in the county can be traced. Minsters were not an additional feature of the Christian mission to the East Angles; at a time before parochial structures they were essential. Like the mission stations of seventeenth- and eighteenth-century New Mexico they provided a measure of safety in numbers for the early missionaries, as well as serving as impressive showcases for the Christian faith.[4]

While the missionaries who accompanied Augustine to England in 597 are sometimes described as Benedictine monks, it is problematic to apply the concept of religious orders to monastic communities in the Anglo-Saxon period. Although some communities chose to observe the Rule of St Benedict, they did so out of choice in the context of an eclectic range of monastic practices. The leaders of monastic communities were 'autonomous rulers of households', beholden to no one except the king and (to a greater or lesser extent) the local bishop.[5] Many early minsters were double houses of both men and women, and might be headed either by an abbot or an abbess. No concept of 'monastic orders' or broader institutions beyond the monastery itself existed, and the exact form of life

---

3   J. Blair, *The Church in Anglo-Saxon Society* (Oxford: Oxford University Press, 2005), p. 3.
4   Hoggett (2010), p. 53 abandons the term 'minster' altogether (owing to its later connotations), preferring 'missionary station'.
5   Blair (2005), pp. 80–3.

followed by early monastics at places like St Fursey's monastery of *Icanho* cannot truly be recovered.

Minsters differed from later monasteries by not following a specific or coherent monastic rule and by including laypeople within their organisation. However, they were also quite different from later parish churches and cathedrals. The early minsters were most thickly clustered on England's east coast, reflecting 'the strong orientation of early English monasticism towards north Francia'. Small monastic sites were especially prevalent in East Anglia at an early date, with one possible reason for the spread of Frankish monastic models being the region's wealth, economic sophistication and close links with trading emporia on the other side of the North Sea.[6] While large minsters were often the norm in other areas of England, small minsters proliferated in East Anglia, in a pattern that anticipated the multiplicity of small religious houses founded in the region later in the Middle Ages.[7]

The early minsters followed no specific architectural plan, and resembled secular assemblages of buildings.[8] Island sites were popular for minsters, with three early Suffolk examples (Burrow Hill, Brandon and Blythburgh) originally encircled by water.[9] However, it can be difficult to tell early minster sites apart from secular enclosures.[10] The archaeological identification of minsters depends, to a large extent, not on the excavation of a ground plan but on the discovery of objects associated with 'minster culture'. For example, writing *styli* seem to have been confined to minsters in the pre-Viking period, and at a site near Brandon these have been found along with a key, imported Frankish pottery, and a gold plaque depicting St John the Evangelist as an eagle that may have come from a richly ornamented Gospel cover. Excavations uncovered the remains of the earliest Suffolk church yet discovered, a timber structure of two to three cells with a western narthex; the nave was 6.5 metres wide with a massive timber threshold, and the remains of an altar base were found at the east end. All of this suggests the existence of a minster at Brandon which was abandoned in the mid-ninth century, but there is no textual evidence to confirm the existence of a minster on the site.[11]

Similarly, an eighth-century whalebone *tabella* (a writing tablet originally filled with beeswax) found at Blythburgh has been taken as evidence of teaching and literacy, and therefore monasticism.[12] A further feature of minsters is the appearance of multiple churches on one site; early Anglo-Saxon monasticism did not so much favour a single monumental church (as later popularised by the Normans) as a multiplicity of small, chapel-sized churches, often arranged axially in a line from east to west.[13] In addition to minsters such as Burrow Hill, Brandon and Blythburgh which have been identified

---

6   Blair (2005), pp. 150–1.
7   Blair (2005), p. 318.
8   Blair (2005), pp. 202–3.
9   Pestell (2004), p. 54.
10   Pestell (2004), pp. 62–3.
11   P. M. Warner, *The Origins of Suffolk* (Manchester: Manchester University Press, 1996), pp. 123–6; S. J. Plunkett, *Suffolk in Anglo-Saxon Times* (Stroud: Tempus, 2005), pp. 162–8; Blair (2005), pp. 206–11; Hoggett (2010), pp. 74–7.
12   Pestell (2004), p. 37 n.77.
13   Pestell (2004), pp. 50–2.

solely by archaeology, Peter Warner proposed Thorney near modern Stowmarket (not to be confused with Thorney in Cambridgeshire) as a potential early monastic site on the grounds that it was an ancient royal demesne at the time of the Domesday Survey and the capital vill of Stow Hundred (the name 'Stow' itself having the connotation of 'holy place').[14]

Sigebert: a monk-king and his minsters

Rædwald died in 624 or 625 and was succeeded by his Christian son Eorpwald. However, Eorpwald's murder by Ricberht, a pagan at his court, shortly after his succession meant that, according to Bede, 'for three years the kingdom relapsed into heathendom'.[15] In 1627 Eorpwald's younger brother Sigebert, who 'had once been a gallant and distinguished commander' returned from Francia (where he may have been studying at a monastery) and assumed the kingship.[16] Shortly afterwards a Burgundian bishop,[17] Felix (whom Sigebert may have known in exile), visited Archbishop Honorius of Canterbury and asked to be made bishop of the East Angles. Honorius sent him to establish his see at a place on the East Anglian coast called *Dommoc*.[18]

Dommoc's exact location remains a mystery, although it was certainly in Suffolk since the place later became the see for the South Folk. The traditional site is Dunwich, but early missionaries to England tended to establish their minsters within the walls of Roman Saxon Shore forts, and Bede described *Dommoc* as a *civitas* (a term he used only for sites with Roman associations). Taken together with several medieval sources that identify *Dommoc* as Felixstowe, the most likely site for the see now seems to be the Roman shore fort of Walton Castle, which was lost to the sea in the eighteenth century.[19] For John Blair, Felix's decision to establish the minster of *Dommoc* within existing Roman walls at Walton Castle was an attempt to evoke 'Christian civic topography';[20] the reuse of Roman sites by early missionaries was a conscious effort to associate themselves with *romanitas* ('Roman-ness') at a time when the trappings of empire were much sought after by rulers. It is unlikely that Roman sites would actually have been defensible by the seventh century, so instead the enclosure marked a boundary between the secular and sacred worlds.[21] St Peter's church, founded by St Cedd at Bradwell-on-Sea in Essex, is the only surviving seventh-century building that may give some sense of what Felix's church at *Dommoc* may have been like.

According to Bede, Sigebert founded 'a school for the education of boys in the study of letters' with the assistance of Felix, because 'he wished to copy what he had seen well

14   Warner (1996), p. 121.
15   Bede, HE II.15, p. 133.
16   Bede, HE III.18, pp. 171–2.
17   A later tradition makes Felix bishop of Châlons-sur-Marne (Hoggett (2010), p. 31).
18   Bede, HE II.15, p. 133). For a discussion of the location of Dommoc see Hoggett (2010), pp. 36–40; Pestell (2004), p. 20 n.8.
19   For the case that Walton Castle is *Dommoc* see Hoggett (2010), pp. 36–40.
20   Blair (2005), p. 68.
21   Hoggett (2010), p. 165.]

contrived in Gaul'. Felix obtained teachers for the school from Canterbury.[22] Although Bede does not specify its location, the school was presumably at *Dommoc* in one and the same place where Felix had his see. Fursey, an Irish missionary, founded a second monastery in an old Roman fort called *Cnobheresburh* (usually identified as Burgh Castle, traditionally located in Suffolk but now in Norfolk), given to him by Sigebert, where Fursey led a successful mission staffed by Irish monks.[23] Royal grants of deserted Roman forts to monastic founders were standard practice in Merovingian Francia at this time.[24] According to Bede, in response to a vision,

> Fursey set himself with all speed to build himself a monastery on a site given him by King Sigebert, and to establish a regular observance in it. This monastery was pleasantly situated in some woods close to the sea, within the area of a fortification that the English call Cnobheresburg, meaning Cnobhere's town. Subsequently, Anna, king of the province, and his nobles endowed the house with finer buildings and gifts.[25]

Fursey was famous for his apocalyptic visions of heaven and hell, and although his *Vita* records that he received these visions in Ireland,[26] Bede suggests that Fursey also experienced visions in England. Fursey introduced a strand of ecstatic spirituality to early East Anglian monasticism; according to Bede, a fellow monk of Jarrow had met a man from East Anglia who had heard Fursey tell the story of his visions, presumably at *Cnobheresburh*. This suggests a monastic culture centred around a charismatic visionary who used his spiritual experiences for preaching and teaching. However, Fursey did not remain in charge at *Cnobheresburh* and became a hermit with his brother Ultan in around 639, handing over the running of the monastery to another brother, Foillan, and two priests named Gobban and Dicuil. It may be significant that Fursey entrusted Foillan with both the monastery and 'the cure of souls', a phrase that may suggest *Cnobheresburh* was the centre of a mission stretching into the Waveney Valley. Fursey's prophetic gifts meant that he foresaw Penda's attack on East Anglia and that 'even monasteries would be endangered'. He accordingly set sail for Francia, where he ended his life at Péronne.[27]

In around 633 Sigebert founded a third monastery and entered it himself as a monk; Bede does not name it, but a single late source (the twelfth-century *Liber Eliensis*) calls it *Betrichesworde* (*Beodericsworth*), the town later known as Bury St Edmunds.[28] While Sarah

---

22 Bede, HE III.18, p. 171.

23 On the identification of *Cnobheresburh* as Burgh Castle see Pestell (2004), pp. 56–8; Hoggett (2010), pp. 44–6 is critical of the identification on the grounds that the language Bede uses indicates that *Cnobheresburh* was a non-Roman site, and therefore not Burgh Castle; however, the excavation of a Middle Anglo-Saxon Christian cemetery suggests that Burgh Castle was an important religious site (pp. 56–60).

24 Blair (2005), p. 188.

25 Bede, HE III.19,pp. 172–3.

26 On Fursey's visions see I. Moreira, *Dreams, Visions, and Spiritual Authority in Merovingian Gaul* (Ithaca, N.Y.: Cornell University Press, 2000), pp. 155–8.

27 Bede, HE III.19, pp. 175–6.

28 E. O. Blake (ed.), *Liber Eliensis*, Camden 3rd Series 92 (London: Camden Society, 1962), p. 11.

Figure 4 Burgh Castle, Norfolk (formerly in Suffolk), a possible site of the minster at *Cnobheresburh*. Engraving by T. Higham, 1819.

Foot identifies Sigebert's monastery as Burgh Castle,[29] Antonia Gransden, the leading scholar of the history of St Edmunds Abbey, has defended Bury as the site of Sigebert's monastery. A large wooden church of St Mary already existed at the time the body of St Edmund was brought to Bury, and St Mary remained part of the dedication of the abbey. The cult of the Virgin Mary also continued at Bury as an important part of the devotional life of the monastery. All of this suggests that an earlier stratum of Christian cult pre-dating the arrival of St Edmund may have existed at *Beodericsworth*,[30] but this is by no means universally accepted, and there is as yet no archaeological evidence to establish the existence of a seventh-century church at Bury.[31]

Wherever it was located, Sigebert retreated to his monastery and left the government of the kingdom to a relative named Ecgric. Unfortunately, effective kingship in Anglo-Saxon England required a king to lead his forces in battle, and when the pagan King Penda of Mercia invaded East Anglia in 640, Sigebert's thegns insisted that he appear on the battle-field. As a monk, Sigebert refused to bear arms and carried only a staff into battle; both he and Ecgric were cut down by Penda.[32] However, Penda's incursion did not bring an end to East Anglian Christianity; Felix ruled as bishop for 17 years from his establishment of *Dommoc*, suggesting he died in 647 or 648.

---

29   S. Foot, *Monastic Life in Anglo-Saxon England, c. 600–900* (Cambridge: Cambridge University Press, 2006), p. 149 n.61.

30   See A. Gransden, 'The cult of St Mary at Beodericsworth and then in Bury St Edmunds Abbey to c. 1150', *Journal of Ecclesiastical History* 55 (2004), pp. 627–53.

31   Foot (2006), p. 149 suggests Burgh Castle as the site of Sigebert's monastery.

32   Bede, HE III.18, pp. 171–2.

Monasticism in an age of turmoil

Sigebert was succeeded by his cousin Anna, the son of his uncle Eni (a brother of Rædwald). Bede, as we have seen, records that Anna richly endowed Fursey's minster at *Cnobheres-burh*. However, according to a life of Foillan (Fursey's successor as abbot of *Cnobheresburh*) composed in around 655, the minster was despoiled by Penda at the time of Fursey's death (c. 650) and King Anna was expelled from the kingdom. Anna and his army returned just in time to save Foillan, and the monks, their relics, ornaments and books were evacuated to Francia.[33]

Owing to the still-perilous position of the Christian faith in England in general and East Anglia in particular, Anna sent his daughters Sæthryth (Sethrida) and Æthelburh (Ethelburga) – the former a stepdaughter, the latter probably illegitimate – to the Frankish monastery of Faremoûtier-en-Brie, where the two women became abbess in succession, beginning with Æthelburh.[34] These two women were probably the first East Anglian women to become nuns (and indeed the first English women), but they are largely forgotten today because they died in France, in contrast to Anna's daughters Æthelthryth (Etheldreda) and Seaxburh (Sexburga) who became abbesses of Ely at a later date. However, Æthelburh continues to be venerated in France as St Aubierge.[35]

Anna was killed by Penda, along with his son Hiurmine (or Jurmin) at the Battle of Bulcamp in 654. Bede records only the bare fact of Anna's death at the hands of Penda,[36] but the twelfth-century *Liber Eliensis* elaborated the account and claimed that the bodies of Anna and Jurmin were enshrined at Blythburgh (from where they were later stolen and taken to St Edmunds Abbey).[37] The presence of this shrine strongly implies that there was a minster at Blythburgh, even if no textual source survives that explicitly states this.[38] In 655 Penda was killed at the Battle of the Winwæd, but so was Anna's successor as king of the East Angles, Æthelhere, who had been fighting alongside Penda (perhaps as a puppet king).[39] Yet in spite of this turmoil, the foundation of new minsters and the spread of the Christian faith continued in East Anglia, aided perhaps by the fact that the new king of Mercia, Peada, adopted Christianity.

Beginning with Dorothy Whitelock, some historians have concluded that there were seven major minsters in the kingdom of East Anglia by the middle of the eighth century, on the basis of a letter of King Ælfwald (reigned 742–9) to the missionary St Boniface in which the East Anglian king promised Boniface the prayers of the seven *monasteria* of East Anglia.[40] However, this interpretation may be based on a mistranslation of the original Latin phrase *in septenis monasteriorum nostrorum sinaxis*, which can be translated in two separate ways depending on the reading of the word *sinaxis* (which can mean both

---

33 Hoggett (2010), p. 45.
34 Bede, HE III.8, pp. 155–6.
35 Young (2018), pp. 161–2 n.60.
36 Bede, HE III.18, p. 172.
37 Hoggett (2010), p. 33.
38 Pestell (2004), pp. 91–2.
39 Warner (1996), pp. 113–14.
40 D. Whitelock, 'The pre-Viking age church in East Anglia', *Anglo-Saxon England* 1 (1972), pp. 1–22, at p. 16; Pestell (2004), p. 21.

Figure 5
An
eighteenth-century
statue depicting
St Aubierge
(Æthelburh),
possibly the first
East Anglian
woman to enter the
religious life, near
Faremoûtier-en-
Brie, France

an assembly and a liturgical act). If the phrase is read as 'in the seven-fold assembly of our monasteries', it refers to a collection of seven monasteries; if, however, it is read as 'in the seven-fold liturgy of our monasteries' it merely tells us that the divine office was typically sung seven times a day in early East Anglian minsters.[41] Since the least problematic reading is clearly that which describes seven liturgical offices, Ælfwald's letter is not reliable evidence for the number of East Anglian minsters in the eighth century.

Icanho, like *Dommoc* and *Cnobheresburh*, is another site whose exact location has been disputed in the past, but since the discovery of a ninth-century cross shaft embedded in the base of the tower of St Botolph's church, Iken in 1977 there has been general consensus among scholars that Iken is indeed *Icanho*. The cross shaft's discoverer, Stanley West, iden-

---

41   For the liturgical interpretation, see Foot (2006), p. 197; Hoggett (2010), p. 165; R. Hoggett, 'The mystery of the seven Anglo-Saxon *monasteria*', *Norfolk Archaeology* 46 (2014), pp. 55–60.

tified it as a possible memorial to Botolph (d. 680).[42] Whether this is true or not, an object of this kind is certainly indicative of a major early ecclesiastical site, and the dedication of Iken parish church to St Botolph, combined with place-name evidence, makes for a strong cumulative case that Iken is *Icanho*.[43] A reference to Iken as *Ycanho* in a fourteenth-century charter of Butley Priory seems fairly conclusive.[44]

Perhaps surprisingly, given Bede's coverage of other early East Anglian monastic founders, St Botolph (Botwulf) makes no appearance in the *Ecclesiastical History of the English People*. Instead, he is first mentioned in the *Vita Ceolfridi* ('Life of Ceolfrith'), which mentions Ceolfrith's visit, in around 669, to *Icanho* to see Botolph's monastic practices, from which he 'returned home abundantly instructed'.[45] Bede's omission of Botolph is a salient reminder that his *Ecclesiastical History* is not an entirely reliable source, promoting as it does the interests of the Northumbrian church. For whatever reason, Bede may have been politically motivated to make no mention of Botolph or the network of monasteries (stretching far beyond East Anglia) that Botolph founded; alternatively, as Richard Hoggett has argued, Botolph was simply irrelevant to Bede's narrative.[46] However, the *Anglo-Saxon Chronicle* records that Botolph began building his minster at Iken in the same year Anna was killed in battle, 654. It is even possible that these two events were connected, and that *Icanho* was founded in honour of the fallen Anna.[47]

In a *Vita* of St Botolph written in 1070–1 (but perhaps based on an earlier source), Folcard of Thorney provided a dramatic account of Botolph's arrival at Iken, then an island in the Alde estuary, which the holy man found infested with demons. This part of Folcard's account recalls the hermit St Guthlac's struggles with demons occupying the island of Crowland in Lincolnshire; while Guthlac raises a cross to banish the unwanted occupants, Botolph drives them away just by making the sign of the cross.[48] Folcard's *Vita* portrays Iken as a remote, demon-infested place, and accordingly the foundation of minsters on island sites has traditionally been seen as a mark of the founders' determination to escape from the world and seek out a retreat. Yet the archaeological evidence suggests quite the opposite. Archaeological evidence of coin finds and other materials of trade on or near minster sites suggests that minsters became – or were deliberately located in – places of trade and assembly. It is important to bear in mind that the best way to travel around Anglo-Saxon Suffolk was not overland but along navigable rivers; Iken, in the Alde estuary, was readily accessible, while Brandon (the site of another early minster) was the main crossing point on the Little Ouse.[49]

42 On the Iken cross shaft see R. J. Cramp, 'The Iken cross shaft', *PSIAH* 35:4 (1984), pp. 291–301.
43 Pestell (2004), p. 25; S. Newton, 'The forgotten history of St Botolph (Botwulf)', *PSIAH* 43:4 (2016), pp. 521–50, at pp. 524–7.
44 Hoggett (2010), p. 47.
45 Newton (2016), p. 523.
46 Hoggett (2010), pp. 47–50.
47 Newton (2016), p. 524.
48 Newton (2016), pp. 529–30.
49 Pestell (2004), p. 55.

It should not be surprising that minster sites were a focus of trade and communication, since minsters were nodes in a European monastic network that facilitated the transmission of rites and devotional practices. Felix, Fursey, Foillan and Dicuil were all international figures who travelled extensively. It was also essential to the ministry of the minsters that they should be readily accessible to visitors and visited frequently. At a time before the establishment of a parochial structure, when individual settlements did not have access to a local priest, many people's contact with the church may have been primarily when they visited minster sites for a mixture of sacred and secular purposes. Bede's narrative suggests that minsters such as *Dommoc*, Sigebert's unnamed foundation and *Cnobheresburh* were primarily centres of education and instruction, rather than monastic retreat; why else would Fursey have felt such a desire to relinquish the administrative burden of running *Cnobheresburh* and become a hermit? A further reason for the laity to visit minsters was the presence of their dead in minster cemeteries, which would have been centres of commemoration.[50] Indeed, some minsters became the nuclei of small towns, as is suggested by the Old English suffix -*burh* ('town') which became a synonym for 'minster' in the eighth and ninth centuries.[51]

The growth of trade between eastern England, Francia and the Low Countries from around 680 put the minsters, which were often located in coastal locations or with good riverine access to maritime trade, at the centre of an economic boom. The archaeological evidence, such as the huge number of ostensibly secular items like pins and belt fittings recovered from the minster site at Brandon, suggests that they took advantage of their positions to become trading hubs.[52] Indeed, Brandon has become a key site in the archaeological and historical reinterpretation of minsters as both sacred and secular sites, very different from some later monasteries that sought to focus exclusively on their internal life as religious communities.[53]

The early success of *Icanho* is evidenced by its ability to found a daughter house at Wenlock in Shropshire not long after the death of Botolph in 680. A foundation charter for Wenlock survives, quoted within the text of a *Vita* of Wenlock's founder, St Mildburg. Æthelheah, who identifies himself as Botolph's successor as abbot of *Icheanog* (Iken), grants Mildburg Wenlock and other estates, 'on condition that the aforesaid *locus* [Wenlock] should remain unalterably under the tutelage of the worshipful abbot Botulf'. Other passages in the charter seem to suggest that Botolph had earlier bought Wenlock from Merewalh, king of the Magonsæte of Shropshire (who was Mildburg's father) and installed a Frankish abbess named Liobsynda.[54] This remarkable document shows not only that *Icanho* was a wealthy institution whose influence reached as far as Shropshire, but also that Botolph aspired to be the founder of a monastic network as well as an individual minster. Once again, it is evidence that challenges the common perception of early monastic houses as isolated, modest institutions sequestered from the world.

---

50   Blair (2005), p. 243.
51   Blair (2005), p. 250.
52   Pestell (2004), p. 34.
53   Pestell (2004), p. 64.
54   Foot (2006), p. 277.

East Anglia remained politically unstable throughout the eighth century and into the ninth, as native leaders sought to throw off the dominance of Mercia. However, there are few indications in either the textual or archaeological record that political events had a direct impact on minsters or monastic life. In 803 the Council of *Clofesho* (another place that cannot now be identified) split the East Anglian diocese into two, with a see at *Dommoc* for the South Folk and a see at *Helmham* for the North Folk. The site of *Helmham* has been disputed for well over a century, with the ruined minsters at North Elmham, Norfolk and South Elmham St Cross, Suffolk usually put forward as the main contenders (although the surviving ruins in those places are actually late Anglo-Saxon, or even Norman).[55] For the purposes of this book, the question of whether the Old Minster at South Elmham St Cross was ever a cathedral is of no real significance; what matters is whether it was a minster and when it was founded. While the former seems highly probable, the latter remains very obscure.

The Viking attack

The year 865 was a momentous one for the kingdom of East Anglia, in which a series of events was set in train that would lead to the end of the kingdom and, apparently, the end of the Christian church in Norfolk and Suffolk. Although raids by Scandinavians had been occurring on the eastern coast of England for nearly 60 years, in the autumn of 865 a 'great army' of Vikings arrived in East Anglia, demanding to be provided with winter quarters and expecting the East Anglians to furnish them with horses. Edmund, the East Anglian king, agreed to these demands and the Vikings remained in the kingdom for a whole year, finally riding north into Lindsey and Northumbria in the autumn of 866. There the Vikings successfully took York but were besieged at Nottingham before returning to East Anglia in the autumn of 869.[56]

The basic outline of these events is given in the *Anglo-Saxon Chronicle*, written in Wessex in the 890s; the Vikings entered East Anglia on horseback and took up winter quarters at Thetford. However, a version of the *Chronicle* copied at Peterborough Abbey added a further detail. The Vikings 'did for all the minsters to which they came. At the same time they came to Medehamstede (Peterborough): burned and demolished, killed abbot and monks and all that they found there, brought it about so that what was earlier very rich was as it were nothing.'[57] Although this only refers to the destruction of Peterborough minster, historians have generally assumed that the Vikings destroyed all the minsters in their path, including Ely, Soham, Brandon, Sigebert's putative early foundation at *Beodericsworth* and the coastal minsters at *Dommoc*, *Cnobheresburh* and *Icanho*. I have speculated elsewhere that the destruction of minsters might explain King Edmund's change in behaviour in November 869. Whereas in 865 he had been willing to make a treaty with the Vikings and permit them to overwinter in the kingdom, in 869 he not only broke his treaty but actively attacked the Vikings in their winter quarters at Thetford.[58]

---

55   For a discussion of this debate see Hoggett (2010), pp. 40–4.
56   Young (2018), pp. 43–5.
57   S. Irvine (ed.), *The Anglo-Saxon Chronicle* (Cambridge: D. S. Brewer, 2004), vol. 7, p. 48.
58   Young (2018), p. 48.]

Figure 6 The 'Edmund Jewel', a ninth-century æstel found at Drinkstone in 2014 and perhaps associated with the minster at *Beodericsworth*. Reproduced by kind permission of the Portable Antiquities Scheme.

Either Edmund had become over-confident during the Vikings' absence in Northumbria and Mercia, or they had done something to significantly alter his behaviour towards them; sacrilege is one possibility. Either way, Edmund was unsuccessful. Defeated at the battle of Thetford, he was killed (either in battle or shot with arrows while tied to a tree), and a new phase began in the history of East Anglia. As the *Anglo-Saxon Chronicle* starkly put it, 'the Danish took the victory, and killed the king [Edmund] and conquered all that land'.[59] East Anglia was now under the rule of ostensibly pagan Scandinavians, although numismatic evidence suggests that the Vikings initially appointed Christian puppet kings to rule East Anglia, perhaps relatives of Edmund.[60]

While the idea of victorious pagan Vikings stamping out Christianity in East Anglia has proved seductive to some historians, there is little or no evidence to justify the idea that the Vikings set out to persecute the Christian faith. Abbo of Fleury's famous account of the death of St Edmund, which introduced a set-piece martyrdom in which Edmund is invited by the Viking leaders to deny the Christian faith and rule as an underking, is unreliable, written over a century after the event, and makes little sense. There are no other indications that Viking leaders required Anglo-Saxon underkings to abandon the Christian faith, and the Vikings' insistence on Edmund's apostasy looks suspiciously

59   J. M. Bately (ed.), *The Anglo-Saxon Chronicle* (Cambridge: D. S. Brewer, 1986), vol. 3, pp. 47–8.

60   Young (2018), p. 70.

61   Young (2018), p. 58.

like an excuse for Abbo to present Edmund like a Roman martyr asked to renounce Christ.[61]

There is no reason to reject completely the idea that the Vikings opportunistically raided and destroyed some minsters in 869, although only the destruction of Peterborough is described in one manuscript of the *Anglo-Saxon Chronicle*. However, there is no convincing evidence for the systematic destruction of minsters imagined by some historians. All that can be demonstrated is that monastic life at some sites, such as Brandon and Burrow Hill, was discontinued in the middle of the ninth century – not that these minsters were destroyed.[62] Clearly, this evidence can be interpreted in a number of ways; perhaps the minsters were abandoned because monastic life was no longer considered safe when monastics did not automatically enjoy royal protection, or perhaps the abandonment of the sites had more to do with changing economic circumstances. The communities may have moved to different, more secure sites rather than disbanding completely. Furthermore, since the abandonment cannot be dated precisely, it is even possible that a decline of monasticism was already under way before 869; we simply do not know.

The chief evidence usually adduced for the destruction of the Church during the period of Viking rule in East Anglia is actually the absence of evidence; specifically, the absence of surviving documentary sources from this period, which were typically produced and preserved in monastic contexts. We know of no episcopal oversight of East Anglia between Bishop Hunberht of Elmham in around 845 and the establishment of an episcopal outpost at Hoxne by Bishop Theodred of London in the 940s; a 'bishop of the East Angles' only appears again in 955.[63] However, the lack of documentation for the East Anglian Church is not a problem confined to the pre-Viking and Viking ages; very little textual material survives before the middle of the eleventh century.[64]

While Viking destruction is one possible interpretation for the disappearance of evidence of the East Anglian church, other interpretations are also possible. The disruption of the Viking age may have allowed lay landowners to take control of church lands both during and after the period of Viking rule, or the character of the minsters may simply have changed (the example of *Beodericsworth* is discussed further below). Many accounts of Viking destruction of religious houses do not pre-date the eleventh century, and the myth of Viking destruction became a *topos* (recurring literary theme) in the telling of monastic history. The real picture may have been more complex, and perhaps more embarrassing for later monastic founders: some minsters may have survived the Vikings, but been abandoned for economic reasons; others may have been seized and secularised by local aristocrats; some communities probably continued, but may have adopted forms of life unacceptable to later monastic founders and re-founders. Most monastic chronicles were written or preserved by Benedictines who looked down on the more eclectic monasticism of their forebears.[65] Stories of Viking destruction ought not to be judged for their historical veracity, but rather for their capacity to legitimise reform and re-foundation in the tenth century and later.

---

62   Pestell (2004), p. 73.
63   Pestell (2004), p. 72.
64   Pestell (2004), p. 74.
65   Pestell (2004), pp. 75–6.

Religious life under the Danelaw

Archaeological evidence suggests that, after a brief period of abandonment, the minster at North Elmham, Norfolk was reoccupied as early as 875, and the fact that several late Anglo-Saxon monastic houses held on to pre-Viking endowments suggests that the institutional existence of these houses was not completely disrupted.[66] Similarly, while the minster at Brandon was abandoned in the last quarter of the ninth century, the church seems to have shrunk (losing its chancel) before it fell out of use, showing that there was no abrupt end to the minster. Furthermore, the site of the present-day Brandon parish church is only 200 metres south of the old minster.[67] Rather than destruction or sudden abandonment, the evidence at Brandon points to the contraction of a minster to a more modest chapel, perhaps because a community was replaced by a single priest, or because the chapel simply became the focus of lay Christian devotion in the absence of clergy.

At least one East Anglian *monasterium* was begun (or at least revived) under Danish rule. According to his earliest hagiographer, the cult of the martyred King Edmund began in Danish East Anglia at the time of the king's death, when a small wooden chapel was built over his burial place in *Hægelisdun* wood (another place whose modern-day location is much disputed). Abbo of Fleury records that, at an unspecified date, Edmund's body was moved from its woodland burial site to the town of *Beodericsworth* (later called Bury St Edmunds). Although the traditional date of this translation is 903, I have argued elsewhere that it probably took place earlier, perhaps on 30 March 889. The cult of St Edmund had gained official approval in Danish East Anglia by around 890, when the kingdom began minting more or less crude replicas of Edmund's original coinage from the 860s bearing variants of the legends SANCTE EADMUNDE REX ('O St Edmund the king!').[68]

Whether the translation of St Edmund to Bury occurred in the late ninth or the early tenth century, it happened while East Anglia was still under Danish rule, yet Abbo of Fleury did not hesitate to describe the church to which Edmund was translated as a *monasterium*.[69] The body of St Edmund was cared for by a community of priests who permitted a laywoman, Oswin, intimate access to the saint's shrine in order to cut the hair and nails on Edmund's supposedly incorrupt body. Exactly what *monasterium* meant in the context of Viking East Anglia seems to have been fluid; a *monasterium* was a religious community, but not necessarily under any religious rule, and might include both clerical and lay members (although this seems to have been the case before the Viking invasion too). It is not even certain that the priests who cared for St Edmund's shrine were celibate.[70] Furthermore, Sarah Foot has argued that Bury's aristocratic patrons considered themselves part of

---

66   Blair (2005), pp. 317–18. See also J. Blair, 'Parochial organisation', in M. Lapidge, J. Blair, S. Keynes and D. Scragg (eds), *The Blackwell Encyclopaedia of Anglo-Saxon England* (Oxford: Blackwell, 1999), pp. 356–8.

67   Warner (1996), p. 126.

68   Pestell (2004), pp. 76–7; Young (2018), pp. 75–6.

69   F. Hervey (ed.), *Corolla Sancti Eadmundi: The Garland of Saint Edmund King and Martyr* (London: John Murray, 1907), p. 48.

70   Young (2018), p. 81.

the extended 'household' of St Edmund even though they did not live in the monastery;[71] the Anglo-Danish minster in tenth-century Bury St Edmunds was as much an idea as a physical building.

While writing and book-production were clearly important in pre-Viking minsters, these activities may have declined in the Viking era; the 'Edmund Jewel', a gold æstel (an object strongly associated with monasticism) discovered at Drinkstone in 2014 may be an exception, if it is right to associate it with the early community at *Beodericsworth*.[72] Because the presence of styli, writing tablets and book covers has been taken as diagnostic of monastic life by many archaeologists, the disappearance of such items from the archaeological record has been taken to mark an end to monasticism. Yet more informal models of religious community based on oral learning and popular devotion focused on saintly relics should not be ruled out. There is abundant evidence, from all parts of the world and from multiple eras, that literacy and access to books are not necessary to sustain the Christian faith or, indeed, religious life. The importance of accumulating relics of saints for tenth and eleventh-century religious houses suggests that the Christianity of the East Anglian Danelaw was very much a relic-focused popular religion.[73]

In addition to Bury St Edmunds, another *monasterium* that may have enjoyed continuity in some form under Danish rule was *Icanho*, albeit not in its original location. According to Botolph's hagiographer Folcard of Thorney, the minster at *Icanho* 'was destroyed by the persecutors of the blessed King Edmund', in other words by the Vikings, in 869. At some point between 955 and 975 Bishop Æthelwold of Winchester received permission from King Edgar the Peaceable to restore the minster at Thorney in the Fens, and to collect 'the bodies of the saints, which were lying unvenerated in sites by that time ruined and neglected'. One of these sites was *Icanho*, although the fact that Æthelwold managed to identify Botolph's tomb suggests that it had not been completely destroyed. As Pestell notes, 'It seems implausible that translations' such as the removal of Botolph from Iken, and Anna and Jurmin from Blythburgh, 'were from churches abandoned after their destruction by Vikings'.[74] Continuity of cult speaks strongly in favour of continuity of community, in one form or another.

Botolph's body was translated to an enclosed hillfort-like structure at Grundisburgh where the church of St Botolph now stands. However, it is possible that Folcard was mistaken about the date at which this translation of Botolph's relics occurred, and it may have happened under the Danelaw in the late ninth century.[75] The fortified nature of the site at Grundisburgh certainly suggests that whoever moved St Botolph's body was looking for a secure location. There is no evidence that a monastic community of any kind was established at Grundisburgh to look after the shrine, but Grundisburgh, like *Beodricsworth*, may have fitted into a new pattern of popular Christian devotion focused on the bodies of saints. By the late tenth century there is evidence that people believed

---

71 S. Foot, 'Households of St Edmund', *Studies in Church History* 50 (2014), pp. 47–58.
72 Young (2018), pp. 65–6.
73 Pestell (2004), p. 89.
74 Pestell (2004), p. 93.
75 Newton (2016), pp. 535–6.

saints' cults had continued throughout the Viking period, 'albeit in unworthy settings'.[76]

Several historians have adopted an adversarial view of the relationship between Danes and Angles in Danish East Anglia that is simply unsupported by any evidence. Some have even gone so far as to argue that the St Edmund memorial coinage, which must have been authorised by the Danish kings of East Anglia, somehow expressed resistance to the Danes. Similarly, the early development of the cult of St Edmund has routinely been interpreted as 'a spiritual focus for opposition and resistance to the Viking elite within East Anglia'.[77] Yet when the East Anglian cult of St Edmund is placed in the context of Edmund's wider cult, it is clear that Edmund quickly came to be considered a Scandinavian saint.[78] The cult of St Edmund was as much a Danish as an English phenomenon, and the minting of the memorial coinage clearly shows that the 'Danish elite' adopted St Edmund as their own at an early period. This is scarcely surprising, given the tendency of colonial elites to assume the cultural identity of the peoples over whom they rule; it is no coincidence that the first Danish king of East Anglia, Guthrum, assumed the English name of Æthelstan.

While the evidence suggests that the Viking rulers of East Anglia adopted the Christian faith within a short while, there was nevertheless a period when church lands passed into pagan hands.[79] There is no evidence that this resulted in persecution of the Church and deliberate destruction of minsters, but it meant that the aristocratic patronage that sustained minsters like Brandon as communal endeavours was gone. This on its own may have been sufficient to bring down institutions integrated into a complex web of religious, social and economic obligations. Even when Viking landowners became Christian (nominally or otherwise), they had little incentive to return land to the church, and since the newly Christian Danes lacked a tradition of monastic foundation, they did not think to express their faith in this way (with the possible exception of Guthrum's putative foundation at Hadleigh). By the last decade of the ninth century Danish East Anglia was undoubtedly a Christian kingdom, and was in the process of developing its own distinctive Christian traditions; the indications are, however, that those traditions did not include monasticism in the form it existed in the pre-Viking kingdom.

Monastic revival in the tenth and eleventh centuries

The Viking kingdom of East Anglia came to an end in 917 when an unnamed Danish king of East Anglia was defeated by the forces of Edward the Elder of Wessex at Tempsford, Bedfordshire.[80] East Anglia was incorporated into what would soon become the kingdom of England, but the state of the church in the region, and monasticism in particular,

---

76   Blair (2005), p. 319.
77   Pestell (2004), p. 77.
78   On the Scandinavian cult of St Edmund see A. Finlay, 'Chronology, genealogy and conversion: the afterlife of St Edmund in the North' in A. Bale (ed.), *St Edmund, King and Martyr: Changing Images of a Medieval Saint* (York: York Medieval Press, 2009), pp. 45–62; E. A. Rowe, *Vikings in the West: The Legend of Ragnarr Loðbrók and his Sons* (Vienna: Faessbender Verlag, 2012).
79   Blair (2005), p. 317.
80   Young (2018), p. 74.

remains very obscure. Hoggett has argued that Theodred, who became bishop of London in around 926, may have established his additional episcopal see at Hoxne not long after this.[81] When Bishop Herbert de Losinga re-founded a chapel at Hoxne in 1100 it was already in ruins, suggesting a very early foundation, and Bishop Theodred's will refers to a community of priests at a minster dedicated to St Æthelberht, king and martyr. Hoxne minster still existed in the 1030s, when Bishop Ælfric of Elmham made bequests to 'the priests at Hoxne'.[82]

However, in spite of the re-foundation of Elmham and the apparent establishment of an episcopal minster at Hoxne, the major Christian centre of the region in the tenth century was undoubtedly *Beodricsworth*. The monastery housing the shrine of St Edmund may or may not have been endowed with the territory around Bury St Edmunds called the *banleuca* in 945, depending on whether an alleged charter of King Edmund I is judged to be genuine.[83] Even if the text of the charter of Edmund I is fabricated, of course, it is possible that the fabrication was itself based on existing oral or textual traditions of a royal benefaction at around this time. We know with certainty of other, smaller benefactions from the local aristocracy at the time.[84] Another minster active by the time Bishop Theodred made his will in the period 942–51 was located at Mendham, although no archaeological remains of the Anglo-Saxon minster at Mendham have yet come to light.[85]

One minster that may have survived the Viking period and into the post-Viking era could have been at Hadleigh, judging from the will of Æthelflæd of Damerham (dating from 962–91), which makes bequests to a community at Hadleigh.[86] It is unlikely that the fact the *Annals of St Neots* identify Hadleigh as the burial place of Guthrum is a co-incidence. There was certainly a minster at Hadleigh by the eleventh century,[87] and given his self-conscious adoption of Christianity, it is possible that Guthrum had himself buried in a church that he himself had founded, or which predated the Viking invasion.

The wills of Æthelflæd and her father Ælfgar refer to a minster at Stoke-by-Nayland, 'the holy foundation at Stoke where my ancestors lie buried' – a phrase that suggests the minster had existed for some time.[88] In her will, Æthelflæd asked for royal protection for the minster at Stoke-by-Nayland, and Cyril Hart and Anthony Syme suggested that Æthelflæd and Ælfgar may have intended Stoke-by-Nayland to be staffed by monks from Bury St Edmunds, which they thought might have been taken over as a 'satellite' of

81 Hoggett (2010), p. 42.
82 Carey Evans (1987), p. 183.
83 On the charter of 945 see A. Gransden, 'The legends and traditions concerning the origins of the Abbey of St Edmund', *English Historical Review* 100 (1985), pp. 1–24, at p. 12; C. Hart and A. Syme, 'The earliest Suffolk charter', *PSIAH* 36 (1987), pp. 165–81; Pestell (2004), p. 79; Foot (2014), pp. 47–8.
84 Hart and Syme (1987), p. 169.
85 E. Martin, J., Plouviez and H. Feldman (eds), 'Archaeology in Suffolk 1984', *PSIAH* 36:1 (1985), pp. 43–57, at p. 47.
86 Knowles and Hadcock (1971), p. 474.
87 Pestell (2004), p. 89.
88 Knowles and Hadcock (1971), p. 483; Blair (2005), p. 318.

the Benedictine abbey at Ramsey by the late tenth century.[89] This speculation, however, is unproven and runs contrary to the traditional chronology of the introduction of the Benedictine rule at Bury in the 1020s or 1030s.

Extensive land grants to churches have been used in an effort to identify potential minsters, since such grants may have been intended to support a community. For example the church of St Gregory in Sudbury received bequests of land in the wills of Æthelric in 961–5 and Ælfflæd in 1000–02, suggesting that it was more than just a parish church.[90] Warner has suggested that St Peter's church, Ipswich (which held six carucates of glebe land in 1086) may have been a minster, and even the church of St Mary at Stoke, south of the River Orwell.[91] The term 'minsterlands' refers to the proto-parochial territories that may have been served by minsters in the tenth century, and perhaps earlier. Whether or not it was ever a cathedral, the Old Minster at Elmham St Cross seems to have served as an ecclesiastical centre for a minsterland that included the Elmhams, Flixton and Homersfield. Just to the south-east, the tenth-century minster at Mendham may have served a minsterland of Mendham, Metfield and Withersdale, while Bungay has been suggested as a possible centre for a minsterland including Bungay, Mettingham and the Ilketshalls.[92] Although there is neither textual nor archaeological evidence for an Anglo-Saxon minster at Bungay, the facts that Bungay was the centre of a soke (an ancient unit of local government larger than a hundred and smaller than a county) and that St Mary's church was shared between parishioners and a later priory suggests lingering rights and privileges associated with an earlier minster site.

Warner suggested that several of the monasteries 'founded' in the post-Conquest centuries were actually revivals of earlier minsters, regularising 'a pre-existing pattern of minster churches and their dependent churches'. Double dedications are sometimes an indication that a later foundation was overlaid upon an old one, as is the survival of the right of local people to worship in the nave of a monastic church. For example, based on the fact that the churches of Reydon and Southwold were once chapels dependent on Wangford, the Cluniac Wangford Priory founded in around 1159 may have been a refoundation of an earlier minster, and Leiston's periodic claims to soke-rights are similarly suggestive.[93]

While it seems reasonable to assume that minsters were distributed at fairly regular intervals through the pre-Conquest Suffolk landscape, in the absence of textual or archaeological evidence any identifications of minster sites must be highly speculative, and there is a potential danger of 'seeing minsters everywhere' if the meagre evidence is over-interpreted. On the other hand, we cannot assume that Anglo-Saxon monastic foundations were sparser than later Norman ones, since early monastic sites left little evidence behind in terms of readily identifiable monastic buildings.[94] Most (if not all) East Anglian

---

89   Hart and Syme (1987), p. 165.
90   Knowles and Hadcock (1971), p. 483.
91   Warner (1996), p. 123.
92   Warner (1996), pp. 132–3.
93   Warner (1996), pp. 133–6.
94   Pestell (2004), p. 2.

minsters before the eleventh century were built out of wood, meaning that they have left little archaeological trace behind.

The Benedictine reform

One of the evidential problems associated with studying early East Anglian monasticism is that all the sources we have come from later Benedictine monasteries.[95] As we have seen, the early minsters did not follow a specific rule of life and their character was eclectic, leading later antiquaries to describe them (rather anachronistically) as colleges of secular priests. Some of these communities may have followed (to a greater or lesser extent) the Rule of St Benedict, but the systematic imposition of the Benedictine rule is primarily associated with the construction of an English kingdom, and the reconstruction of the English church, in the reign of Edgar the Peaceable (reigned 959–75). The monastic reform movement was led by three bishops: Dunstan, abbot of Glastonbury and then archbishop of Canterbury, 959–88; Oswald of Worcester, archbishop of York, 972–92; and Æthelwold, bishop of Winchester, 963–84. The new monastic order was not only a way of imposing greater uniformity of life, but also a means of strengthening royal authority as great royal monasteries wielding secular as well as spiritual power replaced local thegnly foundations.[96]

The tenth-century monastic reform brought not only the Benedictine rule but also, for the first time, distinctive cowled habits which clearly marked out monks as different from the laity and secular clergy. Monks and nuns were separated into different houses, and strict observance of the Benedictine rule meant that, at least in theory, monks held no personal property; they certainly did not hold their own ecclesiastical endowments. Furthermore, the new monasteries followed liturgical calendars that situated them clearly within a spiritual tradition and adopted distinctive forms of script for the copying of manuscripts.[97]

The monastic reform in East Anglia began in the great Fenland monasteries in the late tenth century. It was not until the reign of Cnut that, according to tradition, the monastery at Bury St Edmunds was regularised. There is no reliable evidence for the traditional date of 1020 for the establishment of Benedictine monasticism at Bury; all we know for certain is that there was a Benedictine abbey by 1032 when the rotunda church containing the shrine of St Edmund was consecrated. According to an account from the thirteenth century, Bury was founded by monks from Ely and St Bene't's, Holme, but historians have also suggested the possibility that Bury might have been regularised by Ramsey at an even earlier date, given that the earliest hagiography of St Edmund (Abbo of Fleury's *Passio Sancti Eadmundi*) was written at Ramsey. The idea that an entirely new community was founded at Bury made up of monks from other monasteries sounds suspiciously like Benedictine propaganda, and it is more likely that some or all of the priests at Bury adopted the Benedictine rule. Indeed, we know that at least one of the original priests, the sacrist Æthelwine who briefly took the body of St Edmund to London in 1010–13, was later a Benedictine monk.

---

95 Pestell (2004), p. 99.
96 Pestell (2004), pp. 102–3.
97 Pestell (2004), p. 106.

Ultimately, the origins of Benedictinism at St Edmunds Abbey remain a mystery,[98] but the possibility should not be ruled out that St Edmunds simply 'founded itself' when, in response to a prevailing fashion, the clerics there decided to become Benedictines. However, the late date at which Bury adopted the Benedictine rule in comparison with the Fenland religious houses may be an indication that Benedictine monasticism was politically unacceptable in East Anglia for a long time, perhaps because it was associated with the ambitions of the House of Wessex.[99]

After Bury, the second Benedictine monastery to be founded in Suffolk in the eleventh century was Rumburgh Priory, which was established before 1064 by Bishop Æthelmær of Elmham as a dependent cell of St Bene't's, Holme. There was a cult of St Michael at St Bene't's Abbey, and St Felix was of course the first bishop of the East Angles, so Pestell theorises that the double dedication of Rumburgh to St Michael and St Felix reflected the double patronage of the abbot of St Bene't's and the bishop. Although priors of Rumburgh were appointed by the abbots of St Bene't's, they were presented to the bishop, perhaps because of its foundation by a bishop and perhaps because of its proximity to the bishop's lands at South Elmham.[100] The first prior of Rumburgh was named Blakere, and there were twelve monks at the time of the Domesday Survey, when Rumburgh was listed as Wissett.[101]

Another Suffolk monastery founded shortly before the Norman Conquest, albeit at an unknown date, was the Priory of St John the Baptist in Clare. According to Domesday Book, Ælfric Wihtgarsson founded a community at the church of St John the Baptist under a priest named Leodmær, endowing the community with the manor of Clare (which was worth £40 in 1066). Clare was to be dependent on Bury St Edmunds, under the care of Abbot Leofstan, and the manor of Clare was never to be alienated from the church.[102] Pestell has suggested that Clare's location, on the border of Suffolk and Essex, allowed the community to act as 'a boundary marker of Bury's spiritual authority';[103] at this time Bury was also the guardian of a small community at Dickleburgh in Norfolk.[104] What is uncertain about the community at Clare is whether it followed the Benedictine reform; the principal clue that it may have been a Benedictine priory is Ælfric's stipulation that the endowments could not be alienated – a requirement for Benedictine houses, since the community as a whole was supported by the house's income. If it was ever imposed, the monastic rule does not seem to have endured at Clare, and by the late eleventh century the priory of St John the Baptist was effectively a college of priests, who did not live in community but among the people of the town.[105]

At the time of the Norman Conquest, Bury St Edmunds, Rumburgh and Clare were the only regularised Benedictine monasteries that we know existed in Suffolk. Alongside these reformed communities, it is possible that some minsters of the traditional form, revived in the ninth century, also survived, although clear evidence for them is lacking. However, with St Bene't's foundation of Rumburgh and Bury's foundation of Clare a pattern of large abbeys with dependent houses was beginning to emerge, albeit in embryonic form. The

---

98   For full discussions see Gransden (1985), pp. 1–24; Pestell (2004), pp. 108–19; Young (2016a), pp. 27–9.
99   Pestell (2004), pp. 149–50.
100 Pestell (2004), pp. 125–6.
101 *VCH Suffolk*, p. 77.

Figure 7 Rumburgh Priory

foundations of Bury's later dominance and exercise of secular as well as spiritual authority had already been sown before the Conquest. St Edmunds Abbey came into possession of the eight-and-a-half hundreds of west Suffolk in 1043, and the abbey began minting coinage at around the same time, while its last pre-Conquest abbot, Baldwin, was a key figure at the royal court of Edward the Confessor.[106] Furthermore, although small by later standards, Bury had a stone church that was a major focus of pilgrimage.[107] However, there was 'little drive towards the creation of further monasteries' in eleventh-century East Anglia, where aristocratic patronage was focused primarily on founding churches.[108] All of that was about to change.

---

102 Blair (2005), pp. 358–9.
103 Pestell (2004), pp. 126–7.
104 Blair (2005), p. 360.
105 Blair (2005), p. 363.

Chapter 2

Monasticism in high medieval Suffolk, 1066–1307

In the years after the Norman Conquest, the number of religious communities in Suffolk exploded, transforming the county's physical and religious landscape. The foundation of monastic houses became a conventional expression of piety by aristocratic founders, to a far greater extent than it had ever been in the Anglo-Saxon period. This era also saw the regularisation of previously irregular communities (often as canons under the Augustinian rule) and the introduction of new forms of monasticism, from the Cluniacs and Cistercians in the twelfth century to the mendicants in the thirteenth. By the death of Edward I in 1307, the Suffolk landscape was littered with monastic houses both great and small, in both rural and urban locations. At least 53 houses were founded in the county between 1066 and 1307, making it one of the most plentifully supplied with monasteries in all of England. Indeed, by 1215 10 per cent of all religious houses in England were located in the diocese of Norwich.[1]

In Suffolk, the majority of monasteries were concentrated in the east of the county, in the Sandlings towards the North Sea coast, with a cluster of houses in the Waveney Valley.[2] In some cases, the sites selected for post-Conquest foundations may have been determined by the existence of former (or even still functioning) minsters and communities of priests. In other cases new foundations were established next to the castles and halls of the founder's family.[3] While the foundation of monasteries by aristocratic patrons might seem a tranquil and well-ordered expression of piety, East Anglia periodically experienced ferment and unrest in the two centuries following the Norman Conquest. The Revolt of the Earls in 1075, the Anarchy (civil war between Stephen and Matilda) between 1135 and 1153, and the Revolt of 1173–4 all imperilled the church and its possessions. In 1173 the Abbot of St Edmunds was even forced to defend his monastery in battle when he sent his knights to Fornham St Genevieve carrying the banner of St Edmund, in order to defeat an army of Flemish mercenaries led by the earl of Leicester and intent on sacking Bury.[4]

From the church's perspective, the Papal Interdict of 1208–13 (brought about by King John's intransigence) may have been an even more serious challenge than war and disorder, since it prevented anyone receiving the sacraments; religious who died during this period were not even entitled to a Christian burial. King John's renunciation of Magna Carta produced further chaos in 1215, culminating in the Dauphin Louis' invasion of East Anglia at the end of 1216. Conflict erupted again in the Second Barons' War of 1264–7. Although not all of these wars resulted in fighting in Suffolk, landowners were forced to

---

1   Pestell (2004), p. 155.
2   Pestell (2004), p. 163.
3   Pestell (2004), pp. 216–17.
4   Young (2016a), pp. 60–1.

Figure 8 Clare Castle , where an Anglo-Saxon religious community was relocated within the walls of the castle after the Norman Conquest. Engraving by T. Higham, 1819.

take sides, which sometimes resulted in the destabilisation of local government and the breakdown of law and order.

While the church was theoretically supposed to be immune during secular conflicts, the fates of monastic foundations were intimately tied to those of their patrons, and monastic history cannot be separated from the wider history of medieval England. The preferences of founders and patrons for specific religious orders sometimes also had a political dimension. The Cistercians and Premonstratensians, for example, embodied an ascetic ideal that was sometimes in stark contrast to the worldliness of the older and more established monasteries. Similarly, the appearance of the mendicant orders in England in the thirteenth century allowed people to patronise religious orders with a reforming agenda. Whereas the Benedictines sometimes appeared aloof, power-hungry and inappropriately wealthy, the friars' willingness to promote the interests of the laity made them attractive both to a rising gentry and mercantile class and to ordinary people seeking a church that tended to their pastoral needs.

Post-Conquest monastic foundations in Suffolk

In Suffolk, the social and political changes wrought by the Norman Conquest were less marked than in other English counties, largely because land ownership and ecclesiastical patronage in the western half of the county (the Liberty of St Edmund) were dominated by St Edmunds Abbey. The privileged position of Abbot Baldwin, a French monk of St Denis appointed by Edward the Confessor who became William I's personal physician, ensured that the disruption to St Edmunds and its landholdings was minimal. The challenge to St Edmunds came not from the crown but from the Norman bishops of Elmham, Herfast and Herbert de Losinga, who attempted unsuccessfully to move their see to Bury St Edmunds.[5] St Edmunds Abbey at the time of the Norman Conquest was the subject of a dedicated conference in 2012, whose proceedings were later published as the volume *Bury St Edmunds and the Norman Conquest* (2014).[6]

St Edmunds Abbey stands apart from any other Suffolk monastery on account of its exceptional size, wealth and ability to wield both spiritual and temporal power. Although St Edmunds was not the sole abbey in the county (a distinction it shared with Sibton and Leiston), the abbot of St Edmunds was the only monastic head of house in Suffolk with the right to sit in the House of Lords, and the only abbot to enjoy complete exemption from the jurisdiction of the bishops of Norwich. St Edmunds minted its own coinage and raised its own knights, while the abbot exercised full royal authority within the immediate vicinity of Bury St Edmunds, and the abbey routinely hosted royal visitors, and even Parliament. However, although the other monasteries of Suffolk were minnows when compared with St Edmunds, this did not mean they did not enjoy considerable local influence. The twelfth century was Suffolk's golden age of monastic foundation, when many people wanted to associate themselves with monasticism (often thought to be the surest way to heaven) by founding or patronising religious houses. Many patrons and benefactors were admitted to the confraternity of the monastery, a significant spiritual benefit.

The relative absence of post-Conquest monastic foundations in the western half of Suffolk compared with the eastern half of the county must surely be attributed to the enormous influence and prestige of St Edmunds. Although there were western foundations, such as Ixworth and Chipley, they were few. Pestell has suggested that St Edmunds' dominance of landholdings in the area meant that there was insufficient land available for donors to endow a monastic foundation with an estate large enough to support it. Furthermore, donors in the area gravitated towards Bury rather than considering founding other houses in its orbit.[7] From the abbacy of Baldwin (1065–97) onwards, Bury also established a policy against the foundation of daughter houses.[8]

In spite of Bury's dominance, in the post-Conquest period there were more foundations of Augustinian canons than of any other order, closely followed by foundations of Benedictine monks (although if the pre-Conquest foundations of Bury St Edmunds and Rumburgh are taken into account, Benedictine houses slightly outnumbered Augustinian houses in total). Between them, Norfolk, Suffolk and Essex were home to one-third of all the Augustinian houses in England.[9] By the end of the thirteenth century Suffolk

5   On Bury St Edmunds and the Norman Conquest see Gransden (1981), pp. 65–76; D. Bates, 'The Abbey and the Norman Conquest: an unusual case?' in T. Licence (ed.), *Bury St Edmunds and the Norman Conquest* (Woodbridge: Boydell Press, 2014), pp. 5–21; Young (2016a), pp. 35–42.

6   Licence (2014).

7   Pestell (2004), pp. 169–70.

8   M. Heale, *Dependent Priories of Medieval English Monasteries* (Woodbridge: Boydell & Brewer, 2004a), p. 61.

9   Allen (2018), p. 12.

Table 1 Monasteries founded in Suffolk 1066–1307 (by religious order)

Order	Monasteries	Total
Augustinian canons	Alnesbourn; Blythburgh; Butley; Chipley; Coddenham; Dodnash; Great Bricett; Herringfleet; Ipswich Holy Trinity; Ipswich St Peter and St Paul; Ixworth; Kersey; Letheringham; Woodbridge; possible house at Wherstead	14 (15?)
Benedictine monks	Clare; Creeting St Mary; Creeting St Olave; Dunwich; Edwardstone; Eye; Great Blakenham; Hoxne; Snape; Stoke-by-Clare; Sudbury; Walton; Wickham Skeith	13
Knights Hospitaller	Battisford; Coddenham; Dunwich; Gislingham; Mellis; possible house at Sudbury	5 (6?)
Knights Templar	Cavenham; Dunwich; Gislingham; Mellis	4
Dominican friars	Dunwich; Ipswich; Sudbury	3
Franciscan friars	Bury St Edmunds (Babwell); Dunwich; Ipswich	3
Augustinian canonesses	Campsey; Flixton	2
Augustinian friars	Clare; Orford	2
Benedictine nuns	Bungay; Redlingfield	2
Cluniac monks	Mendham; Wangford	2
Carmelite friars	Ipswich	1
Cistercian monks	Sibton	1
Crutched friars	Whelnetham	1
Premonstratensian canons	Leiston	1

was also home to four houses of religious women (later joined by Bruisyard Abbey in the fourteenth century) and ten houses of friars. Although not all Suffolk houses were valued for their annual income in the 1291 *Taxatio ecclesiastica*, the *Taxatio* reveals that the gap between the wealthiest and poorest monasteries was huge: after Bury, Stoke-by-Clare Priory was the wealthiest, valued at £300, while Hoxne Priory was the poorest, with an income of only 14 shillings. Unsurprisingly, it was generally dependent cells like Hoxne that had the fewest endowments.

It is difficult to establish the extent to which Anglo-Saxon monastic communities other than St Edmunds survived the Conquest. A number of later monasteries were founded on or close to Anglo-Saxon sites, but this may have been because these were sites of reputed sanctity rather than because older communities still lingered in these places. The only other certain survivor was Rumburgh, which seems to have kept its lands intact by surrendering to the Normans. However, the fact that its founder, Bishop Æthelmær, was the brother of Archbishop Stigand of Canterbury may have contributed to the seizure of Rumburgh by Alan, earl of Brittany, when Stigand was deposed in 1070.[11]

---

11   L. B. Cane, 'Rumburgh Priory Church', *PSIAH* 22:2 (1935), pp. 155–69, at pp. 155–6.

Table 2 Monasteries founded in Suffolk 1066–1307 (by foundation date)*

	Monastery	Founded	Order	Value in 1291	Dependency
1	Eye*	before 1087	OSB	–	Bernay
2	Dunwich*	before 1087	OSB	–	Eye
3	Creeting St Olave	before 1087	OSB	£18	Grestein
4	Clare*	1090	OSB	–	Bec
5	Great Blakenham	c. 1092	OSB	£13	Bec
6	Walton*	c. 1105	OSB	£6	Rochester
7	Great Bricett	1114–19	OSA	£21	Saint-Léonard de Noblat
8	Edwardstone	c. 1114	OSB	–	Abingdon
9	Sudbury (St Bartholomew's)*	c. 1115	OSB	–	Westminster
10	Redlingfield	1120	OSB	–	
11	Stoke-by-Clare	1124	OSB	£300	Bec
12	Hoxne*	1130	OSB	14s	Norwich
13	Blythburgh*	c. 1130	OSA	£59	St Osyth's
14	Ipswich Holy Trinity	before 1133	OSA	£135	
15	Wickham Skeith	c. 1135	OSB	–	Colchester
16	Sibton	1150	O.Cist.	£154	Warden
17	Battisford	c. 1154	Kts Hospitaller	–	
18	Mendham*	before 1155	Cluniac	£11	Castle Acre
19	Snape	1155	OSB	–	Colchester
20	Creeting St Mary	before 1156	OSB	£12	Bernay
21	Wangford	before 1159	Cluniac	–	Thetford
22	Ixworth	1170	OSA	£82	
23	Butley*	1171	OSA	£195	
24	Bungay*	1183	OSB	–	
25	Leiston	1183	O.Praem.	£130	
26	Coddenham	before 1184	OSA	–	Royston
27	Dodnash	c. 1188	OSA	–	
28	Ipswich St Peter and St Paul*	before 1189	OSA	£82	
29	Woodbridge	c. 1193	OSA	£23	
30	Campsey	1195	OSA	£107	
31	Dunwich Preceptory	before 1199	Kts Hospitaller	–	
32	Letheringham	before 1200	OSA	£12	Ipswich St Peter and St Paul
33	Alnesbourn	1200	OSA	£71	
34	Kersey	c. 1213	OSA	£33	
35	Herringfleet	c. 1216	OSA	£27	

	Monastery	Founded	Order	Value in 1291	Dependency
36	Gislingham	before 1222	Kts Hospitaller	–	
37	Chipley	before 1235	OSA	£5	
38	Ipswich Greyfriars	before 1236	OFM Conv.	–	
39	Sudbury Blackfriars	before 1248	OP	–	
40	Clare Austin Friars	1248	OESA	–	
41	Dunwich Blackfriars	before 1256	OP	–	
42	Flixton	1258	OSA	£44	
43	Babwell Greyfriars	1263	OFM Conv.	–	
44	Ipswich Blackfriars	1263	OP	–	
45	Ipswich Whitefriars	before 1271	O.Carm.	–	
46	Whelnetham	c. 1274	Crutched		
47	Dunwich Greyfriars	before 1277	OFM Conv.	–	
48	Orford Austin Friars	1299	OESA	–	

**Houses for which no foundation date is known are excluded from this list. Houses marked * are those that might have been located on or close to an Anglo-Saxon monastic site.

The Benedictine monks

The first six foundations made in Suffolk after the Norman Conquest were, unsurprisingly, Benedictine houses. However, in a completely new development, they were also dependent cells of larger monasteries both in England and overseas. Indeed, after 1135 (when Rumburgh became a dependent house of St Mary's, York) Bury St Edmunds was the sole independent Benedictine house in medieval Suffolk. In the eleventh century, mother houses tended not to exercise extensive oversight of their dependent cells in the manner of the later Cluniac and Cistercian reforms. Among the earliest dependent cells was Eye Priory, founded by the lord of the Honour of Eye, Robert Malet, towards the reign of William I.[12] Eye's dependency on the Norman Bernay Abbey was even proclaimed by the priory's imitation of Bernay's groundplan, revealed by excavations in 1926.[13] Clive Paine and Edward Martin argued that Eye Priory replaced an earlier minster on the site of St Peter and St Paul's church, later moving farther east in the period 1100–5.[14]

The discovery of the seal of Bishop Æthelwold of *Dommoc* near Eye in 1822 strengthens

---

12   On the foundation of Eye Priory see Brown (1994), pp. 12–15.
13   Fairweather (1927a), pp. 299–312. On Eye's relationship with Bernay see Brown (1994), pp. 15–18.
14   C. Paine and E. Martin, 'Excursions 2012', *PSIAH* 43:1 (2013), pp. 127–63, at p. 127.

the case for its having been an important ecclesiastical centre in the Anglo-Saxon period,[15] while Eye's early connection with Dunwich is also suggestive. Eye Priory was endowed with all the churches of Dunwich, as well as any future churches that might be erected in the town,[16] and established a lucrative cell at Dunwich. The cell at Dunwich evidently claimed some connection with St Felix's *Dommoc*, spurious or otherwise; at the dissolution a book called the 'Red Book of Eye', supposed to have been the Gospel book of Felix himself, which came to Eye when Dunwich Priory was abandoned owing to coastal erosion, was listed among Eye's possessions and valued at 20 pence.[17]

Like Eye Priory, which was adjacent to Robert Malet's newly built castle,[18] the Priory of St John the Baptist at Clare was located within the walls of Clare Castle. However, whereas Eye's continuity with the Anglo-Saxon past remains uncertain, Clare was certainly a re-foundation of a pre-existing Anglo-Saxon religious community. Clare was the richest religious house in Suffolk at the time of the Domesday Survey, surpassing even Bury St Edmunds with its endowment of 3,000 acres. Gilbert of Tonbridge, son of Richard de Clare, converted the Anglo-Saxon minster (based on individual prebends for priests) into a cell of the great Norman abbey of Bec-Hellouin in 1090, and the community remained within Clare Castle until its relocation to Stoke-by-Clare in 1124,[19] 'probably because proximity to a military household was not conducive to undisturbed religious observance'.[20] The monks may have also needed more space, and the De Clares the opportunity to build a large and impressive church. Clare was not the only cell of Bec established in Suffolk at this time; Great Blakenham, founded in around 1092, was also a dependency.[21]

The Priory of St John the Baptist at Clare, and its successor at Stoke-by-Clare, were essentially the 'honorial monastery' of the Honour of Clare, and the vast extent of their endowments may be partly explained by the fact that tenants of the De Clares who gave land to the priory were exempted from all or part of the military service they owed their feudal lord.[22] The De Clares routinely defended the integrity of the priory's endowment in the honour court,[23] and the priory was a very direct expression of the family's temporal power.

Another house founded by a Norman patron within the curtilage of a castle was Walton Priory at Felixstowe, established by Roger Bigod or his son Hugh at some point between 1087 and 1100 as a dependency of Rochester Cathedral Priory. The priory's original location was within the walls of the Roman fort at Walton (since lost to the

---

15   Young (2018), p. 30.

16   *VCH Suffolk*, p. 72.

17   *VCH Suffolk*, p. 75.

18   Pestell (2004), pp. 199–200.

19   Harper-Bill and Mortimer (1984), pp. 2–3. On these foundations see also J. C. Ward, 'Fashions in monastic endowment: the foundations of the Clare family, 1066–1314', *Journal of Ecclesiastical History* 32:4 (1981), pp. 427–51.

20   Harper-Bill and Mortimer (1984), p. 2.

21   Knowles and Hadcock (1971), p. 88.

22   J. C. Ward, 'The place of the honour in twelfth-century society: the Honour of Clare 1066–1217', *PSIAH* 35:3 (1983), pp. 191–202, at p. 194.

23   Ward (1983), pp. 195–6.

Figure 9 Stoke-by-Clare Priory. Engraving by T. Higham, 1819.

sea), which may have been the original site of Felix's minster of *Dommoc* in the seventh century. However, the destruction of the castle after the Bigods rebelled against Henry II in 1174 forced the community to relocate,[24] although some place the relocation as late as the beginning of the fourteenth century.[25] The second location, around 200 metres north of St Mary's parish church (which doubled up as a conventual church for the monks), was excavated by Stanley West in 1971 and described by Richard Gilyard-Beer and Katharine Davison.[26] In 1998 a series of drawings of the ruins of Walton Priory made in the 1620s surfaced, which have greatly enhanced our knowledge of the material fabric of the monastery.[27]

While Eye, Clare and Walton seem to have been founded in order to gain social prestige, and even as an arm of a local lord's temporal authority, St Bartholomew's Priory in Sudbury was established for more personal reasons. It was founded by the moneyer Wulfric before 1116 as a dependent cell of Westminster Abbey, an unusual choice which may have been related to Wulfric's familiarity with that abbey, or which may simply have reflected Wulfric's desire to be professed as a monk. Although the cell's landholdings always remained

---

24   Pestell (2004), pp. 178–9.

25   J. Fairclough and S. J. Plunkett, 'Drawings of Walton Castle and other monuments in Walton and Felixstowe', *PSIAH* 39:4 (2000), pp. 415–59, at p. 425.

26   S. E. West, 'The excavation of Walton Priory', *PSIAH* 33:2 (1974), pp. 131–8; R. Gilyard-Beer, 'The buildings of Walton Priory', *PSIAH* 33:2 (1974), pp. 138–41; K. Davison, 'History of Walton Priory', *PSIAH* 33:2 (1974), pp. 141–9.

27   Fairclough and Plunkett (2000), pp. 415–59.

Figure 10
Hoxne Abbey House,
on the site of Hoxne
Priory

insignificant,[28] there was a spate of grants in the thirteenth century which, unusually for a small cell, survive in the archives of the motherhouse, Westminster Abbey.[29]

A dependent priory of a monastery closer to home was the Priory of St Edmund, King and Martyr at Hoxne, which was controlled by Norwich Cathedral Priory. Of all the Benedictine houses in Suffolk, Hoxne Priory occupied a unique position as an example of 'episcopal imperialism' which was designed to give the bishop of Norwich an important foothold in Suffolk,[30] a county otherwise at risk of being dominated by St Edmunds Abbey. It is possible that when Bishop Herbert de Losinga gave St Ethelbert's church at Hoxne to Norwich Cathedral Priory in 1100–01 there was still a surviving community of priests there from the earlier Anglo-Saxon minster, but a priory was not formally founded at Hoxne until 1130.[31] The first definite reference to monks living at Hoxne dates from 1205.[32] It is possible that the foundation represented the Benedictine regularisation of a vestigial minster at Hoxne as much as the establishment of an entirely new monastery.[33] On the other hand, the priory was located some distance from St Ethelbert's church in the later Middle Ages, which suggests that the two were distinct institutions.

Although Hoxne had been an episcopal seat of the bishops of Elmham (later Norwich) since at least the tenth century, it was in around 1100 that partisans of the bishop in his long-running feud with St Edmunds Abbey noticed a superficial similarity between the name Hoxne and the name of the unknown place where St Edmund was martyred in

---

28   Pestell (2004), pp. 181–2.
29   C. G. Grimwood and S. A. Kay, *History of Sudbury, Suffolk* (Sudbury: privately published, 1952), pp. 36–7; Mortimer (1996), pp. 1–3.
30   Pestell (2004), p. 185.
31   S. E. West, 'A new site for the martyrdom of St Edmund?', *PSIAH* 35:3 (1983), pp. 223–5, at p. 223 suggested the foundation of a priory at Hoxne came even later, in around 1226.
32   On the foundation of Hoxne Priory see Carey Evans (1987), pp. 185–6.
33   Pestell (2004), p. 189.

869, *Hægelisdun*.[34] If Hoxne was *Hægelisdun* then it was a place of pilgrimage in direct competition with Bury St Edmunds. Hoxne was unusual in this respect among the smaller monasteries of Suffolk, which did not generally attempt to compete with major pilgrimage sites or derive much of their income from pilgrims. In addition to fees from fairs and some manors, Hoxne derived a significant proportion of its income from pilgrims, and over time the cult of St Edmund expanded from a chapel that was supposedly on the site of Edmund's original burial to a second chapel that marked the place where the saint's head was discovered.[35]

Some post-Conquest Benedictine foundations were more successful than others. Edwardstone Priory, founded in around 1114 by Hubert de Monchesney as a cell of Abingdon Abbey, removed to Earls Colne, Essex in 1160.[36] While Edwardstone was not a complete failure, Wickham Skeith Priory was eventually wrapped up entirely by its mother house, St John's Abbey in Colchester. Like Wulfric the Moneyer at St Bartholomew's, Sudbury, the founder of Wickham Skeith, Robert de Sakeville, became a monk of his own foundation. However, after Robert's son Jordan gave the monastery to St John's Abbey, within a few years (perhaps in around 1164) the abbey made the decision to recall the four monks to Colchester, with the proviso that Jordan and his heirs would be entitled to become monks at Colchester if they ever wished to do so.[37]

While Wickham Market was a failure, another Suffolk cell of St John's Abbey, Snape Priory (founded in 1155 by William Martel and his wife Albreda), proved a modest success.[38] On the whole, even the smallest houses managed to survive, although the extent to which a meaningful religious life continued at these tiny houses remains doubtful. One Suffolk village, Creeting St Mary, even had two small priories, both of them cells of different French abbeys: St Olave's, a daughter house of Grestein Abbey, and St Mary's, a cell of Bernay Abbey.[39]

The Augustinian canons

Canons regular are priests who live in community under religious vows. Unlike monks, who may be professed brothers or priests, canons regular are priests; and unlike monks they do not take a vow of stability to a particular monastery. While the primary focus of medieval monks was on the performance of the *opus Dei* in choir, the ministry of the canons regular might be more active and outward-looking towards the wider community. The Augustinian canons regular represented 'a synergy of traditional and new monasticism'.[40] The regularisation of existing communities of priests left behind from the era of Anglo-Saxon minsters as communities of canons regular presented fewer challenges than

---

34 Gransden (1981), p. 70.
35 Carey Evans (1987), pp. 185–90.
36 On Edwardstone see 'Edwardstone: its church and priory', *PSIAH* 15:2 (1914), pp. 87–99.
37 C. Harper-Bill, 'Church and society in twelfth-century Suffolk', *PSIAH* 35:3 (1983), pp. 203–12, at p. 205.
38 *VCH Suffolk*, p. 79.
39 Knowles and Hadcock (1971), p. 87.
40 T. Colk, 'Twelfth-century East Anglian canons: a monastic life' in C. Harper-Bill (ed.), *Medieval East Anglia* (Woodbridge: Boydell & Brewer, 2005), pp. 209–24, at p. 223.

converting these houses into Benedictine monasteries. For example, it was consistent with Augustinian practice for monastic churches to continue as parish churches if necessary, while canons regular might also engage in parish ministry and generally required a smaller endowment than Benedictine monasteries. The flexibility and vagueness of the Augustinian rule compared with the Benedictine may have been attractive to founders and patrons,[41] although it is important not to fall into the trap of thinking the Augustinian canons were less strict religious than monks.[42]

Canons regular began to adopt the Rule of St Augustine in the pontificate of Urban II (1088–99) and it soon became the universal rule of life for canons under vows (as opposed to the secular canons who staffed cathedral and collegiate churches).[43] A first wave of English houses of Augustinian canons regular in the period 1100–35 were foundations in urban areas, often taking over existing parish churches as conventual churches; one Benedictine of the era mocked the canons regular for 'claiming to live the apostolic life in petty parish churches'.[44] The earliest Augustinian foundation in Ipswich, the Priory of the Holy Trinity, was part of this first wave since it was probably founded before 1133. However, Ipswich was unusual in then acquiring a second priory of the same order, the Priory of St Peter and St Paul. Although St Peter and St Paul was not founded until 1188, the priory may have been a regularisation of an Anglo-Saxon minster of St Peter at Bramford, which stood at the heart of the old Anglo-Saxon riverside emporium of *Gipeswic*.[45] However, David Allen has disputed the idea that Holy Trinity was founded or regularised first, arguing for the priority of St Peter's.[46] The Ipswich priories enjoyed equal status, a situation apparently achieved by an agreement to divide the patronage of Ipswich's churches and church lands between them.[47]

Jennie Colk has questioned the extent to which twelfth-century Augustinian canons in East Anglia were actively engaged in pastoral ministry, noting that many houses were so small that they would not have been able to function if canons had spent very much time in pastoral ministry. Instead, the evidence suggests that canons regular rarely directly served the churches in their care, but rather appointed vicars.[48] Instead, the canons became increasingly contemplative and focussed on spiritual life over time.[49]

Whatever their order of foundation, neither of the Ipswich priories was the oldest Augustinian house in Suffolk, an honour that goes to Bricett Priory, founded by Ralph FitzBrien and his wife Emma in the period 1114–19.[50] The fact that Ralph required the

---

41   On the origins of the Augustinian canons regular in Britain see J. Burton and K. Stöber, 'Introduction' in J. Burton and K. Stöber (eds), *The Regular Canons in the Medieval British Isles* (Turnhout: Brepols, 2011), pp. 1–18.

42   Colk (2005), p. 224.

43   Allen (2018), p. 1.

44   Harper-Bill (1980), p. 2.

45   Pestell (2004), pp. 193–4; Allen (2018), p. 2.

46   Allen (2018), pp. 3–6.

47   J. Fairclough, 'The Bounds of Stoke and the hamlets of Ipswich', *PSIAH* 40:3 (2003), pp. 262–77, at p. 272.

48   Colk (2005), p. 213.

49   Colk (2005), p. 214.

50   On excavations of the site of Bricett Priory see Fairweather (1927b), pp. 99–109; E. Owles and N. Smedley, 'Archaeology in Suffolk, 1962', *PSIAH* 29:2 (1963), pp. 166–74, at p. 167.

canons of Bricett to serve as his chaplains when he was in Suffolk suggests that the versatility of canons regular appealed to this patron.[51] An almost unique set of evidence for the foundation of Bricett Priory is a collection of 164 identical copies of a schedule of spiritual benefits promised to donors to the new foundation, now in the library of King's College, Cambridge. Donors were promised remission of 380 days of canonical penance (an indulgence) as well as confraternity with the monks of the cathedral priory of Canterbury (Christchurch). This latter privilege was granted by Archbishop Thomas Becket, showing that the foundation of Bricett had support at the highest levels of the English church.[52] The chance survival of these documents demonstrates that Bricett, and very likely other smaller monasteries, was not a monumental endowment by an individual donor or family but, to a large extent, a 'crowdfunded' enterprise (to use a twenty-first century expression) backed by influential religious figures.

Bricett Priory was also, or soon became, a dependent cell of the French abbey of Saint-Léonard de Noblat. Bricett was the only Augustinian house in Suffolk dependent on a foreign house, but not the only dependent Augustinian priory. Blythburgh Priory, founded in around 1130, was dependent on St Osyth's Priory in Essex, while Coddenham, founded before 1184, was dependent on Royston Priory in Hertfordshire. Unlike Suffolk's Benedictine priories, however, most of the Augustinian houses were independent; Letheringham, as a dependency of St Peter's, Ipswich, was unusual.[53] Furthermore, whereas the last priory of Benedictine monks was founded in the 1150s, Augustinian foundations continued into the 1230s (when the outward-facing ministry of the Augustinian canons was supplanted by that of the mendicants).

It is possible that the Augustinian Rule was used to regularise some existing communities of priests left behind at vestigial minsters surviving from the Anglo-Saxon era; Blythburgh Priory is perhaps the most likely example of such a situation.[54] However, Pestell has suggested that it is also not coincidence that the twelfth-century Augustinian foundation at Butley was so close to the site of an Anglo-Saxon minster at Burrow Hill.[55] Butley Priory was to become Suffolk's greatest Augustinian house and, after St Edmunds Abbey and Stoke Priory, the wealthiest monastic house in the county. The endowment of Butley, like the endowment of his other foundation, Leiston Abbey, was centred on the landholdings of Ranulf de Glanville, and it seems likely that the de Glanville family's monastic foundations were designed to boost their social prestige as part of a climb to high office.[56] Nevertheless, it took 14 years for the foundation of Butley Priory to come to fruition.[57] The appointment of Gilbert, precentor of Blythburgh Priory, as Butley's first prior created a connection with the earlier Augustinian house.[58]

---

51   *VCH Suffolk*, p. 94.

52   R. N. Swanson, 'Fundraising for a medieval monastery: indulgences and Great Bricett Priory', *PSIAH* 40:1 (2001), pp. 1–7, at p. 1.

53   On Letheringham see E. Farrer, 'Letheringham Abbey', *PSIAH* 20:1 (1928), pp. 7–11.

54   On Blythburgh Priory see Harper-Bill (1980), pp. 1–2. On the *Time Team* excavation of the site in 2009 and subsequent investigation see E. Martin, J. Plouviez and D. Wreathal (eds), 'Archaeology in Suffolk in 2012', *PSIAH* 43:1 (2013), pp. 87–116, at pp. 94–5.

55   Pestell (2004), p. 198.

56   Pestell (2004), p. 181.

57   Pestell (2004), p. 158.

Figure 11 Butley Priory. Engraving by T. Higham, 1819.

Butley Priory was endowed by Ranulf with the large complement of 36 canons, and the church was dedicated on 24 September 1188. Butley received some royal patronage (albeit on nothing like the same scale as St Edmunds), and was visited by Henry III in 1235 and 1248. Henry II donated a cope, while the priory was expected to provide a home for royal servants at the end of Edward I's reign.[59] The Priory of St Peter and St Paul in Ipswich likewise received a royal visit from Edward I in 1296, and the king's daughter Elizabeth married John, count of Holland in the priory church.[60] By the end of the thirteenth century, Butley was one of the wealthiest priories in England, with a vast portfolio of lands and patronage.[61] From around 1195 it was granted by the pope the privilege of freely electing its prior, without the need for confirmation by the king or the bishop of Norwich.[62] This was a privilege that even St Edmunds did not enjoy at this time.

Founded at around the same time as Butley, Ixworth Priory was unusual in being located within the Liberty of St Edmund. Originally a modest foundation adjacent to

58   Harper-Bill (1980), p. 3.
59   On the foundation and early years of Butley Priory see J. N. L. Myres, 'Butley Priory, Suffolk', *Archaeological Journal* 90:1 (1933), pp. 177–281, at pp. 177–85; Mortimer (1979), pp. 1–3; Harrison (2000), pp. 5–6.
60   Allen (2018), p. 12.
61   *VCH Suffolk*, p. 95.
62   Myres (1933), p. 179.

Figure 12
Ixworth Abbey House, on the site of Ixworth Priory

the parish church, Ixworth Priory moved to a new site after the first set of buildings were destroyed in civil war – perhaps a reference to the Revolt of 1173–4.[63] As Augustinian life became progressively more focused on obligations to pray for founders and benefactors, and therefore more contemplative, canons regular were less closely connected with parish churches and less involved in outward ministry. Nevertheless, foundations of new Augustinian houses continued into the thirteenth century, long after Benedictine foundations had fallen out of fashion (at least in Suffolk).

Suffolk's smaller Augustinian priories enhanced the prestige of the local families who patronised them, providing these dynasties (and those who followed them as local landowners) with both spiritual benefits and a monumental place of burial. Although these priories were under the episcopal jurisdiction of the bishop of Norwich, they were otherwise independent and autonomous (with the exception of the dependent cells already mentioned). For Harper-Bill, Ranulf de Glanville's foundations at Butley and Leiston, together with John of Oxford's revival of Holy Trinity, Ipswich and Wimer the chaplain's foundation of Dodnash (as well as Herbert Walter's foundation of West Dereham Priory in Norfolk) formed a group of late twelfth-century houses founded in East Anglia by royal servants. The foundations may even have been, to some extent, acts of reparation for acts committed by these men while in royal service.[64]

Alnesbourn, founded at Nacton in around 1200 by Albert de Neville, was one of the wealthier small Augustinian priories in 1291 (with an income of over £71).[65] Kersey Priory, founded in around 1213, was unusual in having a female founder, Nesta de Cockfield.[66] The canons at Woodbridge, founded in around 1193 by Ernald Rufus, were an example

---

63 *VCH Suffolk*, p. 105. On Ixworth see also J. Rowe, *Ixworth Abbey, Bury St Edmunds: A Short and Simple Guide*, 2nd edn (Ixworth: Paul and Mathew, 1965).

64 Harper-Bill (1998), p. 3.

65 *VCH Suffolk*, p. 91.

66 On Kersey see W. B. Grey, 'Kersey. The priory', *PSIAH* 11:2 (1902), pp. 216–19.

of a fairly modest foundation. The canons initially made use of the parish church and the endowments of the priory were largely very local, with no impropriated rectories. Over time, however, Woodbridge significantly expanded its endowment and became a locally influential house.[67] The last two Augustinian houses founded in the county were St Olave's Priory at Herringfleet, in the far north-east of the county (by Richard FitzOsbert in around 1216) and the tiny priory of Chipley, founded at some point before 1235, when it was first mentioned.[68] Chipley was probably Suffolk's last Augustinian foundation, and the fact that foundations of canons regular tail off in the 1230s is no coincidence. The mendicants, who arrived in Suffolk in that decade, largely replaced the original functions of the canons regular as missionary clergy in the parishes (a ministry from which the canons had, in any case, largely withdrawn by the thirteenth century).

The Cluniac monks

Cluny Abbey in France, founded in 910, was the first mother house to retain control and governance of its dependent priories, creating a monastic order that was founded not just on observance of a common rule or historic links between houses, but also on institutional dependence. Cluny's daughter houses were never raised to abbey status, however large or wealthy they became, and could never be independent of the rule of the abbot of Cluny.[69] Cluniacs were Benedictines, in the sense that they followed a strict observance of the Rule of St Benedict (with particular emphasis on the performance of the liturgy), but Cluniac houses differed from other Benedictine houses in England because they both lacked self-governance and belonged to an international network.

Suffolk was home to two Cluniac priories, at Mendham (founded before 1155) and Wangford (founded before 1159). Mendham, as we have seen in Chapter 1, was the site of an Anglo-Saxon minster in the mid-tenth century, which may still have been in existence at the time of the Domesday Survey. By 1155 a cell of Castle Acre Priory had been founded at Mendham by William de Huntingfield, located on an island reached by a causeway in the middle of the marshes of the Waveney Valley.[70] The foundation of Mendham Priory took some time, and a prior (John de Lindsey) was not appointed until around 1170. The convent was to consist of eight monks.[71]

Whereas Mendham was dependent on Castle Acre, Wangford was dependent on Thetford Priory. The priory, which made use of the existing parish church, was apparently founded by 'Ansered of France' before 1160. Wangford was originally in possession of the chapel of Rissemere (later part of Southwold), which was taken over by the monks of St

---

67   *VCH Suffolk*, pp. 111–12; J. Arnott, 'The church and priory of S. Mary, Woodbridge', *PSIAH* 9:3 (1897), pp. 338–46.

68   On St Olave's Priory see W. A. S. Wynne, *St. Olave's Priory and Bridge, Herringfleet, Suffolk* (Norwich: Goose and Son, 1914); K. R. Davis, *St Olave's Priory, Herringfleet, Suffolk* (London: Her Majesty's Stationery Office, 1975). On Chipley Priory see *VCH Suffolk*, p. 99.

69   On the Cluniacs see N. Hunt, 'Cluniac monasticism' in N. Hunt (ed.), *Cluniac Monasticism in the Central Middle Ages* (Basingstoke: Palgrave Macmillan, 1971), pp. 1–10.

70   Pestell (2004), p. 207.

71   *VCH Suffolk*, pp. 86–7.

Figure 13 Wangford Priory

Edmunds Abbey (who had been granted Southwold before the Conquest) in 1206.[72] In spite of its small size, Wangford seems to have had some political importance: in 1226 the prior of Wangford was appointed a papal judge delegate alongside the abbot of Westminster and the archdeacon of Sudbury in order to resolve a dispute about the tithes of Walpole church, and in 1275 the sheriff of Norfolk and Suffolk seized the prior and imprisoned him for a week in Norwich Castle.[73] In the fourteenth century, however, the Cluniac houses would face an existential threat on account of their dependence on a French abbey, a theme which will be explored further in Chapter 3.

The Cistercian monks

The Cistercians, like the Cluniacs, were a Benedictine reform movement, and like Cluny, the French abbey of Cîteaux acted as a motherhouse to all monasteries of the Cistercian reform (although, unlike Cluniac houses, Cistercian houses were abbeys). The Cistercians were centrally governed by a general chapter which met at Cîteaux, but the Cistercian interpretation of the Rule of St Benedict differed from that of the Cluniacs. Rather than prioritising liturgy, the Cistercians advocated a return to manual labour for monks, and Cistercian abbeys eschewed the outward displays of wealth and grandeur of some Benedictine houses. The Cistercians also had a tendency to found their abbeys on virgin sites

---

72   Pestell (2004), p. 98.
73   *VCH Suffolk*, p. 88.

Figure 14 Sibton Abbey. Engraving by T. Higham, 1819.

where a lot of land was available, since the Cistercians originally preferred to farm their own land rather than living off the proceeds of estates farmed by tenants.[74]

Suffolk was home to the sole Cistercian monastery in East Anglia, Sibton Abbey. It remains largely a mystery why the otherwise highly successful Cistercian movement did not take root in East Anglia as it did in other parts of England. Pestell has suggested that the reason usually given for East Anglia's paucity of Cistercian foundations – that the region was lacking in the 'large desolate spaces' the order favoured – does not fully explain the lack of Cistercian foundations. Many British Cistercian houses were not in remote areas, and it seems that, for whatever reason, monastic donors in East Anglia chose not to patronise the Cistercians in the period 1128–54 when most houses were being founded.[75]

In spite of its isolation within the region, Sibton Abbey was a success, and notwithstanding Cistercian aspirations to a simple life, in 1291 it was the fourth wealthiest religious house in Suffolk after St Edmunds Abbey, Stoke Priory and Butley Priory. Sibton was founded by William de Chesney in 1150 as a daughter house of Warden Abbey in Bedfordshire, and the abbey is one of the best documented in Suffolk owing to the fact that Sibton Abbey was owned by the same family from 1610 and the surviving documents were carefully curated. The abbots of Sibton served as papal judges delegate from the late twelfth century, and like St Edmunds Abbey, Sibton Abbey developed an obedientary system in the mid-thirteenth century in which key functions of the monastery were

---

74   On the Cistercian reform see J. Burton, 'The Cistercian adventure' in D. Robinson (ed.), *The Cistercian Abbeys of Britain: Far from the Concourse of Men* (London: Batsford, 1998), pp. 1–33.

75   Pestell (2004), pp. 159–60.

Figure 15 Leiston Abbey. Engraving by T. Higham, 1819.

delegated to the sacrist and cellarer.[76] Sibton was notable for the extent of its ecclesiastical endowments, which extended to over 25 Suffolk parishes, 12 Norfolk parishes and 10 parishes in the city of Norwich. In accordance with Cistercian practice, Sibton remained under the visitatorial jurisdiction of the abbot of Warden throughout its existence.[77]

The Premonstratensian canons

The Premonstratensians were a congregation of Augustinian canons regular founded by St Norbert at Prémontré Abbey in France, but they are often considered an order in their own right because their observance of the Rule of St Augustine was so strict, and because the Premonstratensians were focused primarily on a contemplative life rather than ministry to the outside world.[78] Suffolk's sole house of Premonstratensian canons, Leiston Abbey, was founded by Ranulf de Glanville, also the founder of Butley Priory, in 1183 on a site that is now within the Minsmere nature reserve (the abbey relocated to a different site in 1365). Ranulph asked the abbot of Welbeck for advice about his foundation, and the two men decided on Robert, abbot of Durford, as the first abbot of Leiston. However, Ranulph had to obtain letters from the king to present to the abbot of Prémontré in order to gain the authority to move Abbot Robert to the new foundation. Although Leiston borrowed both canons and books from Durford Abbey in its early days,[79] Ranulph was

---

76   Brown (1985), pp. 1–2.

77   *VCH Suffolk*, pp. 89–90.

78   On the origins of the English Premonstratensians see J. A. Gribbin, *The Premonstratensian Order in Late Medieval England* (Woodbridge: Boydell & Brewer, 2001), pp. 1–19.

79   The possession of a certain number of books was a precondition of foundation for Premonstratensian houses. At least one book from Leiston's library is known to survive; see J. M. Luxford, 'A Leiston document from Glastonbury', *PSIAH* 40:3 (2003), pp. 278–88.

Figure 16 Flixton Priory

insistent that Leiston should owe nothing to any other Premonstratensian house, since he was determined it should become the foremost house of its order in England. By 1185 the abbey church was completed, and Butley transferred the patronage of some churches to Leiston at the insistence of Ranulf.[80]

Houses of religious women

Four houses for religious women were founded in Suffolk in the period 1066–1307: two priories of Augustinian canonesses regular at Campsey (1195) and Flixton (1258) and two priories of Benedictine nuns at Redlingfield (1120) and Bungay (1183). Monasteries of religious women were generally more poorly endowed than monasteries for men; since they were unable to offer masses, women religious were sometimes considered of lesser worth than their male counterparts, and religious women accordingly occupied a rather marginal position within medieval society.[81] Nevertheless, prioresses enjoyed the same manorial and seigneurial rights as their male counterparts, and houses of religious women were funded in much the same way as other monasteries. The main difference was the requirement for women entering a monastery to pay a dowry to the house, a condition

---

80   *VCH Suffolk,* p. 117; Mortimer (1979), pp. 2–4.
81   Gilchrist and Oliva (1993), pp. 24–5.

that effectively limited the social composition of female religious to the daughters (and sometimes widows) of the gentry.

Redlingfield Priory, founded in 1120 by Emma de Guisnes, the heiress of William de Arras, lord of Redlingfield, was the earliest post-Conquest house of religious women in Suffolk. Emma, the first prioress, was perhaps the founder's daughter.[82] Redlingfield's charter of foundation endowed it with the parish church of Redlingfield, which doubled as the community's conventual church throughout its existence. Redlingfield was exempted from the *Taxatio* of 1291, perhaps because it was exceptionally poor.[83] Bungay Priory, founded in 1160 by Roger de Granville and his wife, Countess Gundreda, was likewise apparently exempted, and as at Redlingfield the nuns made use of the choir of the parish church of St Mary (now in ruins). A royal charter of 1235 survives which enumerates all the benefactions to Bungay Priory, but the prioress was not always treated with respect; in February 1299 the prior of Coxford was accused of carrying off the goods and assaulting the men of Prioress Sara de Strafford at Roughton and Thorpe Market, Norfolk. Prioress Sara de Strafford's successor, Joan, was accused in 1301 of carrying off goods belonging to the abbot of Barlings in the town of Bungay.[84]

Campsey (or Campsey Ash) Priory was the wealthiest house of religious women in the diocese of Norwich, with an income of over £107 in 1291.[85] Campsey's founders, the de Valognes family, were a step down socially from the de Clares and Bigods who founded other monasteries in Suffolk.[86] The priory was founded by Agnes and Joan de Valognes on land donated by their brother Theobald. Joan became the first prioress of Campsey, succeeded by her sister, and the foundation was confirmed by King John in 1203–4.[87] While it was not unheard of for male monastic founders and benefactors to enter a monastery (such as Wulfric the moneyer at Sudbury), this seems to have been more common for female founders and benefactors. Pestell has suggested that Gundreda, the founder of Bungay, established the priory as a precaution so that she would have the option of becoming a nun if her husband died on Crusade.[88]

Although Campsey was well endowed for a house of canonesses, the struggle faced by religious women to assert their equality with male religious is well illustrated in Prioress Joan de Valognes's dispute with Prior Robert of Butley Priory over the tithes and mill of Dilham in 1228–9. After papal judge delegates awarded Dilham to Butley, the prioress and convent appealed directly to Rome, as a result of which the canonesses were excommunicated by the papal judges delegate for refusing to accept their judgement. Pope Gregory IX appointed more papal judges, including the prior of Anglesey, who declined to put the excommunication into effect, but Prior Robert petitioned Rome to obtain papal

---

82   *VCH Suffolk*, p. 85.

83   *VCH Suffolk*, p. 83.

84   *VCH Suffolk*, p. 81.

85   Gilchrist and Oliva (1993), p. 40. On the priory's fabric see D. Sherlock, 'Excavation at Campsea Ash Priory, 1970', *PSIAH* 32:2 (1971), pp. 118–39; L. Keen, 'Medieval floor-tiles from Campsea Ash Priory', *PSIAH* 32:1 (1970), pp. 140–51.

86   Pestell (2004), p. 180.

87   *VCH Suffolk*, p. 112.

88   Pestell (2004), p. 181.

confirmation of the excommunication of the canonesses of Campsey. The canonesses appealed to the prior of Yarmouth, another papal judge delegate, who refused to hear the appeal, so the canonesses made a second appeal to Rome. Eventually, in June 1230, Dilham was definitively awarded to Butley – but not before the Prioress of Campsey had caused Prior Robert considerable inconvenience and expense.[89] The episode illustrates the difficulties religious women had in asserting their rights against male monasteries which were almost always better resourced, more powerful and better connected, but also the tenacity with which religious women held their ground.

Several manuscripts belonging to Campsey Priory are known to have survived the dissolution, some from the twelfth and thirteenth centuries, showing that Campsey probably had a library from early in its history.[90] A manuscript collection of saints' lives in Norman French belonging to and perhaps made for Campsey (British Library MS Add. 70513) offers some insight into the devotional interests of the canonesses in the thirteenth century.[91] Annotations within the manuscript state specifically that it was read during meals at Campsey, which shows that Norman French was the language spoken within the monastery (at a time after most people in the outside world, even the gentry, had adopted English as a vernacular).[92] Sara Gorman has argued that the hagiographical collection, begun in the thirteenth century but continued into the fourteenth, was written in such a way that it reinforced Campsey's communal identity.[93]

Suffolk's final house for religious women was founded at Flixton in 1258 by Margery, widow of Bartholomew de Creke. Margery had earlier been given permission to found a monastery on the land she held in fee from Robert de Tatesale in 1256. On the founder's death, Robert de Tatesale granted the tenement Margery de Creke had held in Flixton to Beatrice, the first prioress of the Augustinian canonesses. A survey made in 1292, the year after the *Taxatio*, noted that the convent was limited to 18 and a prioress, and the canonesses were granted 5 shillings a year for the cost of clothing.[94] In addition to these houses, an unsuccessful foundation of Cistercian nuns was attempted at Coddenham in the reign of Henry II by Eustace de Merch, but it seems unlikely that any nuns ever settled there; the foundation had been transferred to Augustinian canons from Royston Priory by 1184.[95]

The mendicants

The emergence of the mendicant orders was arguably the most important development in religious life in the thirteenth century. The term 'mendicant' means 'beggar', and the first mendicant friars (a word that simply means 'brothers') led a life of radical poverty and

---

89   *VCH Suffolk*, p. 112.
90   Sherlock (1971), p. 125.
91   S. Gorman, 'Anglo-Norman hagiography as institutional historiography: saints' lives in late medieval Campsey Ash Priory', *Journal of Medieval Religious Cultures* 37:2 (2011), pp. 110–28.
92   Gorman (2011), p. 114.
93   Gorman (2011), p. 112.
94   *VCH Suffolk*, p. 115. On Flixton Priory's architectural remains see E. Martin, C. Pendleton and J. Plouviez (eds), 'Archaeology in Suffolk 1988', *PSIAH* 37:1 (1989), pp. 59–77, at pp. 67–8.
95   Midmer (1979), pp. 114–15.

Figure 17 Engravings of a Franciscan friar of Babwell from Richard Yates, *An Illustration of the Monastic Antiquities of the Town and Abbey of St Edmund's Bury* (1843)

insecurity that contrasted with the safety of the cloistered life in a conventional monastery. Like monks and canons regular, friars take vows, follow a rule of life, live in community and sing the office in choir; unlike monks, however, friars have no vow of stability to a particular monastery, and move between priories of their order. Furthermore, the friaries were supposed to be not endowed with lands and ecclesiastical livings but supported by the alms of the faithful, and the internal life of the friary is supposed to take second place to the primary ministry of the friars to share the Gospel.

A number of different groups of mendicants emerged in the early thirteenth century. Although the Order of Friars Minor (Franciscans or Greyfriars) and Order of Preachers (Dominicans or Blackfriars) are the best known orders of friars, there were others such as the Order of the Brothers of the Blessed Virgin Mary of Mount Carmel (the Carmelites, who claimed to have been founded by the prophet Elijah on Mount Carmel), the Order of Hermits of St Augustine (Austin friars), and the *Fratres Cruciferi* or Crutched Friars. All of these orders had a presence in Suffolk by the end of the thirteenth century. They brought with them an exciting, charismatic brand of medieval Catholicism. In 1235 a friar preaching Crusade in Clare was said to have blessed a woman who was unable to walk, who immediately regained the use of her limbs.[96] Stories like this brought in alms, and the

---

96   Harper-Bill (1991), p. 4.

friars often prospered on many small grants and donations rather than the monumental endowments of the earlier monasteries.

The friars radically disrupted the established pattern of medieval Christianity because their primary concern was the pastoral needs of ordinary people rather than gaining the patronage and favour of the wealthy (although many friaries achieved the latter as well). The architecture of mendicant churches, which often featured a wide, barn-like nave where people gathered to hear sermons, reflected their missionary aim. To established and ancient monastic institutions the friars represented a threat, not only because they might draw away patrons and pilgrims but also because the friars' preaching might encourage dissent against the spiritual and temporal power wielded by the heads of monastic houses. The friars' unsuccessful attempt to establish themselves in Bury St Edmunds is an important example of the clash between monks and friars in this period.

Bury St Edmunds, as one of Suffolk's largest urban centres, was a tempting target for the friars. The friars prioritised foundations in large towns in order to reach the largest possible audience,[97] and Suffolk's friaries were largely concentrated in towns such as Ipswich, Dunwich and Sudbury. Although Bury St Edmunds was a significant urban centre, the town was governed completely by the Sacrist of St Edmunds Abbey and under the authority of the abbot, which could be overridden only by the pope. The first sign that the friars were attempting to enter Bury came in 1233, when the abbot-elect of St Edmunds sought a bull from Pope Gregory IX confirming that no chapel could be erected within the vicinity of Bury St Edmunds. Both the Franciscans and Dominicans made another unsuccessful attempt to settle in Bury in 1238, which was thwarted by a papal legate.[98] The Franciscans made what was probably their third attempt to enter Bury in June 1257 after obtaining a papal licence to found an oratory. A temporary oratory was smashed by the monks of St Edmunds, who drove the friars out of the town, and although papal judges delegate ruled in favour of the friars, the abbot continued to expel the friars.

The friars then appealed to King Henry III, who instructed a royal justice, Gilbert of Preston, to seize a site on the west side of the town; Gilbert entered Bury with an armed company in April 1258 and put the friars in possession. The friars began building a church, but in 1263 Pope Urban IV once more ordered the friars to withdraw from Bury, and the monks demolished the friary. However, the abbey could not resist the friars forever, and Abbot Simon of Luton reached a compromise whereby the abbey granted the friars a site for a friary at Babwell, just outside the *banleuca* of Bury St Edmunds which marked the immediate area of the abbot's total jurisdiction.[99]

Babwell Greyfriars was the largest Franciscan friary site by area in England, and by 1300 there were about 40 friars – a formidable threat to the spiritual monopoly of St Edmunds Abbey.[100] The site was partially excavated in January 1990 in advance of work to extend the Priory Hotel.[101] In September 1289 the royal justice Sir Thomas Weyland took

---

97   Mattich (1995), p. 15.
98   Young (2016a), p. 76.
99   Young (2016a), pp. 77–80.
100 Midmer (1979), p. 90.
101 *VCH Suffolk*, pp. 124–5; E. Martin, J. Plouviez, and H. Feldman (eds), 'Archaeology in Suffolk in 1990', *PSIAH* 37:3 (1991), pp. 255–79, at p. 266; Mattich (1995), pp. 215–18.

Figure 18 Remains of an altar in the priory church at Clare

refuge at the friary and assumed the Franciscan tonsure and habit when he was on the run from a charge of harbouring a murderer. On the orders of King Edward I, Robert Malet laid siege to the friary until mid-January 1290 in order to starve Weyland out; the fugitive eventually surrendered and spent the rest of his life in exile.[102] This was by no means the last time Babwell Friary would be a refuge for rebels and outlaws.

Although the friars' apparent attempt to enter Bury St Edmunds in 1233 is the first sign of their activity, the first friary to be successfully established in the county was Ipswich Greyfriars, which is first recorded in 1236.[103] The next to be founded was Sudbury Blackfriars, established before 1248,[104] followed by a priory of Augustinian friars at Clare in 1248. Suffolk's only other Austin friary was founded by Robert de Hewell at Orford in 1299.[105] Clare Priory (not to be confused with the earlier priory of Benedictine monks

---

102 P. Brand, 'Weyland, Sir Thomas (c. 1230–1298)' *ODNB*, doi.org/10.1093/ref:odnb/29154, accessed 13 June 2019.

103 B. P. Grimsey, 'The Grey-friars Monastery, Ipswich', *PSIAH* 9:3 (1897), pp. 372–8; N. F. Layard, 'Original researches on the religious houses of Ipswich', *Archaeological Journal* 56:1 (1899c), pp. 232–8; *VCH Suffolk*, p. 126; Mattich (1995), pp. 282–8.

104 *VCH Suffolk*, pp. 123–4; Grimwood and Kay (1952), pp. 37–8; Mattich (1995), pp. 337–40.

105 *VCH Suffolk*, p. 130; Mattich (1995), pp. 333–6.

founded in Clare Castle in the eleventh century) would become one of the county's most important thirteenth-century religious houses, garnering considerable aristocratic and royal patronage. Clare Priory was especially important because it was the first house of the Augustinian friars in England. The friary was founded by Richard de Clare IV, earl of Hertford and Gloucester, perhaps under the influence of Cardinal Richard Annibaldi, the protector of the Augustinian friars.

In September 1249 Henry III took the friars under his royal protection, but the community was not without its teething problems. In 1256 Pope Alexander IV amalgamated a number of smaller groups of Augustinian friars into a single Order of Hermits of St Augustine, who were not really hermits at all but used the term to distinguish themselves from the Augustinian canons. The so-called 'Great Union' of the Augustinian friars may have caused problems at Clare, since in November 1262 a writ was issued for the capture of 'apostate or vagabond friars of Clare' wandering in the countryside. It is possible these were individuals reluctant to accept the Great Union. Curiously, in spite of introducing the friars, Earl Richard made no grants to them, and their principal benefactors were his widow, Countess Matilda and William de Ocstede, steward of the Honour of Clare.[106]

Dunwich, which was probably Suffolk's second largest town until it began to fall victim to coastal erosion in the 1280s, was home to both a Dominican friary (founded in around 1256)[107] and a house of Franciscan friars (founded before 1277).[108] It was Ipswich, however, that had the largest number of houses of friars, since in addition to the Greyfriars, there was a Dominican house founded in 1263[109] and a house of Carmelite friars founded before 1271.[110] Perhaps the most enigmatic of all Suffolk's friaries – partly because its location remains uncertain – was the house of Crutched Friars founded at Great or Little Whelnetham.[111] The friary at Whelnetham was founded before 1274 in the chapel of St Thomas the Martyr, and the friars of Whelnetham established a cell at Barham

106 *VCH Suffolk*, pp. 127–9; Barnardiston (1962), pp. 3–9; Harper-Bill (1991), pp. 2–4; Mattich (1995), pp. 250–9.

107 C. F. R. Palmer, 'The Friar-preachers, or Blackfriars, of Dunwich', *The Reliquary* 26 (April 1886), pp. 209–12; *VCH Suffolk*, pp. 121–2; Mattich (1995), pp. 262–4.

108 *VCH Suffolk*, pp. 125–6; N. E. S. Norris, 'First report on excavations at Grey Friars Monastery, Dunwich, Suffolk', *PSIAH* 22:3 (1936), pp. 287–93; Mattich (1995), pp. 260–1.

109 C. F. R. Palmer, 'The Friar-preachers, or Blackfriars, of Ipswich', *The Reliquary* 27 (April 1887), pp. 70–8; *VCH Suffolk*, pp. 122–3; S. A. Mays, *The Medieval Burials from the Blackfriars Friary, School Street, Ipswich, Suffolk (excavated 1983–85)* (London: Historic Buildings and Monuments Commission for England, 1991); Mattich (1995), pp. 274–81.

110 N. F. Layard, 'Recent discoveries on the site of the Carmelite Convent of Ipswich, and the old River Quay', *PSIAH* 10:2 (1899a), pp. 183–8; V. B. Redstone, 'The Carmelites of Ipswich', *PSIAH* 10:2 (1899), pp. 189–95; B. Zimmerman, 'The White Friars at Ipswich', *PSIAH* 10:2 (1899), pp. 196–204; *VCH Suffolk*, pp. 130–1; Mattich (1995), pp. 269–73.

111 On the Crutched Friars in England see E. Beck, 'The Order of the Holy Cross (Crutched Friars) In England', *Transactions of the Royal Historical Society* 7 (December 1913), pp. 191–208; J. M. Hayden, 'Religious reform and religious orders in England, 1490–1540: the case of the Crutched Friars', *Catholic Historical Review* 86:3 (2000), pp. 420–38.

in the parish of Linton, Cambridgeshire in 1293, but little else is known of this house in the thirteenth century.[112]

The military orders

The military orders developed after the First Crusade as a military adaptation of monastic life. Knights who belonged to military orders were solemnly professed, took vows of poverty, chastity and obedience, and sang the office in choir when they were not engaged in fighting. The military orders were first established in the Holy Land but quickly established commanderies and preceptories in Western Europe whose purpose was to profess and train new recruits and to administer lands and other endowments which funded the orders. The Knights Templar, notoriously, became extremely wealthy in the thirteenth century. While the exact reasons for the suppression of the Templars in France in 1307 remain murky, the suppression was extended to the entire church and all Templar houses in England were dissolved between 1308 and 1312, with their property often passing eventually to another military order, the Knights Hospitaller of St John of Jerusalem.

Suffolk was home to four Templar sites, at Cavenham, Dunwich, Gislingham and Mellis. The preceptory at Cavenham did not survive the suppression of the Templars.[113] The Dunwich preceptory passed to the Knights Hospitaller, although it was demoted to the status of a chapel.[114] Gislingham (founded before 1222) similarly passed to the Knights Hospitaller in the early fourteenth century, as did the Templar chapel at Mellis.[115] The principal house of the Hospitallers in Suffolk, which never belonged to the Templars, was at Battisford (founded in around 1154),[116] which had a subordinate chapel at Coddenham.[117] In addition to the Templars and Hospitallers, one of the smaller military orders, the Brothers of St Thomas the Martyr, seem to have been in possession of a chapel close to Ballingdon Bridge on the road south out of Sudbury.[118] Very little is known of the houses of the military orders in Suffolk in the twelfth and thirteenth centuries, and in several cases we have no information even on their dates of foundation.

Conclusion

By the end of the thirteenth century, few English counties were more abundant in monastic foundations than Suffolk. A clear change in fashions over more than three centuries can be discerned in the county's foundations; the early popularity of Benedictine monks gave way to the Augustinian canons in the twelfth century, who maintained their popularity until the arrival of the friars in the thirteenth century. Thereafter, all religious houses founded in

112 H. F. Chettle, 'The Friars of the Holy Cross in England', *History*, New Series 34:122 (October 1949), pp. 204–20, at p. 211.
113 Knowles and Hadcock (1971), pp. 292–3.
114 *VCH Suffolk*, p. 120.
115 Birch (2004), p. 263.
116 *VCH Suffolk*, pp. 120–1; Martin, Pendleton and Plouviez (1989), p. 70.
117 Knowles and Hadcock (1971), p. 308.
118 Taylor (1821), p. 116.

Suffolk were friaries. As Christopher Harper-Bill noted, a characteristic feature of monasticism in medieval Suffolk was the proliferation of small religious houses, and this became a weakness in later years as these communities were unable 'to maintain a satisfactory liturgical or conventual life'.[119]

Nevertheless, as Chapter 3 will show, the majority of Suffolk's tiny monasteries managed to survive into the fifteenth and even the sixteenth centuries. Monasteries, even small ones, were a great source of local pride, especially to the gentry who patronised them, and both the proliferation and survival of Suffolk's lesser religious houses must surely be attributed to their local significance. The institutional continuity of monastic communities across time, which was largely unparalleled by any other medieval institutions, offered founders and benefactors a chance of social and civic (as well as spiritual) immortality, since the community would always commemorate them and their ancestors. Suffolk's monasteries ranged in size from a great royal abbey at Bury St Edmunds to large institutions founded by royal servants, such as Butley and Leiston, and tiny cells founded by successful individuals and members of the local gentry. While not all were of national or regional significance, all served important functions within their local communities, and the changing fashions of monastic foundation paralleled the social changes of the twelfth and thirteenth centuries – culminating in the emergence of the friars as a potentially rebellious and socially destabilising manifestation of the monastic phenomenon.

---

119 Harper-Bill (1983), p. 205.

Chapter 3

Monasticism in late medieval Suffolk, 1307–1525

Medieval monasticism was by no means a fixed and unchanging phenomenon, and the late medieval period was a challenging one. The survival of a monastery was not guaranteed, and success or failure was subject to devotional fashions as well as political pressures. The dissolution of the Templar houses in 1308–12 marked the start of an ongoing process of suppression that would threaten Suffolk's monastic houses throughout the fourteenth and fifteenth centuries. Houses dependent on foreign priories suffered various sanctions up to and including dissolution, while others, unable to recover from the impact of the Black Death, were so poor they were forced to request dissolution or amalgamation with another religious house. Still other houses were secularised (converted into secular colleges), while some were abandoned due to natural disaster. Only one new monastery (Bruisyard Abbey) was founded in Suffolk in the fourteenth century.

The late Middle Ages was a tumultuous era in English history. Even the largest and most powerful monastery in the county, St Edmunds Abbey, was plunged into crisis by a rebellion against its authority in 1327–9 and then by various outbreaks of plague beginning in 1348–9 and the Peasants' Revolt in 1381. Economic decline and the outbreak of the Wars of the Roses in the 1450s further disrupted civil society, and all of these events had an impact on monasteries. By the beginning of the sixteenth century some of the smaller religious houses had already disappeared, and those that remained were in varying states of health. While the urban friaries thrived, some of the older Benedictine and Augustinian monasteries were struggling to compete with new devotional trends such as the popularity of chantries and the gradual drift of pilgrims away from saintly relics towards holy images. Nevertheless, at the dawn of the sixteenth century there was no reason to believe that the majority of Suffolk's monasteries could not have continued for a considerable time to come.

While information on many religious houses in the twelfth and thirteenth centuries is often scanty, from the fourteenth century it becomes possible to gain a fuller picture of the life, conflicts and traumas of Suffolk's monastic communities. For the first time, extensive accounts and visitation records survive for many monasteries, along with some survivals of books from monastic libraries. Information about religious houses can also be found in papal and state documents. This greater depth of evidence makes it possible to gain a clearer idea of the nature of communal religious life in late medieval Suffolk. This chapter focuses on the particular challenges faced by dependent cells; instances in which religious houses chose or were forced to relocate; the impact of the Black Death; conflicts and scandals, both between monasteries and between monasteries and the wider world; standards of religious life; and the place of monasteries in the wider 'spiritual economy' of late medieval Suffolk. The chapter also deals with religious women.

Dependence, suppression and denizenisation

The impact of external political events on Suffolk's monastic houses intensified in the four-teenth century, especially as a result of England's ongoing wars with France. Although the seizure of the assets of dependent priories of foreign houses (so-called 'alien priories') had been occurring since the 1260s, the financial strain on these cells in the fourteenth century resulted in the denizenisation of several of them – meaning that they cut their links with the foreign motherhouse and became independent houses. While the suppression of 'alien priories' was a gradual process, most of those that did not become denizenised were dissolved by the crown by the Statute of Leicester in 1414.[1]

Creeting St Olave severed its links with its motherhouse, Grestein Abbey, as early as 1347, but the cell seems to have been unable to maintain a conventual life. The priory buildings were sold to Sir Edmund de la Pole in 1460.[2] Creeting St Mary, a cell of Bernay, was seized by the crown in 1378 and seems to have ceased functioning as a religious community not long afterwards, although the crown continued to enjoy the priory's income. Edward IV finally granted the priory's revenue to fund Eton College in 1462.[3] Similarly, the income of Creeting St Mary, suppressed by the act of 1414, was used to endow Eton in 1460.[4] The Augustinian Bricett Priory suffered the same fate, and its income was transferred to the future King's College, Cambridge in 1444.[5]

All Cluniac priories were by definition cells of a foreign house, but the Suffolk Cluniac houses at Mendham and Wangford were treated with particular consideration. In 1337 Edward III ordered the restoration to Mendham Priory of all the lands and endowments alienated from it on the grounds that the prior and monks were all Englishmen and sent no 'apport' (a payment to a foreign motherhouse) to Cluny. Mendham was still under the visitatorial jurisdiction of Cluny in 1405, when the visitors reported there were nine monks and three masses a day, two of which were sung and one said.[6] By severing all links with Cluny, the denizenised Cluniac priories arguably ceased to be Cluniac except insofar as they continued to follow Cluniac observances.

Stoke Priory, Suffolk's largest dependent cell of a foreign monastery, was denizenised in 1395. Stoke became a dependent priory of Westminster Abbey, and the prior was required to pay Westminster 100 marks a year for ten years towards building works at the abbey – although the monks had awkwardly mislaid their charter of denizenisation by 1399.[7] Eye Priory was similarly denizenised, severing its links with Bernay Abbey in 1385.[8] The ease with which Eye received permission to become denizen may have had something to do with the patronage of Richard II's queen, Anne of Bohemia, who had received the

---

1   On the suppression see M. M. Morgan, 'Historical revision no. XCIX: the suppression of the alien priories', *History*, New Series 26:103 (December 1941), pp. 204–12.
2   *VCH Suffolk*, pp. 153–4.
3   *VCH Suffolk*, p. 153.
4   *VCH Suffolk*, p. 153.
5   *VCH Suffolk*, p. 95.
6   *VCH Suffolk*, p. 87.
7   *VCH Suffolk*, p. 145; Harper-Bill and Mortimer (1984), p. 9.
8   C. Paine and P. Aitkens, 'Excursions 1987', *PSIAH* 36:4 (1988), pp. 323–8, at p. 323.

Honour of Eye as part of her dowry.[9] Wangford Priory was granted denizenisation on the one-off payment of a mere 100 marks in November 1393, in consideration of the poverty of the house and the fact that the prior and monks were Englishmen and were not guilty of paying apports to Cluny.[10] While the suppression of cells of foreign houses somewhat pruned Suffolk's monasteries, a number of former 'alien priories' did survive.

The tendency to seek greater independence of action on the part of monasteries was not confined to the foreign cells; even St Edmunds Abbey sought to limit the extent of its dependence on the papacy. In 1398, Abbot William Cratfield obtained permission for abbots of St Edmunds to forgo the lengthy journey to Rome in order to be confirmed by the pope.[11] Snape Priory was less successful in attempting to break free from St John's Abbey in Colchester; the priory obtained papal confirmation of its independence in 1400 but this was bitterly contested by Colchester, with the result that the issue remained unresolved until 1443. Snape's dependence on Colchester was confirmed, and the house never did break free from the mother house.[12] Yet Snape continued to struggle, and in 1499 Henry VII attached Snape to Butley Priory; this too was unsuccessful, and Butley renounced all claim to the house in 1509.[13]

Other cells were also closely tied to their mother houses. Rumburgh Priory's dependence on St Mary's, York meant that no prior was appointed for life, and the entire convent was routinely replaced by different monks from St Mary's – perhaps on a yearly basis. On the other hand, Rumburgh was largely allowed to retain its own revenues.[14] The names of Rumburgh's priors show that they came predominantly from Yorkshire (Benedictine monks traditionally assumed a 'surname' that was usually their place of birth).[15] Likewise, the monks of St Bartholomew's, Sudbury were emphatically monks of Westminster, sent out to serve the outlying cell of the abbey, and their monastic names suggest they largely came from the Westminster area.

Nevertheless, St Bartholomew's seems to have recruited the occasional monk from Suffolk for Westminster. One of these, Richard of Kedington (who was also known as Richard of Sudbury, suggesting he had originally been a monk of St Bartholomew's) was even elected abbot of Westminster in 1308, although his election was vigorously opposed by other monks.[16] At Felixstowe, where Walton Priory was a cell of Rochester Cathedral Priory, Rochester frequently intervened in disputes at the manorial courts of Walton Priory, although for unknown reasons the monks of Walton were forbidden, on one occasion, from participating in the election of a new prior of Rochester.[17]

---

9   J. S. Roskell, 'Sir Richard de Waldegrave of Bures St. Mary, Speaker in the Parliament of 1381–2', *PSIAH* 27:3 (1957), pp. 154–75, at p. 165.

10   *VCH Suffolk*, p. 88.

11   Young (2016a), p. 101.

12   *VCH Suffolk*, p. 79.

13   W. Filmer-Sankey, 'The dissolution survey of Snape Priory', *PSIAH* 35:3 (1983), pp. 213–21, at p. 213.

14   M. V. Heale, 'Rumburgh Priory in the Later Middle Ages: some new evidence', *PSIAH* 40:1 (2001), pp. 8–23, at p. 15.

15   Heale (2001), p. 19.

16   Mortimer (1996), pp. 5–6.

17   Davison (1974), p. 144.

Martin Heale has argued that a strong conservative belief persisted into the sixteenth century that once a site was given over to monastic use it should remain in monastic hands, come what may.[18] This belief goes some way towards explaining the survival of so many small and apparently unsustainable religious houses in Suffolk. Nevertheless, a number of Suffolk houses did not make it to the beginning of major moves towards dissolution in the 1520s. Dunwich Priory, a cell of Eye, was 'swallowed up by the sea' at some point in the reign of Edward I,[19] which caused serious financial difficulties for the mother house of Eye and sent it into terminal financial decline in the fourteenth century.[20] Three more monasteries were simply too small to support conventual life. In 1452 Thomas Turnour, prior of Alnesbourn, asked the bishop of Norwich to annexe Alnesbourn to Woodbridge Priory since he feared Alnesbourn might be turned over to profane use. The bishop willingly complied and Pope Callixtus III issued a bull ratifying the bishop's decision on 18 April 1458.[21] Kersey Priory's income was so slim that the monastery was excused from the payment of tenths (an ecclesiastical tax) in 1347, and in 1444 Sir Henry de Grey, Lord Powys (then patron of the priory) obtained permission to grant it to the future King's College, Cambridge.[22]

Heale suggested that Kersey may have been 'caught up' in the general dissolution of foreign dependencies, implying that perhaps it was classified as an 'alien priory' by mistake.[23] Similarly, in 1455 the little Augustinian priory of Chipley was annexed by the bishop of Norwich to Stoke College (the secularised successor of Stoke Priory), on the grounds that the house's annual income was less than £10 and its buildings were in a ruinous state.[24] Dodnash Priory was threatened with suppression in August 1472 when its patron John de Mowbray, duke of Norfolk, agreed to annex the monastery's income to fund Magdalen College, Oxford. Accordingly, Bishop William Waynflete of Winchester sent an agent to investigate the priory's income, but the annexation never took effect and Dodnash survived until its eventual dissolution by Cardinal Wolsey.[25]

Only one Suffolk monastic house was secularised in the late Middle Ages. Unlike suppression or dissolution, secularisation meant that a monastic foundation passed into the hands of the secular clergy as a collegiate church staffed by canons. In 1414 the earl of March, Richard Plantagenet (who as lord of the Honour of Clare was the patron of Stoke Priory) complained that the priory had not been resettled by English monks according to the wishes of King Richard II. He petitioned the papacy that Stoke should return to its

---

18   M. V. Heale, 'Dependent priories and the closure of monasteries in the late medieval England, 1400–1535', *English Historical Review* 119 (2004b), pp. 1–26, at pp. 2–3.

19   *VCH Suffolk*, p. 76.

20   Brown (1994), pp. 21–3. On the financial state of the Dunwich parishes in 1341 see W. A. Wickham, '*Nonarum Inquisitiones* for Suffolk', *PSIAH* 17:2 (1920), pp. 97–122, at pp. 102–4.

21   Allen (2018), p. 13.

22   *VCH Suffolk*, p. 107.

23   Heale (2004b), p. 11.

24   *VCH Suffolk*, p. 99.

25   Harper-Bill (1998), p. 11.

Figure 19 Leiston Abbey, which moved to a new site in 1365

former status as a secular college in the eleventh century, and the pope granted his request at the Council of Constance in 1415.[26]

Reconstruction and relocation

While several Suffolk monasteries are known to have shifted their location early in their existence, some also moved to completely new sites in the fourteenth century. The most prominent monastery to uproot to a new site was Leiston Abbey, originally founded on a very unsuitable site in Minsmere which was subject to regular flooding. The canons of Leiston decided to move before 1362, and in 1365 they finally obtained a licence from Pope Urban V to move from 'the swampy site near the sea' to a location 1.5 miles away in the town of Leiston. The new monastery was complete by 1380, but then promptly burned down. Judging from some unfavourable visitation records, this series of misfortunes seems to have put the abbey's religious life under considerable strain.[27] Fire was an ever-present hazard in the medieval monastery, as in any medieval building, and St

---

26   Harper-Bill and imer (1984), p. 9.
27   Mortimer (1979), pp. 6–8.

Figure 20 Dunwich Greyfriars

Edmunds Abbey was subject to a number of fires in the late Middle Ages, culminating in the complete destruction of the roof and interior of the abbey church in 1465.[28]

The gradual loss of Dunwich to the sea caused the removal of the Greyfriars to a new site outside the town as early as 1289, and in 1328 the friars obtained a licence to enclose the site of their former monastery, on the grounds that a site once used for Christian worship where bodies were buried should not be converted to a secular use.[29] Today, the second site of the Dunwich Greyfriars is Dunwich's only surviving ecclesiastical ruin. Another monastery that shifted site was Walton Priory, which began next to Walton Castle within the walls of the ruined Roman shore fort of Walton Castle (the probable location of St Felix's *Dommoc*). At some point before 1500 the priory was relocated to a new site next to Walton church, but no documentary evidence survives to give an indication of when this was; Katharine Davison thought it was in the early fourteenth century.[30] Once again, coastal erosion seems the most likely reason for the move.

Some monasteries considered shifting site but never executed this. In 1384 the Dunwich Blackfriars considered moving their friary to Blythburgh. The friars obtained a papal licence to do this, but the move seems never to have occurred.[31] Butley Priory also suffered from periodic chronic flooding of both the monastery and its lands, but although this was a subject of frequent complaints, the prospect of moving the priory altogether seems to have been too daunting.[32]

---

28   Young (2016a), pp. 110–13.
29   *VCH Suffolk*, p. 125.
30   Davison (1974), p. 146.
31   *VCH Suffolk*, p. 122.
32   Harrison (2000), p. 25.

The impact of the Black Death

Although archaeologists now reject the old idea that bubonic plague first came to Britain in 1348, the outbreaks of bubonic and pneumonic plague in that year and subsequent outbreaks (especially in 1361) had a devastating demographic effect on East Anglia, especially in urban areas. The loss of life did lasting demographic, economic and institutional damage even to the largest monastic houses. Half of Bury's 80 monks died in 1349, and in 1351 Pope Clement VI exempted Bury monks from the canonical requirement to be at least 25 years old before proceeding to ordination to the priesthood. St Edmunds Abbey was left with insufficient labour to farm its lands, and its income fell. When the economy began to recover in the 1370s it was centred on the production of linen cloth. The abbey's failure to capitalise on this new economic trend would result in long-term decline.[33]

Smaller houses were even more severely affected. While Walton Priory had a prior and 13 monks in 1307, this number was down to only three monks by 1381.[34] The number of Augustinian friars at Clare in the 1460s (15) was half what it had been in the 1330s (30).[35] Likewise, Blythburgh Priory never regained the same number of canons after the Black Death as it had had before.[36] Women religious were similarly affected, with the number in the diocese of Norwich dropping from around 1,500 between 1150 and 1349 to about 300 between 1350 and 1400.[37] The impact of plague continued to be felt in the fifteenth century, and the prior of Alnesbourn blamed 'pestilence' and 'plague' for the priory's inability to support itself when he asked for Alnesbourn to be united to Woodbridge Priory in 1452.[38] At St Edmunds Abbey the plague killed two abbots, the prior and the sacrist in the course of just one year in 1361–2, and by 1369 (when the plague returned yet again) there was a severe breakdown of monastic order when one monk was murdered by his confreres in the dormitory and ineptly buried in the churchyard.[39]

In the face of recurrent outbreaks of plague and the social changes the plague produced, the quiet observance of religious life must have been a challenge in the late Middle Ages. Nevertheless, there were signs of recovery. At St Edmunds Abbey, Prior Henry of Kirkstead was responsible for building up and organising a fine monastic library in the 1360s and 1370s,[40] while an indication of Butley Priory's growing status at the end of the fourteenth century was the permission granted to Prior William de Haleworth to wear a mitre in 1398. Prior Haleworth was permitted to wear a ring, carry a pastoral staff and administer solemn benediction.[41] These were privileges normally confined to abbots, and mitred priors were unusual; the grant was a recognition that Butley was one of Suffolk's most important monastic houses.

33 Young (2016a), pp. 94–5.
34 Davison (1974), pp. 142–3.
35 Harper-Bill (1991), p. 10.
36 Harper-Bill (1980), p. 3.
37 Gilchrist and Oliva (1993), p. 46.
38 Allen (2018), p. 13.
39 Young (2016a), p. 95.
40 Young (2016a), p. 96.
41 Myres (1933), p. 193.

Conflicts and scandals

While monks and canons were supposed to lead an apostolic life, their behaviour did not always live up to the ideals they espoused. Where monastic influence intersected with political power there was significant potential for conflict, and the relationship between the townsfolk and abbey of Bury St Edmunds deteriorated significantly in the fourteenth century. As the abbey accumulated ever greater wealth its administration became more complex and burdensome for the townsfolk, whose own prosperity was booming owing to the success of the abbey. Yet the town of Bury St Edmunds, under the thumb of the abbey's sacrist, was prevented from forming its own local government. Real trouble began in January 1327, when the abbey failed to repay a debt of £2,000 to the townsfolk. The burgesses took an oath against the abbot and gathered support from the countryside, bursting into the abbey with a crowd of 3,000 people, looting and destroying documents.

The rebels captured and imprisoned the prior (the abbot was absent in London) and deposed the alderman of the town, Richard of Berton, replacing him with his more radical brother John. The townsfolk took control of government of the town, and when the abbot returned, they forced him to sign a charter of liberties. When the abbot then attempted to repudiate the charter, the townsfolk laid siege of the abbey precinct. By May both the parish clergy and the friars of Babwell had joined in looting the abbey, and the parish churches of St James and St Mary were attacked as well. By October the monks were giving as good as they got, kidnapping burgesses and attacking the townsfolk with siege engines mounted on the walls and gates of the precinct.

In retaliation, the townsfolk stormed the abbey again and set large parts of it alight, while roving bands in the countryside attacked the abbey's manors. Finally, the abbot managed to obtain permission from the pope to excommunicate the rebels, and the earl of Norfolk entered the town to subdue the townsfolk. The role of the friars in resisting the abbey was not over, however; the rebel alderman John of Berton escaped gaol in January 1329 and sought sanctuary at Babwell Friary, which he used as a base to foment further rebellion in Bury. A group of outlaws seized control of the town gates, and in October 1329 John of Berton launched a daring raid on the manor of Chevington in which he captured the abbot, stuffed him in a sack and sent him to Brabant.[42]

The level of violence between laypeople and monks witnessed in Bury St Edmunds in the 1320s was exceptional, even for the fourteenth century. However, disturbances returned in 1381 when Bury became caught up in the Peasants' Revolt. This time, although the prior and others were assassinated by the rebels, the restoration of order was much swifter and took only a few days.[43] Incidents of this kind had the effect of undermining the authority of the abbey, however, since the abbots were forced to call in external assistance; they also emboldened the friars and the parish clergy in their campaign against the monks. St Edmunds was not the only house attacked during the Peasants' Revolt; at Walton Priory the library was burned, along with the warden's house.[44]

---

42   Young (2016a), pp. 87–92.
43   Young (2016a), pp. 98–101.
44   Davison (1974), p. 142.

WEST FRONT *of the* ABBEY GATE

Figure 21 The Abbey Gate at Bury St Edmunds, built before 1346 to protect against future rebellions

The friars clashed not only with the older religious orders but also with the parish clergy. During the rebellion against St Edmunds Abbey, the parish clergy would not permit the friars to move their friary inside the limits of the town because they perceived them as pastoral rivals.[45] Conflicts arose between the parish clergy and the friars not only over preaching, but also over the hearing of confessions. Theologians were divided on whether the laity could only confess their sins to the parish priest, or whether friars could take confessions instead. The vicar of Clare, Richard Shoreditch, clashed with the Augustinian friars on this issue in the 1320s.[46]

St Edmunds Abbey and Babwell Friary were not the only monasteries to clash with one another so badly that it spilled over into physical violence. Dunwich Priory and Leiston Abbey came into conflict over tolls levied on ships arriving at the harbour of Minsmere (long since vanished through coastal erosion). People from the town of Dunwich attacked

---

45   Young (2016a), p. 91.
46   Harper-Bill (1991), pp. 9–10.

Leiston Abbey in 1235, and the bad relations between Leiston and the town and priory of Dunwich continued into the fourteenth century, when papal judges delegate had to decide a dispute between Dunwich Priory and Leiston over the latter's manor of Westhouse in the parish of Knodishall.[47]

While a number of abbots of St Edmunds were famous for clashing with the crown, some smaller houses also dared to defy the king. A major financial strain on small religious houses was the expectation that they provide corrodies: a pension, with board and lodging, for royal servants. Sometimes the burden of corrodaries (the recipients of corrodies) was so great that monasteries resisted their imposition. When Edward II sent Henry de Grundisburgh, an usher of the royal kitchen, to be maintained at Eye Priory in November 1316 the prior refused to act, resulting in the temporary confiscation of the priory's goods by the sheriff of Norfolk and Suffolk.[48] A similar situation arose at Eye in March 1338, when the prior was ordered to pay £80 to Robert of Artois and failed to comply, so the priory and its goods were seized (this was in addition to regular seizures of Eye's goods as an alien priory). The priory remained in the custody of guardians appointed by the Crown until 1348.[49]

As well as suffering institutional scandals, individual religious sometimes behaved in scandalous ways and brought disrepute on the monastery. While few went so far as to murder fellow monks, as happened at St Edmunds in 1369, fugitive monks were a problem. It was forbidden for religious to leave their monastery without permission. A monk of Rumburgh, John de Gisburne, fled the priory in 1311/12,[50] and in 1500 a canon of Leiston, Thomas March, was sentenced to 20 days of penance for 'apostasy', but this was remitted at the request of the other canons.[51] In 1509 a Crutched Friar of Brandenburg, John Millendonck, was sent to the friary at Whelnetham in the hope of reforming his conduct. Millendonck had been removed from his original monastery and sent to England for reform, but the attempt does not seem to have been successful since Millendonck was removed from Whelnetham and sent to Donnington Priory a year later, in 1510.[52]

An episcopal visitation of the Priory of St Peter and St Paul, Ipswich dating from the second quarter of the fourteenth century provides some colourful illustrations of the sorts of accusation that might be levelled against a monastic official, but also the ease with which it was possible for an official to defend himself against unsubstantiated claims. Thomas Verdoun, the cellarer, was accused of having carnal relations with numerous women, but he informed the visitors he had already confessed this fault to the prior and received a penance. Verdoun was also accused of attacking a subdeacon, Thomas Makel and an acolyte, John Wylde, in the cellary, 'even to the shedding of blood', and of attacking Peter Belleward and John Scriveyn in the priory church; he even attacked Richard of Hecham, the prior of Letheringham. Verdoun was accused of eating meals in a private room and of 'running about commonly and frequently in the town, drinking and eating with suspect

---

47　　Mortimer (1979), p. 6.
48　　Brown (1994), p. 20.
49　　Brown (1994), pp. 21–2.
50　　Heale (2001), p. 16.
51　　*VCH Suffolk*, p. 119.
52　　Hayden (2000), p. 428.

laypersons in common taverns'. On one occasion, his accusers alleged that Verdoun had been found in bed with two Ipswich women by the rector of St Matthew's, Ipswich, the rector of Holbrook and Geoffrey Hemmyng, and had attempted to attack the men before he was dragged out of the house. Another accuser alleged Verdoun was a glutton who frequently vomited in choir during the office.[53]

The accusations against Verdoun are so numerous – and range so widely between the petty and the grave – that it seems highly unlikely that most of them were true. The level of accusations speaks, rather, to a spiteful atmosphere within the monastery where grudges were fostered and burst out at the time of an episcopal visitation. Verdoun may well have been corrupt, but he was also clearly an unpopular figure whom the other canons were doing their level best to discredit. The fact that Verdoun's denials and excuses seem to have been accepted by the visitors suggest that the visitors realised the accusations were malicious; on the other hand, as an experienced cellarer Verdoun may have been too useful to the monastery for his offences to be taken seriously, or he enjoyed protection in high places. However, the range of accusations is also a reminder of the wide variety of temptations available to religious living in a fast-growing urban environment like four-teenth-century Ipswich.

The suicide of Prior Robert Brommer of Butley in 1509 was gravely scandalous, resulting in the exhumation of the prior's body from consecrated ground, but it also produced a dispute between the canons and the bishop of Norwich about Brommer's successor. Sheila Harrison has suggested that Brommer's suicide may have been connected with the burden imposed on the house by supporting the financially struggling Snape Priory.[54] The canons elected William Woodbridge as prior and even obtained royal assent, but the bishop of Norwich cancelled the election and appointed Augustine Rivers to lead the house instead, although the bishop's reasons for the intervention remain obscure.[55] Prior Rivers proved a success as a manager, eliminating Butley's substantial debts to the Crown.[56]

Houses of religious women

All of Suffolk's four houses of religious women survived throughout the late Middle Ages, being joined by a fifth, Bruisyard Abbey, in 1366. Popular stereotypes over the centuries have tended to suggest that medieval nuns were reluctant recruits, perhaps daughters given to a convent at a young age or widows with few other options. Yet the evidence suggests that, far from being compelled to join a religious community, the majority of women who became nuns and canonesses in medieval East Anglia did so because they felt a genuine vocation.[57] Among other things, the monastic life offered educational opportunities for women that they could obtain nowhere else.

---

53   C. R. Cheney, 'A visitation of St. Peter's Priory, Ipswich', *English Historical Review* 47:186 (April 1932), pp. 268–72.
54   Harrison (2000), pp. 22–3.
55   Harrison (2000), p. 12.
56   Harrison (2000), p. 24.
57   Gilchrist and Oliva (1993), p. 51. See also M. Oliva, 'Counting nuns: a prosopography of late medieval English nuns in the Diocese of Norwich', *Medieval Prosopography* 16:1 (1995), pp. 27–55.

Campsey Priory was the largest, wealthiest and most elite of Suffolk's female religious houses. While the other houses had only local endowments, Campsey's possessions were more extensive and reached beyond manors in the immediate locality.[58] Campsey also experienced the least decline in numbers of professed women in the late Middle Ages.[59] In 1347 Matilda of Lancaster, countess of Ulster, entered Campsey as a canoness. Matilda was of royal blood, being the daughter of Henry, third earl of Lancaster (a grandson of Henry III), and she spent much of her life in Ireland, being married first to William de Burgh, earl of Ulster and Connacht, and then to Ralph Ufford, justiciar of Ireland. Her first husband was murdered and her second died in Dublin, forcing her to flee the English colony. Matilda's arrival at Campsey was a major boost for the house, not only on account of her social prestige but also because her brother the earl of Lancaster agreed to pay 200 marks to the priory while she was there.[60] However, Matilda did not stay long, and in 1364 she obtained papal permission to enter her own new foundation of Bruisyard Abbey as a Poor Clare nun, but when she died on 5 May 1377 she was nevertheless buried in the priory church at Campsey.[61] Campsey became 'an Ufford mausoleum', and Robert, earl of Suffolk was buried there in 1369.[62]

In the case of Bungay Priory, we have surviving household accounts for Prioress Elizabeth Stephenson, beginning in 1490. This shows that Bungay's income rose in the late fifteenth and early sixteenth centuries, along with expenditure, and the prioress made sure there was always a narrow margin between the two. The house suffered from no hefty arrears during the period of Stephenson's rule, and from the limited evidence available it appears that she managed the priory's finances very effectively.[63]

Flixton Priory was the poorest house of religious women in the diocese of Norwich.[64] Nevertheless, in 1414 the priory accommodated 16 corrodaries, two chaplains and 20 household servants.[65] Some of the corrodarians were men.[66] In 1370 Flixton Priory became embroiled in a lengthy dispute with the parishioners of Fundenhall over repairs to the church (impropriated to Flixton), which was litigated in the papal curia. An episcopal visitation in 1493 found nothing to reform, although the canonesses were at the time obliged to hear mass at the parish church because their chaplain had broken his arm. A visitation of 1514 was less sympathetic; Prioress Margaret Punder was accused of capricious behaviour and of granting frequent access to a relative, John Wells, who may also have been the chaplain. Bishop Nykke ordered Wells to leave the priory and banned him from the town of Flixton. A visitation of 1520 found mainly administrative issues with

---

58   Oliva (1998), p. 209.
59   Oliva (1998), p. 39.
60   VCH Suffolk, pp. 113.
61   R. Frame, 'Matilda [Maud] of Lancaster, countess of Ulster', ODNB, doi.org/10.1093/ref:odnb/50027, accessed 26 July 2019.
62   D. Allen, 'A newly-discovered survival from the muniments of Maud of Lancaster's Chantry College at Bruisyard', PSIAH 41:2 (2006), pp. 151–74, at p. 151.
63   Oliva (1998), pp. 95–6.
64   Oliva (1998), p. 121.
65   Gilchrist and Oliva (1993), p. 36.
66   Gilchrist and Oliva (1993), p. 65.

Figure 22 Bungay Priory

the priory's accounts; likewise, visitations of 1526 and 1532 were uneventful, and the fall of Cardinal Wolsey meant that Flixton escaped plans for its dissolution in the 1520s.[67]

The most serious infraction of monastic discipline known to have occurred in a female religious house in Suffolk occurred at Redlingfield Priory in 1427, when Prioress Isabel Hermyte was accused of a sexual relationship with her bailiff, Thomas Langlond. Hermyte was accused of liaisons with Langlond 'under hedgerows and in woods', 'in the small hall', and 'out in the summer fields when the prioress sent the nuns one way to look for herbs'. In her trial at the bishop's visitation, Hermyte offered the bizarre defence that she was a Lollard heretic, as well as insisting that Langlond was a freeborn man rather than a villein. Hermyte was unwise to admit to Lollardy at a time when heresy had recently become punishable by death by the statute *De haeretico comburendo* of 1401. However, the court was most concerned by whether or not Langlond was a freeborn man, the implication being that a liaison with a villein was a much more serious offence. Redlingfield's court rolls were scrutinised, but it was found that all references to Langlond's family's status had been erased, perhaps by Hermyte herself.[68]

Sexual impropriety was not the only accusation against Prioress Hermyte. She admitted that she had not been to confession since 1425, that she slept in a separate chamber from the others nuns along with a novice, Joan Tate, and that she had physically attacked another

---

67   *VCH Suffolk*, p. 116.

68   M. Fisher, '"A thing without rights, a mere chattel of their lord": the escape from villeinage of a Suffolk family', *PSIAH* 42:1 (2009), pp. 32–7, at pp. 32–3.

Figure 23 Redlingfield Priory

nun, Agnes Brakle. Furthermore, the prioress had kept no accounts, obits (commemorations of past members of the community) had been neglected, and the convent's goods had been sold and trees cut down without its consent. The bishop's commissary, Dr Ringstede, ordered the whole convent to fast on bread and water on Fridays in order to repent the situation that had arisen, while Prioress Hermyte was compelled to resign and sent to Wykes Priory for correction. Joan Tate, who confessed to sexual immorality inspired by the prioress's bad example, was ordered to do public penance by walking in front of the convent procession on Sunday, wearing no veil and only a shift of white linen.[69]

Bruisyard Abbey, a house of Poor Clare nuns, was the sole religious house founded in Suffolk in the fourteenth century. It was unusual in being founded first as a chantry college by Matilda, countess of Ulster, before becoming a monastery in 1366. The chantry was originally founded in 1347 within Campsey Priory, where Maud was then a canoness, to pray for the souls of her husbands. However, the chantry priests, who were elderly, complained of having to walk all the way from the village of Campsey Ash to the priory. They also claimed that it was

> more in accord with honourable usage to … say service where there is no conversation of women, rather than near the choir of the nuns where it happens at times that they mutually impede one another by the noise of voices … [and] because the dwelling of clerks and women should be separate lest sinister suspicion arise.[70]

Accordingly, in 1354 the chantry was moved to the manor of Rokehall in the parish of Bruisyard. However, in 1364 Lionel, duke of Clarence arranged for the chantry college to be handed over to the Poor Clares (or Minoresses) as a monastery, although this was not

---

69   *VCH Suffolk*, pp. 83–4.
70   Quoted in Allen (2006), p. 153.

enacted until October 1366.[71] Matilda of Ulster was not the only aristocratic woman to enter Bruisyard as a nun; in May 1423 a niece of the earl of Suffolk joined the convent.[72] Maud de Vere, countess of Oxford (another member of the dynasty of the dukes of Suffolk), was buried at Bruisyard when she died in 1413.[73]

Unlike some monasteries for women, which required dowries, or at the very least that novices brought certain possessions with them to the convent, Bruisyard maintained a fund for women who wished to join the community but were unable to meet these requirements.[74] The Poor Clares of Bruisyard also remained true to the mission of the founder of their order, St Clare of Assisi, towards the poor, and the monastery spent around 17 per cent of its total income on alms – the largest proportion of any Suffolk house.[75] Campsey, in spite of being the wealthiest female house, spent only 22 shillings on alms.[76] Perhaps on account of this careful observance, Bruisyard accrued special spiritual privileges; Pope Urban V remitted 140 days of penance to anyone who contributed to the sustenance of the nuns of Bruisyard,[77] while Pope Sixtus IV granted the nuns and their benefactors a plenary indulgence which permitted them to choose any priest as their confessor.[78] Bruisyard enjoyed special papal protection, meaning that aristocratic women who wished to retreat to the monastery had to obtain special papal permission to do so.[79]

The social composition of Suffolk's houses of religious women ranged from the high aristocracy to the 'parish gentry' and urban middle class. Dorothy Calthorp, daughter of the sheriff of Norfolk and Suffolk, was a nun at Bruisyard in the sixteenth century, while another nun, Alice Cook, was the daughter of a mayor of Norwich.[80] The daughters of the countess of Suffolk boarded as pupils at Bruisyard and Bungay in 1416 and 1417,[81] and monasteries routinely took in temporary aristocratic guests.[82] Bruisyard's most controversial nun was Jane Wentworth, the 'maid of Ipswich', who as a twelve year-old girl in 1515 had manifested signs of demonic possession at the shrine of Our Lady of Grace in Ipswich. Wentworth's possession drew huge crowds of onlookers, including Lord Curzon and Abbot John Reeve of St Edmunds Abbey.[83]

71   *VCH Suffolk*, p. 131.
72   J. Watts, 'Pole, William de la, first duke of Suffolk', *ODNB*, doi.org/10.1093/ref:odnb/22461, accessed 26 July 2019.
73   J. Ross, 'Vere, Thomas de, eighth earl of Oxford', *ODNB*, doi.org/10.1093/ref:odnb/101271, accessed 26 July 2019.
74   Gilchrist and Oliva (1993), p. 52.
75   Gilchrist and Oliva (1993), p. 64.
76   Oliva (1998), p. 144.
77   Oliva (1998), p. 164.
78   Gilchrist and Oliva (1993), p. 57.
79   Oliva (1998), p. 122.
80   Gilchrist and Oliva (1993), p. 48.
81   Gilchrist and Oliva (1993), p. 58.
82   Gilchrist and Oliva (1993), p. 65.
83   R. Rex, 'Wentworth, Jane [Anne] [called the Maid of Ipswich]', *ODNB*, doi.org/10.1093/ref:odnb/47141, accessed 26 July 2019.

In theory, nuns did not need to reach a level of education beyond the point where they could sing the office in choir. However, nuns often owned books, such as the finely decorated psalter owned by Anne Felbrigge, a nun of Bruisyard, who added the obits of her parents to the feast days of the saints.[84] The survival of *ex libris* inscriptions in Norman French in some surviving books from Campsey Priory strongly suggests that there was a proper library at Campsey of the kind that existed in some male religious houses.[85] It is possible that a manuscript life of St Etheldreda now in Cambridge University Library (MS Add. 2604) was associated with Flixton Priory, since it was later owned by the Tasburgh family of Flixton Hall who received the property of the priory after the dissolution.[86]

Alongside late medieval Suffolk's nuns and canonesses, there was also an 'institute of recluses' in Ipswich in the fifteenth century. Recluses were women who secluded themselves from society in cells in urban areas.[87] In Ipswich, the female recluses were connected with the Carmelite friary and sought to follow as closely as possible the Carmelite rule of life. 'A certain devout woman' named Agnes may have been the initiator of this group of recluses, who were effectively 'third order' Carmelites.[88]

Standards of religious life

Some historians have been tempted to assume that just because monasteries were small, their standard of religious observance was lax,[89] but the real picture is more complex than this. Both wealth and poverty presented temptations to depart from the rigours of apostolic life; religious in wealthy houses might behave little differently from the lay gentry, while the inmates of poor houses were forced to make their living in inventive ways, often by leaving the monastery. It was also difficult to enforce discipline in a house that could barely support itself. However, the majority of Suffolk's religious houses fell between these two extremes, and visitation records reveal that standards of religious life were generally satisfactory, if not always exemplary.

The constant round of confiscations and expulsions during England's wars with France took their toll on the 'alien priories'. By 1378 the annual value of Eye Priory, once a wealthy house, had dropped to £100 a year (£30 of which went on supporting corrodaries), and the buildings were in such a poor state of repair that they required 1,000 marks of expenditure.[90] After denizenisation, however, Eye's fortunes improved. Late building works such as the construction of what is now one of the only surviving monastic brewhouses show

---

84   Gilchrist and Oliva (1993), p. 53.

85   Gilchrist and Oliva (1993), p. 54.

86   V. Blanton, *Signs of Devotion: The Cult of St Æthelthryth in Medieval England, 695–1615* (University Park, Pa., Pennsylvania State University Press: 2007), pp. 259–60.

87   A. B. Mulder-Bakker, *Lives of the Anchoresses: The Rise of the Urban Recluse in Medieval Europe* (Philadelphia, Pa.: University of Philadelphia Press, 2005), pp. 3–6.

88   Zimmerman (1899), p. 198. The recluse named Amabille who allegedly bore two children by Thomas Verdoun (cellarer of St Peter and St Paul, Ipswich) in the visitation accusations against Verdoun may also have been part of this institute (Cheney (1932), p. 272).

89   Heale (2001), p. 16.

90   Brown (1994), p. 22.

that the priory was still thriving at the time of the dissolution.[91] Stoke Priory did not fare so well after its denizenisation in 1395; in 1397 the priory was taken into the custody of the bishop of London, probably owing to laxity of observance, and in 1410 the abbot of St Edmunds received a papal commission to investigate the monks' allegations that the prior was guilty of dilapidating the goods of the monastery. The last prior, William Easterpenny, was installed in 1411 but moves to secularise the priory were set in motion soon afterwards.[92]

Monastic houses were, at least in theory, centres of learning. While the contents of the vast library of St Edmunds Abbey are well known to scholars, the only surviving list of books belonging to another Suffolk monastery catalogues the modest collection of Rumburgh Priory, which also doubled as a parish library. It is a list that gives some idea of the contents of the library of a smaller religious house, with a focus on necessary pastoral texts and standard pastoral manuals. Advanced texts such as biblical commentaries or philosophical works make no appearance.[93] Some houses seem to have struggled to maintain standards of education and monastic learning in the Middle Ages, Rumburgh perhaps among them. Even Butley, in spite of its relative wealth, struggled to maintain educational standards by sending its religious to study at the universities, and by the 1520s Butley had no scholars at Oxford or Cambridge.[94] Nevertheless, Prior William Woodbridge was still in possession of a copy of Aristotle's *De anima* in the early years of the sixteenth century.[95]

The friars, by contrast, maintained high educational standards throughout the Middle Ages. Clare Priory had an impressive library and was the place where foreign Augustinians studying at Oxford and Cambridge were supposed to spend their vacations.[96] Unfortunately, few books survive from Suffolk's friaries: nine from Babwell Greyfriars, two from Ipswich Greyfriars, and one from the Augustinian friars at Clare.[97] A list of benefactors to Ipswich Greyfriars mentions 49 books, and a few books are mentioned in Clare's cartulary.[98] Some friars became noted writers, such as Osbern Bokenham (1392/3–1464), an Augustinian friar of Clare who wrote popular verse lives of the saints,[99] and the Suffolk-born Carmelite and pastoral writer Richard Lavenham.[100] Bokenham may have been the author of a surviving poem, 'The dialogue at the grave', in which an Augustinian friar of Clare

91   E. Martin, C. Pendleton and J. Plouviez (eds), 'Archaeology in Suffolk in 2008', *PSIAH* 42:1 (2009), pp. 61–88, at p. 82.

92   Harper-Bill and Mortimer (1984), p. 9.

93   On Rumburgh's books see J. Middleton-Stewart, 'The provision of books for church use in the Deanery of Dunwich, 1370–1547', *PSIAH* 38:2 (1994), pp. 149–66, at pp. 151, 153.

94   Harrison (2000), p. 14.

95   Harrison (2000), p. 23.

96   Harper-Bill (1991), p. 11.

97   Mattich (1995), p. 166.

98   Mattich (1995), p. 167.

99   D. Gray, 'Bokenham, Osbern', *ODNB*, doi.org/10.1093/ref:odnb/2785, accessed 23 July 2019.

100   P. V. Spade, 'Lavenham [Lavyngham], Richard', *ODNB*, doi.org/10.1093/ref:odnb/16135, accessed 23 July 2019.

and a layman recite the descendants of Joan of Acre.[101] Katherine Barnardiston thought the poem might have been a 'catechism' learned by the friars in order to remember the lineage of their benefactors in commemoration.[102] The Ipswich Whitefriars were especially renowned for their learning, producing such voluminous writers as Thomas Yllea, John Polsted, John Kynyngham, John Barmingham and Nicholas Kenton.[103] However, the true extent of the libraries and learning of the friars of medieval Suffolk has largely been lost.

Late medieval visitations tend to reveal neglect rather than flagrant violation of religious rules of life and liturgical commitments. A 1520 visitation of Blythburgh Priory reported that mass was no longer sung, but said; otherwise, however, 'religion was as well observed as it might be by so small a number'.[104] At Butley the canons struggled to maintain the buildings and keep water out of the refectory in the early sixteenth century, and the rood beam in the church was rotten with damp.[105] The canons of Dodnash failed to keep up their obligation to say masses for the soul of William le Newman, whose chantry was endowed in 1351, and in 1506 his descendant Thomas Fincham launched a legal attempt to seize the priory's lands until it made satisfaction.[106] The canons of Dodnash also bungled the election of Prior William le Newman in 1346, rendering it uncanonical, although the bishop of Norwich appointed him anyway.[107]

In 1448 the prior of Rumburgh was in possession of a large collection of arms and armour (clerics, especially monks, were not supposed to bear arms),[108] although it is unlikely these were for his personal use; a monastic head of house, as the greatest magnate of a hundred, might be expected to raise and equip troops just like a secular lord in time of war. At least two prioresses of Bungay apparently enjoyed watching performances by travelling players, who received payment from the priory in 1405/6 and 1443/4,[109] but it was not uncommon for heads of religious houses to behave like the rest of the gentry. After all, they were an integral part of the local gentry community, exercised the same seigneurial rights and presided over manorial courts just like lay gentry.

In spite of the large endowment they received from Simon of Sudbury, the monks of St Bartholomew's struggled to make ends meet and managed to obtain a papal indulgence for anyone granting alms to the monastery on the grounds of its poverty. Westminster Abbey did its best to rid itself of the cell, but although conventual life had probably ceased there before the dissolution, Westminster Abbey continued to supply a chaplain to say divine service in the chapel of St Bartholomew's until the nineteenth century, and the chapel survives to this day, the only monastic church in Suffolk to survive complete and with its original roof.[110] St Bartholomew's was arguably the only Suffolk house that escaped disso-

---

101 For the text of the poem see Barnardiston (1962), pp. 65–9.
102 Barnardiston (1962), p. 63.
103 *VCH Suffolk*, pp. 130–1.
104 Harper-Bill (1980), p. 4.
105 Harrison (2000), p. 9.
106 Harper-Bill (1998), p. 13.
107 Harper-Bill (1998), p. xix.
108 Heale (2001), p. 14.
109 J. Stokes, 'Women and performance in medieval and early modern Suffolk', *Early Theatre* 15:1 (2012), pp. 27–43, at p. 32.
110 Mortimer (1996), pp. 4–6.

lution altogether – merely deteriorating into a proprietary chapel of the secularised mother house.

At Clare Priory the *peculium*, a sum of money permitted to individual friars in spite of their vow of poverty, steadily increased, and some friars were allowed private chambers and even servants in the fifteenth century. However, while it is easy to see these developments as manifestations of spiritual decline, they also reflected broader changes in society such as a trend towards privacy and the subdivision of larger buildings for multiple purposes.[111] The fourteenth and fifteenth-century rolls of Hoxne Priory give some insight into the domestic arrangements of a typical small monastery. In addition to the usual kitchen, bakery, dairy and brewery, Hoxne had a hall with glazed windows, subdivided by a painted curtain, a glazed parlour, and a parclose in the chamber of the hall. There was a dormitory for the monks and a chamber above it. In 1454 the monks commissioned a clock, presumably so that they could more accurately know the times when they should be singing offices. Hoxne also had an orchard and garden, stables, closes for threshing and winnowing corn, a malthouse and a dovecote.[112]

The fourteenth-century inventories of an even more tiny monastic house than Hoxne, St Bartholomew's, Sudbury, show that it was in possession of a chapel containing a relic of St Bartholomew and a handful of liturgical books, a hall and chamber, and a kitchen, larder, bakehouse and barn; the chapel and barn survive to this day. The hall contained tables for the prior and his servants, with bronze candlesticks, a salt-cellar of tin and a pepper mill. There were large vats in the bakehouse for brewing beer.[113]

In addition to the domestic service buildings they required, the Hoxne monks had to get water from somewhere (probably piped from nearby Chickering Beck to a cistern).[114] The need for a properly engineered water supply was particular to religious houses, where a number of people lived in community, and in the case of Benedictines, there were hygiene requirements in the rule of life they followed. During their attempt to lay siege to St Edmunds Abbey in 1327 the townsfolk of Bury St Edmunds destroyed an aqueduct built in the twelfth century by Abbot Samson which brought water from Horringer into the abbey precincts,[115] and the plumbing system that supplied and emptied the monastic lavatorium was impressive.[116] So durable was the monastic plumbing of St Peter and Paul's Priory in Ipswich that it remained in use to supply the parish of St Peter until the early nineteenth century.[117]

The standard ground plan of a medieval monastery was unsuitable when it came to the large urban friaries, which showed a high degree of adaptability while usually adhering to the basics of the traditional monastic groundplan.[118] At Ipswich Blackfriars, for example,

---

111 Harper-Bill (1991), pp. 10–11.
112 Carey Evans (1987), p. 186.
113 Mortimer (1996), p. 6.
114 Carey Evans (1987), p. 186.
115 Young (2016a), p. 90.
116 Hoggett (2018), p. 196.
117 Allen (2018), p. 11.
118 Mattich (1995), pp. 52–5.

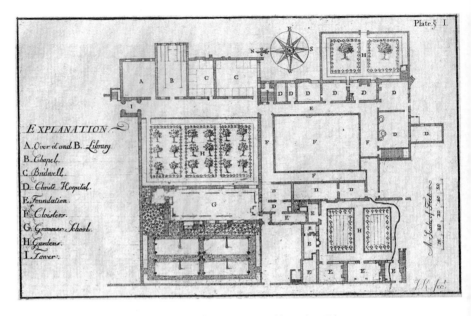

Figure 24 Groundplan of Ipswich Blackfriars. Engraved by John Kirby, 1735.

there were as many as 25 novice friars in residence at any one time, studying to be licensed as preachers. These novices required study cubicles in a shared study-dormitory. Furthermore, the friars wanted their refectories to be open to the laity, meaning that these needed to be larger and located close to the edge of the monastic precinct.[119] An eighteenth-century plan of the surviving buildings of the Ipswich Blackfriars by John Joshua Kirby illustrates some of these arrangements.[120]

The friars of Ipswich took a full part in the town's civic life, and a sixteenth-century document describes the order of procession at Corpus Christi. The Carmelites always came first in procession, followed by the Franciscans, the Dominicans, the secular clergy with the Blessed Sacrament, the canons of Holy Trinity and the canons of St Peter and St Paul.[121] Since those first in order of precedence walk at the back of processions, this indicates the canons of St Peter and St Paul were considered the most senior religious of the town and the Carmelites (as the latest arrivals) the most junior.

Perhaps surprisingly, at a time when even the Augustinian canons had largely withdrawn from the parish ministry which was originally one of their chief functions, the Benedictine monks of Rumburgh seem to have been serving as parish priests not only to the priory-cum-parish church of St Michael and Felix at Rumburgh but also at South Elmham.[122] This suggests the survival into the late Middle Ages of practices at Rumburgh derived

---

119 On lay access to friaries see Mattich (1995), pp. 55–9.

120 R. Gilyard-Beer, 'Ipswich Blackfriars', *PSIAH* 34:1 (1977), pp. 15–23, at pp. 18, 20.

121 Allen (2018), pp. 5–6.

122 Heale (2001), p. 17.

from the Anglo-Saxon minster and suppressed in many other places at the outset of the Benedictine reform in the tenth century.

The Knights Hospitaller of St John were prevented by external events from taking a very active role in their Suffolk houses in the late Middle Ages. In the later fifteenth century the Knights were preoccupied with the defence of the island of Rhodes from the Turks. John Malory was granted permission to leave Rhodes in December 1469 to visit Battisford, which he had been granted almost two years earlier, in January 1468.[123] This long delay suggests that the Knights' focus may have been elsewhere for much of the period.

Monasteries in the spiritual economy

Masses, prayers and communities living the religious life were commodities of economic as well as spiritual value in late medieval England, and patrons and benefactors were often keen to receive the best value for the financial commitment they made to support religious institutions. While monastic houses were generally the sole recipients of benefactions (along with parish churches) in the twelfth century, the development of chantries funded by the nobility and gentry in the thirteenth century created competitor institutions. A chantry was created when a patron gave instructions for mass to be sung for his or her soul, either for a fixed term or in perpetuity, in a church, monastery or dedicated chantry chapel. Although most chantries were not perpetual, endowing a chantry was cheaper than founding a monastery. However, whereas a chantry was simply designed to offer masses for a patron's soul after death, a patron could benefit from the merits accrued by the religious lives of the monks or nuns of the monasteries they patronised during life, especially if enrolled in the confraternity. Monasteries were still an attractive option for patrons, therefore, but by no means the only one.

Among the gentry, houses of religious women were particularly popular destinations for bequests in the late Middle Ages. Bruisyard Abbey, as a new foundation in the 1360s, attracted particular attention, but the older houses were also popular. Bequests to communities of religious women in gentry wills outnumber those to male monasteries by five to one.[124] While the small size of these bequests meant that female monasteries remained poor in comparison with male monasteries of a similar size, they are an indication that the prayers, intercession and almsgiving of nuns and canonesses were particularly valued by some late medieval patrons. People also preferred to be interred inside the churches of female monasteries.[125] Likewise, bequests to friaries among Ipswich's urban elite were twice as common as bequests to other religious houses. In Bury St Edmunds, bequests to Babwell Greyfriars were much more popular than bequests to St Edmunds Abbey, and by the period 1512–39 only around 10 per cent of testators left anything to the abbey.[126]

Monasteries in areas crowded with religious houses, chantries and secular colleges,

---

123 P. J. C. Field, 'Sir Robert Malory, Prior of the Hospital of St. John of Jerusalem in England (1432–1439/40)', *Journal of Ecclesiastical History* 28:3 (1977), pp. 249–64, at p. 260.
124 Gilchrist and Oliva (1993), pp. 59–61.
125 Gilchrist and Oliva (1993), p. 62.
126 MacCulloch (1986), p. 135.

such as the area around Ipswich, faced stiff competition for the patronage of the laity.[127] Religious houses sometimes had chantries within them, or functioned as chantries. The foundation of a chantry within Campsey Priory has already been mentioned. This also occurred in 1349 at the Benedictine cell of St Bartholomew's, Sudbury when Simon Thebaud, bishop of London (better known as Simon of Sudbury, the archbishop of Canterbury murdered during the Peasants' Revolt of 1381) endowed St Bartholomew's with a considerable amount of land in return for masses for the soul of his brother Nigel and other relatives.[128] The canons of St Peter and St Paul's Priory undertook to distribute food and drink on the anniversaries of important benefactors 'as for a professed canon'; the canons also undertook to sing multiple masses for the souls of benefactors.[129] The heads of wealthier religious houses also behaved in much the same way as the nobility, sometimes establishing personal chantries to sing masses for their souls. In 1337 the prior of St Peter and St Paul's, Ipswich, had a personal chantry attached to his manor of Hintlesham.[130]

Beyond the competition they faced from chantries, changes in devotional fashions took their toll on monastic finances. Hoxne Priory, which relied to some extent on the donations of pilgrims, saw a significant downturn in donations from the second half of the fifteenth century,[131] perhaps because Anglo-Saxon saints like St Edmund were losing their appeal in comparison with miraculous images. The monks of St Edmunds sought to cash in on the new fashion, taking control of the holy well and chapel of Our Lady of Woolpit, which featured a famous image of the Virgin and was the most visited Marian shrine in Suffolk after Our Lady of Grace in Ipswich.[132]

Rumburgh Priory was a centre of the cult of the Northumbrian virgin martyr St Bee (Bega), called 'Seynt Bory' by visitors in 1528. This cult seems to have come to Rumburgh from its mother house of St Mary's, York. Around Michaelmas (29 September) offerings of money and cheese were made to the image of St Bee, decorated with a tunic of black velvet and jet beads. The church also featured a 'table' of hymns and prayers to St Bee, which may have been something like a wooden triptych.[133] In spite of the fact that she had no connection whatsoever to the locality, local people in Suffolk seem to have venerated St Bee enthusiastically, and the value of gifts to her shrine was almost equal to the revenue generated by pilgrims to St Bee's Priory where Bega was actually buried.[134] Rumburgh's surviving accounts show that the monastery sometimes struggled to make ends meet toward the end of the fifteenth century; nevertheless, its finances remained stable and it

---

127 Harper-Bill (1998), p. 13.
128 Mortimer (1996), pp. 3–4.
129 Allen (2018), p. 15.
130 Allen (2018), p. 12.
131 Carey Evans (1987), p. 191.
132 C. Paine, 'The Chapel of Our Lady at Woolpit', *PSIAH* 38:1 (1996), pp. 8–12.
133 On the cult of St Bee at Rumburgh see Middleton-Stewart (1994), p. 152. *VCH Suffolk*, p. 78 misidentifies Bory as a possible corruption of St Birinus, while Cane (1935), p. 160 even suggested 'Bory' might be a corruption of Eboracum, the Latin name for the city of York. The Welsh St Baruc, anglicised as St Barry, has his feast day on 27 September (two days before Michaelmas) but it is highly unlikely that a Welsh saint would have had a cult centre in Suffolk.
134 Heale (2001), p. 18.

is remarkable that such a small monastic house (which rarely exceeded three members) remained financially viable at all.[135]

Detailed visitation records for the diocese of Norwich survive for the year 1499, when Archbishop John Morton exercised jurisdiction over Norfolk and Suffolk during a vacancy. One problem encountered by the visitors was the poor standard of pastoral oversight in parishes impropriated to monasteries. Heads of religious houses, who formally exercised the cure of souls, were employing chaplains to discharge clerical duties in the parishes who sometimes lacked sufficient learning or failed to perform their duties.[136] At Ellough, near Beccles, the chaplain was found to be a Cistercian who did not wear the habit of his order. Although the chaplain was ordered to resume the habit, he was not sent back to his monastery even though he was in breach of the Benedictine vow of stability. Little Glemham also had a monk serving as chaplain, while two monks were reported to be at large celebrating occasional masses – something expressly forbidden by the Rule of St Benedict.[137] Incidents such as these suggest that some monasteries who impropriated cures were cutting corners pastorally in order to ensure that the impropriations were as lucrative as possible.

Conclusion

The fourteenth and fifteenth centuries were a challenging period for Suffolk's monasteries, which struggled to maintain numbers even as wealth flooded into the region from the burgeoning wool industry. The new wealth was not always directed towards monasteries, nor were fashionable devotions, and small monasteries sometimes found themselves the 'poor relations' of richly endowed parish churches and chantry colleges. The demographic catastrophe of the Black Death not only diminished monastic numbers, but also made it harder for monasteries to gain a viable income from endowments of land, since there were not always enough people available to work it. Some of the older, smaller monasteries struggled to maintain educational and liturgical standards, while the friaries and Bruisyard Abbey, the county's only house of Poor Clares, were thriving.

This pattern of thriving 'reformed' orders while more established monasteries experienced slow and steady decline is characteristic of late medieval Britain and Ireland as a whole. Patrons were attracted to the most observant houses, since they believed they might derive the greatest spiritual benefit from funding the most devout monastics. However, the decline of older monasteries against newer religious movements should not be overstated, since wealthier monasteries had vast reserves of land and a considerable hold over their locality, meaning that financial decline rarely threatened their very existence. Visitation records suggest that, by the late fifteenth century, monastic life was recovering and generally in a healthy state across the board. The scandalous behaviour uncovered in some Norfolk monasteries was absent in Suffolk, and 'the general picture is one of conscientious if uninspired and pedestrian observance of the Rule, marred by occasional minor scandal

---

135 Heale (2001), pp. 10–13.
136 C. Harper-Bill, 'A late medieval visitation: the diocese of Norwich in 1499', *PSIAH* 34:1 (1977), pp. 35–47, at p. 44.
137 Harper-Bill (1977), p. 45.

and a good deal of run-of-the-mill ill-nature in the cloister'.[138] What is perhaps most remarkable is that so many of the smaller monasteries, whose continued existence was often in doubt, made it through to the beginning of the sixteenth century. In the 1520s Suffolk's friaries and houses of religious women had never been stronger; its more traditional monasteries were slightly fewer than they had been a century earlier, and some were moribund, but the majority were in a slightly reduced but nevertheless strong condition.

---

138 MacCulloch (1986), p. 133.

Chapter 4

The dissolution of the monasteries in Suffolk, 1525–1540

The dissolution of the monasteries is commonly associated with Henry VIII's lord privy seal, Thomas Cromwell, and located in the late 1530s. However, in the diocese of Norwich a determined campaign of dissolution began a whole decade earlier in the 1520s, as Cardinal Wolsey sought to appropriate the revenues of many of the diocese's smaller monasteries for his new foundations at Ipswich and Oxford. Although Wolsey's fall in 1529 meant that some of these dissolutions were not carried through at the time, Wolsey succeeded in dissolving five Suffolk monasteries. The process of dissolution formally resumed in 1536, albeit for different reasons, when any religious house with an income below £200 a year was targeted for closure. The dissolution was not formally complete in Suffolk until early in 1540, and even then not every monastic institution came to an end: St Peter's Hospital in Bury St Edmunds, for example, was still functioning as late as 1637,[1] and St Bartholomew's Priory in Sudbury never technically ceased to exist.

The dissolution of the monasteries was a complex process rather than a single event. As was shown in Chapter 3, dissolution and secularisation were threats faced by smaller religious houses from the 1440s onwards, and by dependent cells of foreign houses long before that. Yet both 'dissolution' and 'suppression' are ambiguous terms, since they imply a complete eradication of a religious house which rarely occurred. Technically, 'dissolution' meant the break-up of a religious community, which might involve sending the religious to live in other communities or sending them out into the world. Dissolution, in and of itself, did not end a religious institution. For example, the dissolution of Stoke Priory in 1415 changed the character of the institution rather than ending it, as the monks were replaced by secular canons. Even if the religious were not replaced, however, a monastery might continue a kind of legal existence for centuries after the departure of the last religious and long after the conventual buildings had fallen into ruin, since the monastery's spiritualities (its impropriated parishes) continued to exist. In the case of St Edmunds Abbey, both the spiritual and temporal jurisdictions of the abbey survived for centuries after its dissolution, so the abbey did not cease to exist in every respect in 1539. Furthermore, some houses were never technically dissolved because they were abandoned by their communities before this could take place, such as Bungay Priory, Sibton Abbey and Hoxne Priory.

Rather than the total elimination of Suffolk's monasteries, the dissolution process should be seen as a sliding scale of institutional erasure. Some monasteries truly ceased to exist in every possible way, as the land was given over to secular possession and use

---

1   Milner (2013), p. 35.

and the spiritualities dispersed. Some houses survived as nothing more than a collection of spiritualities, perhaps transferred as an endowment to another institution; in the case of St Edmunds Abbey, the abbey's spiritual and temporal jurisdiction continued to exist, defining the character of the locality for centuries to come. And, in the case of St Bartholomew's, Sudbury, the religious house was never dissolved but simply faded away. Owing to the ambiguity of the term 'dissolution', 'deconventualisation' might be a more accurate term to use when discussing the end of religious communities. A religious house was deconventualised when the convent ceased to exist, even if the rights of the head of house remained in some sense intact or the institution continued to exist in a non-monastic form. The subject of this chapter is, first and foremost, the deconventualisation of Suffolk's monasteries, whatever their subsequent fate as institutions.

An analysis of the dates of dissolution of Suffolk houses reveals that the largest concentration of dissolutions in the shortest time occurred in February 1537, when no fewer than nine houses were dissolved in a period of less than ten days. The dissolution of the friaries was likewise very concentrated, occurring in November and December 1538. St Edmunds Abbey was the sole house dissolved in 1539, with the last remaining dissolutions occurring in February 1540.

The dissolution of the monasteries was a process of reform, but it was emphatically not a harbinger of the arrival of Protestantism in England. The religious justification for dissolution was not new; episcopal visitations throughout the fifteenth century denounced small religious houses that were barely able to support themselves as a potential source of scandal to the church. Bishops routinely dissolved unsustainable religious houses in the late Middle Ages, either uniting them with larger houses or applying their revenues to the foundation of colleges. The popularity of the writings of Erasmus among the Christian humanist clerical elite made dissolution even more likely. Erasmus was suspicious of 'superstitious' pilgrimages and veneration of relics and extolled the virtues of education, and bishops of a reforming bent were unsympathetic to institutions whose sole purpose was singing the office and attracting pilgrims to dubious saints' cults. These bishops, like Erasmus himself, were scrupulously orthodox Catholics.[2] The Erasmian agenda of expunging superstition played a key role in Henry VIII's justification for the suppression of the monasteries,[3] although Henry's agenda clearly evolved during the process of dissolution, and it is difficult to discern anything other than financial motives by the end.

Although the dissolution of the monasteries in the 1530s was not unprecedented, therefore, the manner in which it proceeded was. Although most monasteries in the fifteenth and sixteenth centuries were suppressed under episcopal or legatine authority, the suppression of monasteries by parliamentary statute had occurred at the time of the dissolution of cells of foreign houses during the Hundred Years War. However, during the suppression of the so-called 'alien priories' the crown's appropriation of monastic income had only been temporary; the idea that the crown might permanently appropriate

2   E. Duffy, *Saints, Sacrilege and Sedition: Religion and Conflict in the Tudor Reformations* (London: Bloomsbury, 2012), pp. 135–6.

3   M. V. Heale, 'Training in superstition? Monasteries and popular religion in late medieval and Reformation England', *Journal of Ecclesiastical History* 58 (2007), pp. 417–39, at pp. 420–2.

Table 3 Suffolk monasteries dissolved 1525–40

Monastery	Order	Dissolved	Value at dissolution	Last head of house
Dodnash	OSA	1 Feb 1525	£44 18s 8½d	Thomas
Snape	OSB	1 Feb 1525	£99 1s 11½d	Richard Parker
Ipswich St Peter and St Paul	OSA	May 1528	–	William Brown
Walton	OSB	9 Sep 1528	£33 9s 10½d	–
Rumburgh	OSB	March 1529	–	John Halton
Bungay	OSB	Abandoned before dissolution (April 1536)	£61 11s 9¼d	Cecilia Falstolf
Campsey	OSA	1536	£182 9s 5d	Elizabeth Buttry
Ipswich Greyfriars	OFM Conv. Conv.	Unknown (1536?)	–	–
Leiston	O.Praem.	1536	£181 17s 1¾d	George Carleton
Sibton	O.Cist.	Alienated before dissolution (1536)	£250 15s 7½d	William Flatbury
Herringfleet	OSA	3 Feb 1537	£49 11s 7d	William Dale
Flixton	OSA	4 Feb 1537	£23 4s ½d	Elizabeth Wright
Letheringham	OSA	7 Feb 1537	£26 18s 5d	William Basse
Ipswich Holy Trinity	OSA	9 Feb 1537	£82 6s 9d	John Thetford
Redlingfield	OSB	10 Feb 1537	£81 2s 5½d	Grace Sampson
Blythburgh	OSA	12 Feb 1537	£48 8s 10d	John Righton
Eye	OSB	12 Feb 1537	£161 2s 3¼d	William Parker
Ixworth	OSA	Feb 1537	£204 9s 5¼d	William Blome
Woodbridge	OSA	Feb 1537	£50 3s 5½d	Henry Bassingbourne
Mendham	Cluniac	1537	–	Thomas
Butley	OSA	1 Mar 1538	£218 17s 2¼d	Thomas Manning
Clare Austin friars	OESA	29 Nov 1538	–	John Halybread
Dunwich Blackfriars	OP	Nov 1538	–	–
Dunwich Greyfriars	OFM Conv.	Nov 1538	–	–
Ipswich Blackfriars	OP	Nov 1538	–	Edmund
Ipswich Whitefriars	O.Carm.	Nov 1538	–	–
Babwell Greyfriars	OFM Conv.	Dec 1538	–	Peter Brinckley
Hoxne	OSB	Alienated before dissolution (1538)	£18 1s 0d	William Castleton
Sudbury Blackfriars	OP	1538	–	John Hodgkin
St Edmunds	OSB	4 Nov 1539	£1,656 7s 3½d	John Reeve
Wangford	Cluniac	16 Feb 1540	£30 9s 5d	John
Bruisyard	OSC	17 Feb 1540	—	Mary Page
Battisford	Kts Hospitaller	1540	£52 16s 2d	Giles Rusel

monastic lands and income, rather than transferring monastic assets to new pious uses, was a new one in the 1530s. Furthermore, while the dissolution of the lesser religious houses was justified in terms familiar from the late Middle Ages, the dissolution of great royal foundations like St Edmunds Abbey was a radical act that profoundly changed the relationship between the monarchy and the church.

Dangerous ideas

Although the doctrinal debates of the Reformation cannot be blamed for the dissolution of the monasteries, the new ideas nevertheless had an impact on Suffolk's religious houses. The ideas of Martin Luther reached Bury St Edmunds as early the 1520s, when the Lutheran convert Robert Barnes visited the monastic library and managed to recruit two monks, Edward Rougham and Richard Bayfield, then the abbey's chamberlain. Although Rougham would later turn against Lutheranism, Bayfield was convinced by the new ideas. A few years later, Abbot John Reeve found Bayfield out and he was imprisoned until Rougham persuaded the abbot to release him; Bayfield then fled to the Continent, and on his return he was tried, convicted and burned as a relapsed heretic and fugitive monk.[4] Another Bury monk, John Salisbury (1501/2–73), was also imprisoned for holding Lutheran views in the 1520s, but survived to be appointed bishop of Sodor and Man under Elizabeth I.[5]

No monastic community in Suffolk was more strongly influenced by the new ideas than the Augustinian priory at Clare. It is unclear whether the popularity of Lutheranism among English Augustinian friars had anything to do with the fact that Luther himself had belonged to this order; it is more likely that Augustinian interest in doctrinal reform arose from the friars' careful study of the works of St Augustine, whom Luther generally held in high regard. In May 1528 a layman, Thomas Hensted testified before the bishop of London that three friars of Clare (John Wygger, Thomas Topley and William Gardiner) all held a memorialist view of the eucharist, believing that the consecration of the elements of bread and wine was a mere commemoration and did not result in a substantial change (it should be noted that this was a doctrinal position associated with Lollardy rather than Lutheranism). The friars also denied the efficacy of pilgrimage, and another friar, Robert Topley, had run away from the friary and was roaming Essex preaching against the veneration of images and auricular confession. By the late 1520s, over a quarter of the friars at Clare were said to be Lutherans, although it might be excessive to describe Clare as 'little better than a Lutheran "cell"'.[6] On the other hand, the last pre-Reformation prior of Clare, John Halybread, was sent to preach against Thomas Bilney and the dean of Stoke College, Matthew Parker (Elizabeth I's future archbishop of Canterbury).[7]

Clare was not the only Suffolk friary where reformist ideas were in circulation. The Dominican friar John Hodgkin (d. 1560), who taught theology at Sudbury Blackfriars, was elected prior provincial of the English Dominicans in 1527, and lived in a house west of the priory church in Sudbury between 1530 and 1536, when he was deposed as

---

4   Young (2016a), pp. 120–1.
5   I. Atherton, 'Salisbury, John', *ODNB*, doi.org/10.1093/ref:odnb/24538, accessed 28 July 2019.

Figure 25 Remains of the cloister at Clare Priory

provincial. As a vocal supporter of the royal supremacy, in 1536 Hodgkin was consecrated suffragan bishop of Bedford. Hodgkin married and participated in the consecration of bishops in Edward VI's reign, although he later repudiated his wife in the reign of Mary I.[8] Hodgkin was not the only former religious from Suffolk to be elevated to the episcopacy; in March 1536 Thomas Manning, the prior of Butley, was nominated by the bishop of Norwich as his suffragan and consecrated bishop of Ipswich; George Carleton, abbot of Leiston, was also nominated to the episcopate but never consecrated. The appointment did not, however, prevent the dissolution of Butley Priory, and in 1538 Manning was deprived of his suffragan bishopric and appointed warden of Mettingham College.[9]

The most prominent of all former Suffolk religious in the ranks of the new reformed church was the controversialist John Bale (1495–1563). Bale was a native of Suffolk, having been born in the coastal village of Covehithe, and he entered the Carmelite order at Norwich when he was only 12 years old. Bale studied at Cambridge, Louvain and Toulouse and served as prior of the Carmelite houses at Maldon, Ipswich and Doncaster. Although Bale served as prior of Ipswich for less than a year, he came under the influence of a key figure in Reformation Suffolk, Lord Wentworth, who converted him to Protestantism. By 1536 Bale had renounced his Carmelite habit and taken a wife. He would subsequently become the most vociferous and vituperative controversialist of the early

6   G. Baskerville, 'Married clergy and pensioned religious in Norwich Diocese, 1555 (continued)', *English Historical Review* 48:190 (April 1933), pp. 199–228, at p. 209.

7   Harper-Bill (1991), p. 17. On this incident see G. R. Elton, *Policy and Police: The Enforcement of the Reformation in the Age of Thomas Cromwell* (Cambridge: Cambridge University Press, 1972), pp. 139–41.

8   *VCH Suffolk*, p. 134; A. A. Chibi, 'Hodgkin, John', *ODNB*, doi.org/10.1093/ref:odnb/47308, accessed 28 July 2019.

9   *VCH Suffolk*, p. 98.

English Reformation, and was appointed bishop of Ossory in Ireland during the reign of Edward VI.[10] In spite of his full-throated support for reform and implacable opposition to monasticism, Bale recognised the learning of the friars and emphatically opposed the destruction of monastic libraries, writing that:

> To destroy all without consideration, is and will be unto England forever, a most horrible infamy among the grave seniors of other nations. A great number of them which purchased those superstitious mansions [i.e. monasteries], reserved of those library books, some to serve their jakes, some to scour their candlesticks, and some to rub their boots. Some they sold to the grocers and soap sellers, and some they sent over sea to the bookbinders, not in small number, but at times whole ships full, to the wondering of the foreign nations.[11]

Bale was not alone in seeking to preserve what he considered good in the legacy of the monasteries. The royal librarian John Leland, who subscribed to elite Erasmian scepticism about the utility of monasteries, nevertheless made strenuous efforts to save what remained of the library of St Edmunds Abbey both before and after the dissolution.[12] However, in the 1530s monasteries were threatened not only by officials of the crown but also by a popular trend towards iconoclasm that may have been, at least in part, a revival of long-suppressed Lollard hostility to orthodox Catholicism. The 1531 execution of the preacher Thomas Bilney, who denounced pilgrimages, relics and the veneration of saints (but otherwise remained an orthodox Catholic), was followed by a wave of iconoclastic violence in Suffolk and Essex. In 1532 a group of Eye shoemakers threatened to burn the great rood in Eye Priory church, although no monastery was actually attacked.[13] In 1538 an ex-monk of Eye was burned for heresy at Norwich for denouncing an image carried in processions at Eye and for advocating communion under both kinds (the administration of both host and chalice to the laity) – a reminder of the rigorous doctrinal orthodoxy of the Henrician regime.[14]

Wolsey's dissolution

Cardinal Thomas Wolsey, who was born in Ipswich in 1473, had little to do with his home county during his meteoric rise to power in church and state. However, Wolsey's plan to found a splendid new college in Ipswich brought him back to Suffolk on a progress in 1517, and with the help of his assistant Thomas Cromwell he soon began to identify religious houses in East Anglia whose revenues might be redirected to support Cardinal College and its sister foundation in Oxford. Since the college was to be in Ipswich, and colleges were generally endowed with lands in their vicinity, it made sense to fund it by suppressing Suffolk houses; in doing this, Wolsey was simply following the pattern set in the fifteenth

---

10   J. N. King, 'Bale, John', *ODNB*, doi.org/10.1093/ref:odnb/1175, accessed 28 July 2019.
11   Quoted in Middleton-Stewart (1994), p. 159 (spelling modernised).
12   Young (2016a), pp. 129, 151–3.
13   MacCulloch (1986), p. 155.
14   Baskerville (1933), p. 209.

Figure 26 Gateway to
Cardinal's College, Ipswich,
on the site of the former
Priory of St Peter and St Paul

century by the suppression
of Creeting St Mary, Great
Bricett and Kersey to endow
Eton and King's colleges.
However, the cardinal's
grandiose plans made him
many enemies in Suffolk;
for the chronicler of Butley
Priory, Wolsey's suppres-
sions were 'to the shame,
scandal, destruction and
ruin of all the monks and
nuns of England'.[15]

Dodnash Priory, surren-
dered on 1 February 1525,
was the first religious house
in Suffolk dissolved as part
of Wolsey's campaign.[16]
Snape Priory was dissolved
on the same day. Snape
had been struggling to be a
sustainable religious house
for well over a century,
although by 1520 it seems
to have largely recovered financially, but remained tiny. When they were expelled by Dr
John Allen, there were only two monks and a prior.[17] Snape's detailed dissolution survey
survives, giving a detailed breakdown of the possessions of a small religious house.[18]

The religious house central to Wolsey's plan was the Priory of St Peter and St Paul in
Ipswich, since Wolsey planned to use its site for his Cardinal College. Wolsey obtained a
separate papal bull dissolving St Peter and St Paul in May 1528.[19] He managed to bungle
the dissolution of the small Benedictine priory of Walton in Felixstowe. The decision was
announced to the monks on 9 September 1528 by Stephen Gardiner, then archdeacon of
Worcester, serving as the cardinal's commissary (later, as bishop of Winchester, Gardiner

---

15 MacCulloch (1986), p. 151.
16 *VCH Suffolk*, p. 100.
17 Filmer-Sankey (1983), p. 213.
18 Filmer-Sankey (1983), pp. 213–19.
19 *VCH Suffolk*, p. 103. See also N. F. Layard, 'Remarks on Wolsey's College and the Priory of St.
    Peter and St. Paul, Ipswich', *Archaeological Journal* 56:1 (1899), pp. 211–15.

would be a key figure in the Tudor state). However, since the duke of Norfolk claimed to be the priory's founder by descent, Wolsey was forced to obtain a grant of the monastery from the duke in early 1529, after the monks had already been expelled.[20]

The sensitivities surrounding the dissolution of Walton Priory are a reminder that monasteries were a source of ancestral pride to the families who regarded themselves as their founders; any dissolution, therefore, had to be carefully negotiated with local magnates if it was not to alienate them. When it came to the major dissolutions in the period 1536–40, the acquiescence of the gentry and nobility was bought by the crown's willingness to re-grant monastic land to the landowning class. Similarly controversial was Wolsey's dissolution of Rumburgh Priory, the ancient Anglo-Saxon monastery that became a daughter house of St Mary's, York in the twelfth century. Abbot Whalley of St Mary's offered Wolsey 300 marks if Rumburgh could be saved,[21] but Wolsey was immoveable. However, Wolsey's fall meant that houses earmarked for dissolution, such as Blythburgh and Flixton,[22] received a reprieve.

The dissolution of the lesser religious houses, 1535–7

With the enactment of the Act of Supremacy in 1534, those heads of religious houses who were willing to subscribe to the royal supremacy (as most were) separated their monasteries from any allegiance to Rome. This had the effect of removing automatically any spiritual privileges conferred on any monastery by the papacy. Even before Henry VIII moved to dissolve the monasteries, therefore, the supremacy greatly weakened them as institutions – especially those which, like St Edmunds Abbey, were directly dependent on the Holy See.[23] The removal of Roman authority made it possible for Henry, as Supreme Head of the Church of England, to appoint Thomas Cromwell as his vicar general in spirituals. Cromwell's lay commissioners accordingly conducted a visitation of all the monasteries in England in 1535–6, compiling the *Valor Ecclesiasticus* (a valuation of their incomes) and seeking out – some might say fabricating – evidence of monastic vice. The *Valor* was presented to Parliament in February 1536, which shortly afterwards approved a bill for the suppression of all monasteries with an income of less than £200 a year.[24] The first act of suppression declared that

> … it is and shall be much more to the pleasure of Almighty God and for the honour of this his realm that the possessions of such spiritual religious houses, now being spent, spoiled and wasted for increase and maintenance of sin, should be used and converted to better uses, and the unthrifty religious persons so spending the same to be compelled to reform their lives.[25]

20 *VCH Suffolk*, pp, 80–1; MacCulloch (1986), p. 151.
21 MacCulloch (1986), p. 151; Heale (2001), p. 15.
22 *VCH Suffolk*, pp. 93, 116.
23 Young (2016a), p. 123.
24 On the visitation and dissolution of the lesser religious houses see C. W. Bernard, *The King's Reformation: Henry VIII and the Remaking of the English Church* (New Haven, Conn.: Yale, 2005), pp. 243–7, 433–52.
25 J. R. Tanner (ed.), *Tudor Constitutional Documents AD 1485–1603 with Historical Commentary* (Cambridge: Cambridge University Press, 1930), p. 60.

Figure 27 Broken sedilia in the choir at Leiston Abbey

Before the end of 1536 four Suffolk monasteries would be gone: Bungay, Campsey, Leiston and Sibton. The nuns of Bungay anticipated the dissolution by abandoning their house, so that the duke of Norfolk 'as founder, lawfully entered thereunto'.[26] Nothing is known of the dissolution of Campsey Priory beyond the inventory drawn up by the commissioners.[27] The dissolution was particularly devastating for religious women, since unlike religious men (most of whom were priests), they had no place and no means of sustenance in a post-monastic world. The dissolution thus removed the only economic alternative to marriage for most women.[28]

The commissioners arrived at Leiston Abbey on 21 August 1536 and assessed the value of the abbey's goods at £42 16s 3d; the value of vestments and ornaments was significantly exceeded by the abbey's cattle and corn. Abbot George Carleton was granted a pension of £20, but the other canons received nothing; at this early stage of the dissolution, it was expected that religious would join a larger monastery of their order whose income exceeded £200.[29] Sibton Abbey was never dissolved because its last abbot, William Flatbury, connived in the demise of the monastery as a client of the duke of Norfolk. Keen to secure a non-resident incumbency, Flatbury hastened the end of his house by granting it to Thomas, duke of Norfolk, Antony Rous and Nicholas Hare before he was required to surrender to the crown; according to the *Valor*, Sibton's income exceeded £250 and the house should not, therefore, have been dissolved until 1539.[30]

26 *VCH Suffolk*, p. 82.

27 F. Haslewood, 'Inventories of monasteries suppressed in 1536', *PSIAH* 8:1 (1892), pp. 83–116, at pp. 113–16; *VCH Suffolk*, pp. 114–15.

28 B. J. Harris, 'A new look at the Reformation: aristocratic women and nunneries, 1450–1540', *Journal of British Studies* 32:2 (1993), pp. 89–113, at p. 90.

29 Haslewood (1892), pp. 10; L. Brown *Three Worlds, One Word: Account of a Mission* (London: Collings, 1981), p. 1.

30 *VCH Suffolk*, p. 90; Brown (1981), p. 1.

The dissolution picked up pace early in 1537, and no fewer than nine Suffolk houses were dissolved in the month of February alone, most of them Augustinian: Herringfleet,[31] Flixton,[32] Letheringham,[33] Ipswich Holy Trinity,[34] Redlingfield,[35] Blythburgh,[36] Eye,[37] Ixworth[38] and Woodbridge.[39] Blythburgh Priory, as a cell of St Osyth's Priory, did not technically fall under the terms of the Act of Suppression, but it was dissolved anyway – presumably because the mother house made no protest.[40] There was no provision for pensions for anyone other than the head of house under the Act of Suppression, although the nuns of Redlingfield each received a one-off sum of 23s 4d. The commissioners found little of worth in these monasteries, although Eye yielded a number of relics: an arm of St Blaise, the rib of an unidentified saint, and the famous 'Red Book of Eye', which was supposedly the Gospel book of St Felix from Dunwich. We receive a glimpse of the personal cost of these dissolutions to the ejected religious in the fate of the last prior of Woodbridge, Henry Bassingbourne. Bassingbourne secured the position of rector of Wyck Rissington in Gloucestershire but, according to his parishioners in 1548, he failed to celebrate divine service and sat all day in the local alehouse.[41]

Although its income exceeded £200 a year, Butley Priory was dissolved on 1 March 1538. The last prior, Thomas Manning, who had also been suffragan bishop of Ipswich since 1536, made several attempts to bribe and grovel his way out of dissolution, even asserting at one point that 'with the King's favour I would never resign [the priorship]'.[42] It fell to the grantee of the dissolved monastery, the duke of Suffolk, to provide pensions for the ejected canons; the duke was initially reluctant to take on Butley on the grounds that the pensions might exceed the value of the site, but he eventually agreed to do so. In addition to the priory, the free school attached to the monastery was closed as a result of the dissolution.[43]

The dissolution of the friaries, 1538

While it was possible for the government to justify the dissolution of religious houses with an income under £200 a year as the pruning of unsustainable communities, the dissolution of the friaries was quite obviously the suppression of vibrant and successful monastic houses. The dissolution of the friaries must have made it clear to all that the government would leave no religious house undissolved. The friars were the object of particular

---

31   Haslewood (1892), pp. 85–7 (inventory); *VCH Suffolk*, p. 101.
32   Haselwood (1892), pp. 88–90 (inventory); *VCH Suffolk*, pp. 116–17.
33   Haslewood (1892), p. 101 (inventory); *VCH Suffolk*, p. 108.
34   Haslewood (1892), pp. 91–4 (inventory); *VCH Suffolk*, p. 104.
35   Haslewood (1892), pp. 95–8 (inventory); *VCH Suffolk*, p. 84.
36   Haslewood (1892), pp. 99–100 (inventory); *VCH Suffolk*, p. 93.
37   Haslewood (1892), pp. 105–8 (inventory); *VCH Suffolk*, p. 75.
38   Haslewood (1892), pp. 109–12 (inventory); *VCH Suffolk*, p. 106.
39   *VCH Suffolk*, p. 111.
40   Harper-Bill (1980), p. 4.
41   Harrison (2000), p. 29.
42   Myres (1933), pp. 210–11.
43   Harrison (2000), pp. 27–31.

hostility from the government. Unlike Benedictines and Augustinians, mendicant friars were part of orders with an international organisational structure. Friars in England often had close links with foreign friaries and with Rome, and in spite of their subscription to the royal supremacy, friars were sometimes seen as ongoing agents of Roman authority in England. Rather than being entrusted to Thomas Cromwell's usual lay commissioners the suppression of friaries was a specialist task handled by Richard Yngworth, suffragan bishop of Dover, who was himself an ex-Dominican friar.

Yngworth arrived in Suffolk in November 1538 or earlier, reporting the dissolution of both the Franciscan and Dominican houses in Dunwich. Conveniently, because the Dunwich houses lay so close to the sea, Yngworth reported that it would be easy for the lead stripped from the friaries to be taken away by ship for the king's use.[44] Yngworth also managed to dissolve Ipswich's two remaining friaries (Blackfriars and Whitefriars) in November.[45] Ipswich Greyfriars had been an early target of Yngworth, dissolved perhaps as early as 1536 after its patron, Lord Wentworth, denounced it as an 'idle nest of drones' and asked to take possession of it.[46] Although the inventory of Ipswich Greyfriars from 1535 survives (the friary had no fewer than 20 service books in the choir),[47] no record of its actual dissolution survives. Similarly, although the dissolution of Sudbury Blackfriars took place in 1538 (and probably in the month of November), no exact date survives.[48]

At the end of November Yngworth moved to dissolve Clare Priory. The house was in a poor condition and so much in debt that the value of the priory's goods did not cover the debts. The priory's jewels were pledged as security to a number of people to whom the priory owed debts, and it is possible that this was a device to prevent these treasures falling into the commissioners' hands.[49] The last friary to be visited and dissolved by Yngworth was Babwell Greyfriars in Bury St Edmunds, in December 1538.[50] Dr Peter Brinckley was the warden of Babwell Greyfriars at the time of its dissolution. Brinckley seems to have joined Wingfield College after the dissolution of Babwell, since he had a pension of £5 from the dissolution of Wingfield; he was also rector of Great Moulton 1543–6 and vicar of Shottisham St Martin in 1558. He died at Earsham in 1559, having taken a wife and subsequently divorced her.[51]

The final phase of dissolution, 1539–40

At the start of the year 1539 only four religious houses remained in Suffolk: the great Benedictine abbey of Bury St Edmunds, the house of Poor Clare nuns at Bruisyard, the Cluniac Wangford Priory, and the preceptory of the Knights Hospitaller at Battisford. The commissioners had visited St Edmunds Abbey in 1535, when they produced a mocking inventory of the abbey's relics, forbade new novices, sent away all monks under the age

44   *VCH Suffolk*, p. 122.
45   *VCH Suffolk*, pp. 123, 131.
46   *VCH Suffolk*, p. 126.
47   L. J. Redstone, 'Notes on Suffolk manuscript books', *PSIAH* 20:1 (1928), pp. 80–92, at p. 81.
48   *VCH Suffolk*, p. 124.
49   *VCH Suffolk*, p. 129; Barnardiston (1962), pp. 24–5; Harper-Bill (1991), pp. 17–18.
50   *VCH Suffolk*, p. 125.
51   Baskerville (1933), p. 215.

Figure 28 Ruins of the north transept, St Edmunds Abbey

of 24, and confined the monks to the monastic precincts. The commissioners were back in 1538, this time to strip the shrine of St Edmund itself.[52] However, the commissioners were powerless actually to dissolve the abbey in the absence of new legislation that tackled religious houses with an income that exceeded £200 a year.

Whereas the 1536 act for the suppression of the lesser religious houses had attempted to offer some semblance of moral justification for dissolution, the text of the 1539 act for the suppression of the greater houses simply noted that since so many heads of greater religious houses had already freely surrendered to the crown, it made sense to suppress them all.[53] This line of reasoning shows that the connivance of abbots who voluntarily surrendered their houses even before the law required them to do so – such as Abbot Flatbury of Sibton – was of immense propaganda value for the Henrician regime. These abbots set an example that others were expected to follow, or else they would be compelled to do so. St Edmunds Abbey prepared for dissolution by disposing of its splendid library to various lay recipients, and apparently by concealing the body of the eponymous St Edmund in an unknown location.[54] The surrender itself was signed by Abbot John Reeve on 4 November 1539, and the dismantling of the vast Romanesque abbey church – possibly the largest in Europe at the time – began immediately.[55]

---

52 Young (2016a), pp. 127–9.
53 Tanner (1930), pp. 64–5.
54 Young (2018), pp. 145–53.
55 Young (2016a), p. 131.

In spite of its dissolution, the shadow of St Edmunds Abbey continued to loom large in the locality. The jurisdictions created by the abbey remained: the Liberty of Bury St Edmunds (the immediate locality of the town or *banleuca*) remained judicially and ecclesiastically separate from the rest of Suffolk until the nineteenth century, while the Liberty of St Edmund (the eight-and-a-half hundreds of West Suffolk) also retained its own justices and courts. The bishop of Norwich continued to be excluded from exercising any jurisdiction over Bury, and the archdeacons of Bury St Edmunds were directly appointed by the archbishop of Canterbury. Ironically, the bishop of Norwich's inability to intervene in Bury made the town a focus of dissident Puritan activity – a state of affairs indirectly caused by St Edmunds Abbey. Local elites stepped into the vacuum left behind by the abbey, clinging onto offices created by the abbots and excluding the townsfolk from power; Bury St Edmunds did not receive a royal charter to become a corporation until 1606, and the hereditary stewards of the Liberty of St Edmund continued to contest the authority of the corporation long after that.[56]

With St Edmunds Abbey dissolved, the commissioners moved against the Knights Hospitaller in Suffolk – their preceptory at Battisford and its various subordinate chapels or 'members'.[57] When the commissioners visited in December 1539, they found that Battisford Preceptory was in possession of some service books of moderate value, and the house seems to have been in a healthy financial state.[58] The late dissolution of Wangford Priory was a technicality, since the surrender of this house was included in that of its mother house, Thetford Priory, on 16 February 1540. In reality, conventual life at Wangford probably ceased long before this; in March 1537 the duke of Norfolk had reported to Cromwell that the prior of Thetford had recalled the monks from Wangford to the mother house and let out the property to farm.[59]

Bruisyard Abbey, which was probably the very last religious house in Suffolk to be dissolved, on 17 February 1540, was a special case. Although Bruisyard should have been dissolved under the first act of suppression, Abbess Mary Page had paid £60 to the crown in 1537 in order to stave off dissolution. Abbess Page was confirmed by royal letters patent on 4 July 1537.[60] However, after the second Act of Suppression nothing could save Bruisyard. It is possible that the abbey's royal connections and popularity among the local gentry may have contributed to its special treatment.

Hints of resistance

Suffolk witnessed no major acts of resistance to the royal supremacy or the dissolution of the monasteries of the kind seen in northern England. The small size of Suffolk's monasteries, the influence over them of gentry patrons who largely supported the dissolution, and the self-interest of the heads of the religious houses themselves (whose generous pensions depended on their acquiescence) probably explain why no open resistance

---

56   Young (2016a), pp. 136–42.
57   *VCH Suffolk*, p. 121.
58   Redstone (1928), p. 81.
59   *VCH Suffolk*, p. 89.
60   *VCH Suffolk*, p. 132.

occurred. In spite of the absence of major resistance, however, there are hints of reluctance and obstruction. Early in 1538, anticipating dissolution, Prior William Castleton of Hoxne alienated the priory to Sir Richard Gresham and recalled the monks to the mother house of Norwich Cathedral Priory. In so doing he was depriving the crown of the income of dissolution and required a royal pardon on 1 April 1538.[61] Given that Castleton later became the first dean of Norwich Cathedral, it seems unlikely that his actions represented deliberate defiance; it is possible that the prior simply did not understand the process of dissolution and that he did not have the right to dispose of Hoxne Priory as he chose.

In September 1538 John Hilsey, bishop of Rochester, was at Babwell Greyfriars, whose warden had been reported for 'treasonable utterances' but now expressed remorse and offered the surrender of the house.[62] In a letter to Thomas Cromwell of 23 December 1536, Sir Thomas Russhe alluded darkly to 'matter against my lord suffragan prior of Butley [Thomas Manning, prior of Butley and bishop of Ipswich] ... for concealing treason of a canon of Butley'. Misprision of treason (knowing about a treasonous act and not reporting it) was a serious offence, but we nothing more about the unnamed treasonous canon of Butley; it is highly likely that both this canon and the warden of Babwell had denied the royal supremacy. However, Prior Manning's gift to Cromwell of two swans, six pheasants and a dozen partridges four days later may have been intended to curry favour.[63]

The last pre-Reformation prior of Clare, John Halybread (alias Stokes), although he accepted the royal supremacy, preached against Matthew Parker, dean of Stoke College, thereby violating an explicit injunction of the bishop of Norwich not to engage in controversy (although Halybread later expressed the desire to relinquish his Augustinian habit).[64] Another Augustinian friar of Clare clearly felt differently: Stephen Luskyn was the only priest known to have paid a fee of £4 for permission to continue to wear his Augustinian habit under the dress of a secular priest.[65] If not an act of resistance, this was certainly an act of nostalgia for his former monastic state.

The fate of the ex-religious

The dissolution had many social effects, including loss of local employment, the restructuring of local elites and the loss of alms for the poor. It also sent out into the world a group of men and women who no longer had a defined place in society. Ex-religious were forced to find new identities and occupations for themselves. This was easier for men than for women, and easier for younger religious than for those who had spent almost their entire lives within a monastery, but the transition must have been traumatic for all involved. The majority of male religious were also priests, so in theory they could join the parish clergy or become chantry priests. However, the chantries were abolished in 1548 and obtaining a benefice required patronage – something hard enough for the secular clergy, and even more so for ex-religious. Historians have been divided on the extent to which the former

61   *VCH Suffolk*, p. 76.
62   *VCH Suffolk*, p. 125.
63   Myres (1933), p. 210.
64   Elton (1972), p. 141.
65   Harper-Bill (1991), p. 18.

religious were harshly treated;[66] clearly some were very generously rewarded, but others seem to have been left to fend for themselves. Blackwood calculated that only 13 per cent of Suffolk's ex-religious obtained ecclesiastical preferment.

After the dissolution of the lesser religious houses, male religious did not automatically gain the right to join the secular clergy (since, in theory, they were supposed to join larger houses of their own order), and they had to obtain dispensations to assume secular garb from the archbishop of Canterbury. Such dispensations survive for William Reeve, a canon of Leiston and for William Downaby, a canon of Woodbridge.[67] It was in the interests of the acquirers of monastic land after the dissolution of the lesser houses to find benefices for ex-religious, because they were otherwise liable to pay them pensions.[68] Thus the duke of Norfolk, who acquired Sibton Abbey after the dissolution, presented the ex-abbot William Flatbury to the living of Brockdish, Peter Hutchinson to Westleton and William James to Cransford.[69]

Blackwood calculated that, of 273 ex-religious from Suffolk houses, only 57 (21 per cent) received pensions from the crown (although others may have received pensions from recipients of grants of monastic land).[70] Following the dissolution, the receiver of the Court of Augmentations for Norfolk and Suffolk established himself at Bury St Edmunds, which became the centre for the distribution of pensions to East Anglian ex-religious.[71] Officials working for the Court Augmentations, such as Sir Robert Southwell and Nicholas Bacon, seem to have taken advantage of their positions by enriching themselves with monastic lands.[72] It is noticeable that a large number of ex-religious who obtained livings did so in the same parishes that had formerly been in the gift of their dissolved house, which may indicate that private arrangements with new patrons of livings were reached before the dissolution.[73] Some ex-religious used inventive means to obtain livings: Thomas Cole, an ex-monk of Bury, obtained the rectory of Flempton by legally reassigning his pension to Ambrose Jermyn, on condition that Jermyn persuaded the patron of the living (Thomas Lucas of Little Saxham) to nominate Cole – which he did on 15 November 1541.[74]

The group of ex-religious who did best out of the dissolution were the 44 monks of St Edmunds, all of whom received pensions from the crown (usually £6 13s 4d) because the abbey was dissolved under the second Act of Suppression (and was also a royal foundation).[75] Of those Bury monks whose subsequent careers we know, eight retired and 20 obtained a position in the church as secular clergy. Eight monks entered secular employment.[76] Those ex-monks who obtained ecclesiastical livings often had a long wait; some

66 Blackwood (2001), pp. 81–2.
67 Baskerville (1933), p. 202.
68 Baskerville (1933), p. 203.
69 Baskerville (1933), p. 203 n.2.
70 Blackwood (2001), pp. 82, 309–10.
71 Baskerville (1933), p. 204 n.2.
72 Blackwood (2001), p. 87.
73 Baskerville (1933), p. 206.
74 Baskerville (1933), p. 199 n.4.
75 Blackwood (2001), pp. 210–11.
76 Blackwood (2001), pp. 310–11.

did not achieve this until the 1550s. A few monks went into teaching, some into law, and one was a humble weaver in the 1550s.[77] Another ex-monk of Bury, William Blomfield, became an alchemist and was allegedly dabbling in necromancy in the 1540s; magic was sometimes a last resort for former religious.[78]

Former religious women faced particular challenges in the post-dissolution world. Unless they received a pension or their families were prepared to support them, marriage was virtually their only option. However, former female religious were forbidden from marrying until 1549.[79] No evidence survives of female ex-religious from Suffolk houses marrying, but it is likely that at least some did. Only the heads of house received official pensions. Elizabeth Wright, the last prioress of Flixton, died at Bramfield, Suffolk on 23 November 1549; Ela Buttry, the last prioress of Campsey, died in the parish of St Stephen, Norwich, on 27 October 1546; Cecilia Falstoff, the last prioress of Bungay (whose pension was paid by the duke of Norfolk) died at Nawton, Norfolk, on 12 May 1552; and Grace Sampson, the last prioress of Redlingfield, was still alive in 1556.[80] These women's wills suggest that they were not wealthy at the time of their deaths: Grace Sampson left everything to the Bedingfield family who owned the site of her former priory of Redlingfield.[81] The prioress of Campsey received the extraordinarily generous pension of £23 a year, second only to the abbot of St Edmunds,[82] but other religious women were forced to make their own way. Two former Campsey canonesses, Isabella Norwich and Bridget Cocket, set up a school together in Dunwich. The nuns of Bruisyard were more fortunate; in his will of 1557 Nicholas Hare, who had purchased Bruisyard after the dissolution, required his wife to support four ex-nuns.[83] Since the Hare family became recusants after the accession of Elizabeth, this injunction was presumably honoured.

The fate of monastic sites

Legally, all the land and property of monasteries dissolved under the first and second acts of suppression went to the crown – but, as we have seen, some monastic sites were alienated to or seized by their 'founders' before they could actually be formally dissolved, so these houses were never in the hands of the crown. The government was chiefly interested in any valuable materials that could be salvaged from the dissolved houses: precious stones and metals that were part of reliquaries and others treasures, the vast quantity of lead used to roof monastic buildings, and the high-quality freestone from which the monasteries were sometimes built. Monastic sites, monastic lands and monastic spiritualities (impropriated parishes and rights of presentation to benefices) were soon bestowed by the crown on the nobility and gentry in a vast exercise of patronage distribution.

---

77   Blackwood (2001), p. 82.

78   F. Young, 'The dissolution of the monasteries and the democratisation of magic in post-Reformation England', *Religions* 10:4, 241 (2019), doi.org/10.3390/rel10040241, accessed 2 August 2019.

79   Blackwood (2001), p. 83.

80   Baskerville (1933), p. 205.

81   Gilchrist and Oliva (1993), p. 49.

82   Blackwood (2001), p. 82.

83   Blackwood (2001), p. 83.

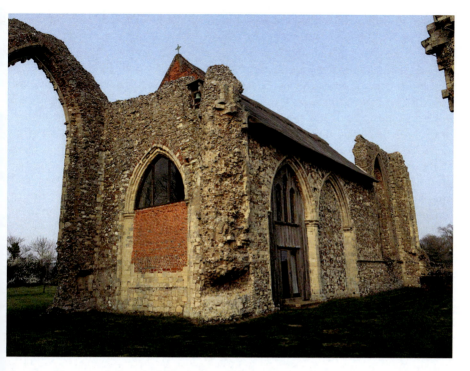

Figure 29 The re-roofed north aisle at Leiston Abbey

Perhaps the most systematic post-dissolution destruction took place at Bury St Edmunds, where stone was stripped from the abbey so effectively that only the rubble cores of walls were left. Although it is possible that some of this stone was taken by the townsfolk once the commissioners were finished, most of it went to help build Henry VIII's fortifications.[84] However, demolishing a building in order to sell its materials was labour-intensive and expensive, and often exceeded the value of the building itself; it seems most likely that most monastic churches (which were not also parish churches) were simply abandoned and allowed to fall into ruin. The residences of heads of religious houses, on the other hand, were often converted directly into secular dwellings. Similarly, monastic domestic and farm buildings often continued in use but structures like cloisters that now served no use went to ruin. In later years many converted dwellings of heads of religious houses fell into ruin too, as they were deemed too small or unfashionable in style; some dwindled into mere farmhouses.

Blackwood has exhaustively analysed the social make-up of the recipients of grants of monastic land in Suffolk.[85] The greatest single recipients were the dukes of Norfolk and Suffolk, receiving 16 and 15 monastic manors respectively. Between them, royal officials

---

84   Young (2016a), p. 131.
85   Blackwood (2001), pp. 310–17

obtained 25 manors while the local gentry obtained 42. London merchants purchased 11 manors.[86] Blackwood cautions against viewing the dissolution as the key factor in the rise of the gentry in Tudor Suffolk, since only 31 of the county's 166 gentry families made some purchase of monastic property.[87] While the crown could have let some of the confiscated monastic property, Henry's desperate need for ready money meant that most properties were sold outright at 20 years' purchase (meaning the buyer paid 20 times the property's annual value). Thus when Sir Edmund Bedingfield bought Redlingfield Priory for £561 19s 0d he paid almost exactly 20 times the priory's annual value according to the 1535 *Valor Ecclesiasticus*.[88]

The church obtained little monastic land, with the dean and chapter of Ely's acquisition of the manor of Lakenheath from St Edmunds being one of the few examples.[89] One of the most prolific purchasers of monastic lands was Sir Thomas Kytson the elder, a London mercer who had bought the manor of Hengrave in 1522 and built a magnificent house there. Kytson assisted in the dissolution of Ixworth Priory, some of whose stone was supposedly used to face Hengrave Hall, which was completed in 1538. In 1540 Kytson purchased eight monastic manors for the sum of £3,710;[90] ironically, the house he built was itself destined to become a religious house later in its history.

Conclusion

In Suffolk, the dissolution occurred in four stages: Cardinal Wolsey's dissolution of small religious houses in 1525–8; the dissolution of the lesser religious houses in 1536–7; the dissolution of the friaries in 1537–8; and the final dissolution of St Edmunds Abbey and some monastic outliers in 1539–40. The dissolution of the monasteries was, without doubt, the most destructive event in the history of the East Anglian church since the Viking invasions of the ninth century. It resulted in the greatest redistribution of property since the Norman Conquest and triggered significant social changes, as well as removing the purpose of a whole class of people.

The completeness of the dissolution of the 1530s was new, shocking and transformative. However, the idea of dissolution was not new, and this may have contributed to the complacency of some heads of monastic houses who naively thought they might buy or bribe their way out of suppression. Although the tragedy of the dissolution is often framed in terms of the ruination of monastic buildings – Shakespeare's 'bare ruined choirs' – there was little deliberate and direct destruction. Most buildings just fell into ruin since they could not be converted to domestic use. The true loss was arguably not architectural, but human and intellectual. The dissolution broke up communities of men and women which, in some cases, had existed with a corporate identity for over 500 years. The dissolution was, above all, a loss of memory and a turning away from the past, symbolised most of all in the breaking-up of monastic libraries containing books as old as the apparently

---

86   Blackwood (2001), p. 85.
87   Blackwood (2001), p. 89.
88   Blackwood (2001), p. 84.
89   Blackwood (2001), p. 85.
90   Blackwood (2001), p. 86.

seventh-century 'Red Book of Eye'. The losses inflicted by the dissolution of the monasteries on England's cultural memory are both incalculable and irrecoverable.

Yet the monasteries also left behind traces that were hard to eradicate, and not only in the form of monumental ruins in the landscape. The lingering survival of some monastic institutions, such as St Peter's Hospital in Bury St Edmunds and St Bartholomew's chapel in Sudbury, Ipswich's dependency on plumbing left behind by the Priory of St Peter and St Paul, and the various jurisdictional anomalies created by the Abbey of St Edmund in West Suffolk made it impossible to forget the monastic legacy entirely. Even the smaller monasteries left ghostly traces in the form of clusters of spiritualities inherited by the acquirers of monastic lands and their descendants; until the nineteenth century, and even beyond, the old territories of the monasteries could be traced by the pattern of impropriated parishes, especially in eastern Suffolk. The monasteries were also more actively remembered, a theme that will be considered in the next chapter.

Chapter 5

Modern monasticism in Suffolk

English monasticism did not come to an end with the dissolution of the monasteries – although it came very close indeed to extinction. Only a handful of monasteries were revived in the reign of Mary I (1553–8), when Catholicism was restored, although none of them were in Suffolk. Not restoring monastic lands to the church was the most significant compromise Mary and the papacy made with the Henrician Reformation, since expropriating the acquirers of monastic lands would surely have unleashed rebellion against the crown. However, it is possible that at least one Bury monk became a monk of the revived Benedictine foundation of Westminster Abbey,[1] and Edward Rougham, an ex-monk and former sacrist of St Edmunds Abbey, was appointed archdeacon of Bury St Edmunds in 1555, exercising exactly the same spiritual jurisdiction over the town of Bury as he had as sacrist.[2] The few re-founded monasteries were dissolved once again in 1559 following the accession of Elizabeth, but Mary's brief revival had given English monasticism the impetus it needed to regroup and survive in exile.

The strength of recusant Catholicism among the Suffolk gentry in the sixteenth, seventeenth and eighteenth centuries meant that a steady stream of Suffolk-born men and women travelled to monasteries on the Continent to train as religious, while some Catholic families employed monastic chaplains. At the end of the eighteenth century an important community of Augustinian canonesses took refuge in Suffolk from the French Revolution, and in the nineteenth century an abbey of Benedictine nuns was established at East Bergholt; the county also witnessed the arrival of several congregations of religious women in the second half of the nineteenth century, as well as a pioneering experiment in Anglican monasticism at Claydon. Since the dissolution of the monasteries five of the religious orders present in medieval Suffolk (Benedictines, Dominicans, Franciscans, Augustinian canonesses and Augustinian friars) have returned to the county at one time or another. Most remarkably of all, in 1953 Clare Priory was re-founded as the mother house of the Augustinian friars in England and Scotland. To date, Clare Priory remains the only one of Suffolk's medieval monastic houses to be re-established on its original site.

Suffolk's Catholic families continued to provide men and women to the English exiled monastic houses on the Continent throughout the seventeenth and eighteenth centuries. While 19 Suffolk-born men joined monastic religious orders, the number of Suffolk-born women to enter the religious life was much higher: 86 women joined convents in exile (see Appendix 2). Although we have no figures for the number of women who joined the priories of Campsey Ash, Flixton, Redlingfield and Bungay in the Middle Ages, given the small size of those houses it seems unlikely that the number of women from Suffolk

---

1   Young (2016a), p. 142.
2   Young (2016a), p. 141.

entering the religious life fell very much in the post-Reformation period. It is also note-worthy that the religious women of post-Reformation Suffolk came from a small number of gentry families, two of whom acquired the lands of female monasteries at the dissolution: the Bedingfield family of Redlingfield, who acquired Redlingfield Priory, supplied 18 vocations, and the Tasburgh family of Flixton, who acquired Flixton Priory, supplied three.

Some of these religious women achieved prominence. Frances Bedingfield (1616–1704) joined Mary Ward's Companions of Jesus and founded the Bar Convent in York in 1686, which is still functioning to this day.[3] Trevor Warner of Parham, who became a Carmelite nun, became famous through a biography by Edward Scarisbrick published in 1691.[4] Likewise, Catherine Burton (1668–1714), a Carmelite nun from Beyton, was the subject of a widely disseminated spiritual biography by Thomas Hunter.[5] Books like these ensured that the absence of actual monastic communities from Suffolk during the era of penal laws against Catholics did nothing to lessen the interest of Suffolk's Catholic women in the religious life.

Remembering monasticism

When William Camden visited Bury St Edmunds in the 1580s he viewed the 'carcasse ... of that auncient monument', which was now 'altogether deformed'. Camden complained of the 'goodlie pretense of reforming religion' that led to the dissolution. Nevertheless, Camden was impressed: 'I assure you [the ruins] make a faire and goodlie shew, which who soever beholdeth, hee may both wonder there at, and withall take pity thereof'.[6] Harriet Lyon has argued that Camden 'combined elements of an older critique of the avarice of the Henrician regime with a new sense of aesthetic outrage and material loss'.[7]

The dissolution of St Olave's Priory, Herringfleet is a good example of a suppression that made vanishingly little difference to its locality. A little over a year after its dissolution St Olave's was vested in Sir Henry Jerningham, whose family had controlled the priory and whose ancestors were buried there.[8] In Elizabeth's reign the recusant Jerningham family would turn Lothingland (the remote corner of north-east Suffolk where St Olave's was located) into a Catholic stronghold, and in 1572 Sir Henry arranged in his will for the re-foundation of St Olave's Priory as an almshouse and the restoration of the priory church, although his wishes were never carried out.[9]

---

3   F. Young, 'Appendix 1: Notable East Anglian Catholics' in F. Young (ed.), *Catholic East Anglia: A History of the Catholic Faith in Norfolk, Suffolk, Cambridgeshire and Peterborough* (Leominster: Gracewing, 2016b), pp. 221–66, at pp. 225–6.

4   [Scarisbrick, E.], *The Life of Lady Warner* (St Omer, 1691).

5   F. Young, 'An horrid popish plot': the failure of Catholic aspirations in Bury St Edmunds, 1685–88', *PSIAH* 41:2 (2006), pp. 209–25, at pp. 215–17.

6   W. Camden, *Britain,* trans. P. Holland (London, 1610), p. 461.

7   H. K. Lyon, 'The afterlives of the dissolution of the monasteries, 1536–c. 1700', PhD thesis, University of Cambridge, 2018, p. 108.

8   *VCH Suffolk,* p. 101; R. Houlbrooke, *Love and Dishonour in Elizabethan England: Two Families and a Failed Marriage* (Woodbridge: Boydell & Brewer, 2018), pp. 21, 27.

9   Houlbrooke (2018), p. 37.

St Olave's was not the only monastic property that passed, ironically, into the hands of committed Catholics. Flixton Priory passed to the Tasburgh family, who heavily incorporated architectural features from the dissolved Flixton Priory (including holy monograms in flint flushwork) into their home at St Peter's Hall.[10] Although the Tasburghs initially embraced the Reformation, they returned to Catholicism in the early seventeenth century. However, the Bedingfield family of Redlingfield, who acquired Redlingfield Priory after the dissolution, never conformed to the Church of England. They may also have continued to support the former nuns of Redlingfield, judging from the fact that Grace Sampson, the last prioress of Redlingfield, left everything to the Bedingfields in her will;[11] perhaps this was an act of gratitude. Whether the fact that so many members of the Bedingfield family of Redlingfield travelled to the Continent to enter houses of religious women was an act of conscious or unconscious reparation for the dissolution of Redlingfield Priory is something we may never know.

Some Suffolk recusants hinted that they desired or expected to see a restoration of the monasteries one day. Robert Hare of Bruisyard (c. 1530–1611), the second son of the purchaser of Bruisyard Abbey, Sir Nicholas Hare, was a noted antiquary and collector of manuscripts who inherited Bruisyard Hall from his brother Michael shortly before his own death. Robert Hare was also a Catholic recusant, and felt some anxiety about books he had acquired from dissolved monasteries; in a note in one book, acquired by Hare at the dissolution of St Augustine's, Canterbury, Hare instructed that the book should be returned 'if hereafter, by God's favour, the monastery should happen to be rebuilt' – suggesting that Hare wanted to see a restoration of the monasteries.[12] Similarly, Edward Gage of Hengrave Hall, who owned the site of St Saviour's Hospital just outside Bury St Edmunds, drew up a formal agreement with the English Benedictine Congregation in 1661 that he would return the hospital to the Benedictine Order 40 years after any restoration of the Catholic faith in England.[13]

While the restoration of the monasteries may seem far-fetched to us in hindsight, England twice came close to a Catholic restoration in the seventeenth century: in the early 1620s, when it looked as though the future Charles I would marry the Spanish infanta and introduce toleration for Catholics (or even convert to Catholicism), and in the reign of James II (1685–88) when a Catholic king did all he could to try to overturn legislation against Catholics. At the start of James's reign many people assumed there would be a restoration of Catholicism and the monasteries, including the then owner of the abbey precincts in Bury St Edmunds, who offered the property for sale to the monks of St Edmund's Priory in Paris. On the advice of James himself, who thought it would be inflammatory for the monks to reacquire the site, the monks of St Edmund's abandoned their plan.[14]

Whatever their view of the monasteries, families in possession of monastic lands were

10   Crouzet (2007), p. 8.
11   Gilchrist and Oliva (1993), p. 49.
12   E. Leedham-Green, 'Hare, Robert', *ODNB*, doi.org/10.1093/ref:odnb/12306, accessed 1 August 2019.
13   Young (2015), pp. 38–9.
14   Young (2006), p. 213.

S? SAVIOUR'S HOSPITAL.

Figure 30 St Saviour's Hospital, Bury St Edmunds. Engraving from Richard Yates, *An Illustration of the Monastic Antiquities of the Town and Abbey of St Edmund's Bury* (1843).

compelled to retain and preserve some monastic records in order to demonstrate their legitimate titles to land. Individual quires from Bury's fifteenth-century Curteys Register, which listed the manors of the abbey's cellarer in alphabetical order, were torn out and parcelled out between different landowners, and in the seventeenth century Sir Simonds D'Ewes of Stowlangtoft and Sir Thomas Eden both owned monastic registers from St Edmunds.[15]

Some families cherished monastic relics for more pious reasons. The Mannocks of Giffords Hall in Stoke-by-Nayland somehow came into possession of the pectoral cross worn by the last abbot of St John's Abbey, Colchester, Thomas Beche (alias Marshall) at his execution on 1 December 1539 for refusing to surrender his abbey. In the twentieth century, the Mannocks gave the pectoral cross to the Benedictine monks of Buckfast Abbey, Devon with the proviso that they should return it in the event of the restoration of St John's Abbey.[16] Further afield, the Tasburgh family may have been responsible for preserving one of Ireland's greatest treasures, the Cross of Cong. The Tasburghs purchased Cong Abbey in County Mayo in 1667 and thereafter placed it in a trust administered by

---

15   Young (2016a), pp. 153–4.
16   J. Ashdown-Hill, *Mediaeval Colchester's Lost Landmarks* (Derby: Breedon, 2009), p. 46.

a group of Catholics,[17] thereby making it possible for a community of Augustinian canons to survive at Cong into the nineteenth century.[18]

Monasticism and folklore

As Martin Heale has argued, the idea that once in monastic use a site should remain monastic was so deeply held in late medieval England that it aided the survival of otherwise unsustainably tiny monasteries.[19] It is unsurprising, therefore, that anxiety about the potential sacrilege of living in monastic buildings or on monastic land was hard to shake after the dissolution. In 1632 the Norfolk antiquary Sir Henry Spelman completed his *History and Fate of Sacrilege* (although it would not be published until 1698), which catalogued the misfortunes of families who acquired monastic lands in East Anglia, attributing all of them to divine displeasure at the dissolution of the monasteries. According to Spelman, Henry VIII had plunged England into an

> Ocean of Iniquity and Sacrilege, where whole thousands of Churches and Chapels dedicated to the Service of God ... together with the Monasteries and other Houses of Religion and intended Piety, were by King Henry VIII. in a temper of indignation at the Clergy of that time mingled with insatiable Avarice, sacked and rased as by an Enemy.[20]

Spelman recounted meeting one man who recounted the violent deaths suffered by the owners of one unnamed monastic property in Suffolk,[21] and the fact that only two owners of the site of St Edmunds Abbey between 1560 and 1720 managed to pass the property from father to son must have given some pause for thought.[22] The anxiety about sacrilege voiced by Spelman was not inconsistent with supporting the Reformation in and of itself; conservative Anglicans like Spelman did not advocate monasticism, but they were well aware that some secular collegiate churches and hospitals had been permitted to survive, and believed that all of the monasteries should have been converted into parochial or collegiate churches, thus keeping the buildings in the hands of the church. The sacrilege was committed not by expelling monks and nuns, but by alienating lands properly belonging to the church to profane use.[23]

---

17 F. Young, 'The Tasburghs of Bodney: Catholicism and politics in South Norfolk', *Norfolk Archaeology* 46 (2011), pp. 190–8, at pp. 192–3.

18 C. Galban, 'The regular canons in Early Modern Ireland' in M. Browne and C. Ó Clabaigh (eds), *Households of God: The Regular Canons and Canonesses of St Augustine and of Prémontré in Medieval Ireland* (Dublin: Four Courts, 2019), pp. 266–74, at pp. 268–74.

19 Heale (2004b), pp. 2–3.

20 H. Spelman, *The History and Fate of Sacrilege, discover'd by examples of scripture, of heathens, and of Christians; from the beginning of the world continually to this day* (London, 1698), pp. 182–3.

21 G. Parry, *The Trophies of Time: English Antiquarians of the Seventeenth Century* (Oxford: Oxford University Press, 1995), p. 282.

22 Young (2016a), p. 156.

23 On Spelman and sacrilege narratives see Lyon (2018), pp. 184–7.

Yet even though those who regretted the sacrilege of the dissolution officially supported the ejection of the monks and nuns, some monks and nuns seemingly refused to go away. Lyon has argued that the memory of religious not only persisted after the dissolution but also that the vanished religious 'acquired a form of agency in the form of ghost stories long after their death'.[24] Monastic ghost stories were 'a particular species of narrative developed to make sense of a difficult past'.[25] However, since many ghost stories were first recorded in the nineteenth century (or even later) it is often difficult to judge whether they are romantic confections or represent a genuine tradition of unease about the sacrilege of dissolution; Alan Murdie may be right that it was the discovery of the burials of several abbots of St Edmunds in 1901–2 that led to a spate of twentieth-century sightings of ghostly monks in Bury St Edmunds.[26] Margaretta Greene's 1861 story *The Secret Disclosed*, which placed the ghost of a nun in Bury's Great Churchyard, was clearly a fiction – although it has nevertheless fed into local ghostlore.[27]

One of Suffolk's best-known examples of monastic folklore may have developed as an explanation for a stain on some steps in Clare Priory. Clare Priory House was created from the Cellarer's Hall and other domestic buildings of the priory; the 'Legend of Clare' was first recorded in 1902 and tells the story of an unscrupulous sacrist, Hugh of Bury, who finds himself in debt to Jewish moneylenders. The devil appears to Hugh in the form of a friar and offers to help him make money from the sacristy, provided Hugh keeps a candle for him and never lights it. Of course, the sacrist forgets his promise and lights the candle; the devil kills the friar on the refectory steps, leaving a bloodstain that can never be removed.[28] It seems very unlikely that this story was passed on orally from before the dissolution; rather, the story probably developed to explain an otherwise unexplained stain on some steps.

The Benedictine monks

Westminster Abbey was dissolved for a second time under Elizabeth I in July 1559, and Abbot Feckenham and those monks who failed to conform to the Church of England were imprisoned. Among them was Sigebert Buckley, who spent 40 years imprisoned in various places until his release from Framlingham Castle (which had been a prison for recusants since 1580[29]) in 1606.[30] If conditions at Framlingham were anything like those at Wisbech Castle, where most captured priests were imprisoned, then Buckley would

---

24 Lyon (2018), p. 178.

25 Lyon (2018), p. 179.

26 A. Murdie, *Haunted Bury St Edmunds* (Stroud: Tempus, 2006), pp. 14–22.

27 [M. K. Greene], *The Secret Disclosed: A Legend of St Edmund's Abbey* (Bury St Edmunds: Samuel Gross, 1861).

28 Barnardiston (1962), pp. 52–62.

29 J. Ridyard (ed.), *Medieval Framlingham: Select Documents 1270–1524*, SRS 27 (Woodbridge: Suffolk Records Society, 1985), p. 7.

30 J. McCann and H. Connolly (eds), *Memorials of Father Augustine Baker and Other Documents Relating to the English Benedictines*, Catholic Record Society 33 (London: Catholic Record Society, 1933), p. 160.

Figure 31 Framlingham Castle, where Sigebert Buckley was imprisoned. Engraving by
T. Higham, 1819.

have been able to conduct some sort of ministry to local and visiting Catholics from his
prison.

The first English monk professed after 1559 was born in Suffolk, and he was also
probably the most influential English monk of the second half of the sixteenth century.
Robert Sayer of Redgrave (1560–1602) studied at Gonville and Caius College, Cambridge,
where he came under the influence of the college's Catholic butler, John Fingley (who was
later executed). After he graduated from Peterhouse in 1581, Sayer went to the English
Colleges at Douai, Rheims and Rome (seminaries established to train Catholic priests
for missionary work in Protestant England), where he was ordained priest. Sayer briefly
returned to England in 1586 and narrowly evaded capture. He returned to the Continent
and, in 1589, he was professed a Benedictine monk of Monte Cassino, taking the name
Gregory. Sayer devoted the remainder of his life to moral theology, becoming the Catholic
church's foremost authority on the subject until his writings were surpassed by those
of Alphonsus Liguori; nevertheless, his writings remained in print until the nineteenth
century.[31]

Not all Englishmen interested in the monastic life wanted to join foreign monasteries,
however, and not long after his release from Framlingham Castle, in 1607 Sigebert Buckley
clothed two young men in the Benedictine habit and thus revived (or perpetuated) the
English Benedictine Congregation. The post-Reformation English Benedictines were very

---

31   T. Cooper (rev. D. D. Rees), 'Sayer, Robert [name in religion Gregory]', *ODNB*, doi.
     org/10.1093/ref:odnb/24769, accessed 2 August 2019.

Figure 32 Hintlesham Hall. Engraving by T. Higham, 1819.

different from their pre-Reformation confreres, and the congregation was structured as a missionary organisation whose purpose was to send priests to England to convert the country back to the Catholic faith. When on the Continent, the monks lived in a number of priories whose priors owed obedience to the president of the congregation, elected by a general chapter. In England, the monks rarely lived any kind of communal life and served as secret missionary priests to Catholic families, under the authority of two priors who claimed jurisdiction over the ecclesiastical provinces of Canterbury and York. In theory, from 1633 there were other 'cathedral priors' (including a cathedral prior of Norwich) who claimed jurisdiction over the territory of the medieval dioceses, but in practice these were titular offices.[32]

In addition to Robert Sayer in the sixteenth century, during the seventeenth and eighteenth centuries 12 men from Suffolk became Benedictine monks. The best known of them is undoubtedly Bartholomew Roe (1583–1642), who was executed for treason at Tyburn during the English Civil War and later canonised as one of the Forty Martyrs of England and Wales in 1970. Roe was born in Bury St Edmunds and was converted to Catholicism while a student at Cambridge, when he visited a Catholic priest imprisoned at St Albans. Roe initially joined the English College at Douai to train for the secular priesthood but was expelled for insubordination; he then joined the Benedictines at St Laurence's Priory, Dieulouard in Lorraine, and was one of the founders of St Edmund's Priory, Paris in 1615 – a house that, in 1621, claimed to be the legal successor of the dissolved St Edmunds Abbey. Roe returned to England as a missionary priest but was soon captured and spent many years in prison before his execution.[33]

---

32 On the re-establishment of the English Benedictine Congregation see D. Lunn, *The English Benedictines 1540–1688* (London: Burns & Oates, 1980), pp. 90–120.

33 G. Scott, 'Three seventeenth-century Benedictine martyrs' in D. H. Farmer (ed.), *Benedict's Disciples,* 2nd edn (Leominster: Gracewing, 1995), pp. 266–81, at pp. 275–8.

Figure 33 Flixton Hall. Engraving by T. Higham, 1819.

The first Benedictine mission in post-dissolution Suffolk was that of William Palmer (1575–1655) at Hintlesham Hall, the home of the recusant Timperley family. Like Robert Sayer, Palmer seems to have been professed into the Italian Benedictines, but he later joined the English Benedictines and was sent to Hintlesham in 1622; it is unclear how long he stayed with the Timperleys, but he died at Longwood, Hampshire in 1655.[34] Another Suffolk gentleman to have a Benedictine chaplain in the seventeenth century was Sir Edward Gage of Hengrave, whose chaplain at his London home was Jerome Hesketh – although it is unclear whether Hesketh was also Sir Edward's chaplain at Hengrave Hall.[35]

The decision of the Tasburgh family to appoint a Benedictine chaplain at Flixton Hall in 1657 would have far-reaching consequences. After the death of the first Benedictine missioner, William Walgrave, in a fall on the stairs in 1665, no chaplain was appointed until 1704.[36] However, in his will of 1706 Richard Tasburgh attempted to establish a permanent chaplaincy at Flixton by setting aside a fund of £400 a year to support a priest. Felix Tasburgh, himself a Benedictine monk, made similar efforts to endow a chaplain, but it was not until the death of George Tasburgh in 1736 that the mission was permanently established, with the proviso that the chaplain should be a Benedictine monk, and preferably from St Edmund's Priory in Paris.[37]

34 N. Birt, *Obit Book of the English Benedictines 1600–1912* (Edinburgh: Mercat Press, 1913), p. 35.

35 Young (2015), pp. 53–4.

36 Crouzet (2007), pp. 24–8; F. Young, 'The Tasburghs of Flixton and Catholicism in North-East Suffolk', *PSIAH* 42:4 (2012), pp. 455–70, at p. 460.

37 Crouzet (2007), pp. 35–8; Young (2012), pp. 463–4.

The Benedictine monk Maurus Rigmaiden arrived at Coulsey Wood House, a property owned by the Bedingfields of Redlingfield in the parish of Stoke Ash, in 1715, and stayed until his death in 1759.[38] In 1717 Francis Howard, a monk of St Gregory's Priory, Douai, was sent to Coldham Hall, the home of the Rookwood family. By 1720 Howard was based in Bury St Edmunds, and in 1749 he was appointed titular cathedral prior of Norwich, making him the most senior monk in East Anglia (at least symbolically).[39] By the 1730s Howard was functioning as chaplain to the Gage family at Hengrave Hall, where he kept a mission register which still survives – a rare document from the period.[40] However, Howard's role changed yet again in 1741 when the death of a secular priest in Bury St Edmunds left Howard in charge of the main Catholic mission in the town, which he would serve until his death in 1755.[41] In 1738 Howard was joined in Bury by Alexius Jones, a monk of St Laurence's Priory, Dieulouard.[42] Remarkably, Jones's detailed diary for the first four years he spent in Bury still survives; Jones posed as tutor to the Bonds' son 'Jemmy' (James), since the penal laws against Catholic priests still remained in force.

In 1753 Howard and Jones were joined by a third monk, Maurus Heatly,[43] but the death of Howard and Jones in 1755 marked the end of the Benedictine mission, which was taken over by the Jesuit John Gage. While the two monks collaborated closely, their freedom of action was limited by the fact that Jones was chaplain to the Bond family and Howard was treated as a personal chaplain by Delariviere Gage, the mother of Sir Thomas Gage, 3rd baronet of Hengrave. There is no evidence that Howard, Jones and Heatly were ever able to say the office together or live any kind of conventual life. The monks had to balance their pastoral duties towards the Catholic population of Bury St Edmunds and the surrounding area against their dependence on the patronage of their respective gentry families.

The most prominent Suffolk Benedictine of the eighteenth century was probably John Anselm Mannock (1681–1764) of Giffords Hall, Stoke-by-Nayland. Mannock joined St Gregory's, Douai in 1700 after he accidentally killed his brother by dropping a cannon-ball from a window, and was filled with remorse. Mannock, who served as a chaplain at Kelvedon Hall in Essex, became a hugely popular writer on Catholicism whose *Poor Man's Catechism* (1752) was reprinted many times and even into the nineteenth century, anticipating the later apologetic works of John Henry Newman.[44]

The monk-chaplains at Flixton, freed from subservience as domestic chaplains to the Tasburgh family by the separate endowment they secured in 1736, were able to remain at Flixton even after the estate was bought by an Irish Protestant family, the Adairs, in 1753.

---

38   Young (2015), p. 144.
39   Young (2015), p. 110.
40   Young (2015), p. 113.
41   Young (2015), p. 114.
42   Young (2015), p. 117.
43   Young (2015), p. 141.
44   P. Jebb, 'Mannock, John [name in religion Anselm]', *ODNB*, doi.org/10.1093/ref:odnb/17984, accessed 6 August 2019; J. Gillow, *A Literary and Biographical History, or Biographical Dictionary of the English Catholics* (London: Burns & Oates, 1885–1902), vol. 4, pp. 458–61.

Figure 34
St Edmund's church,
Bungay

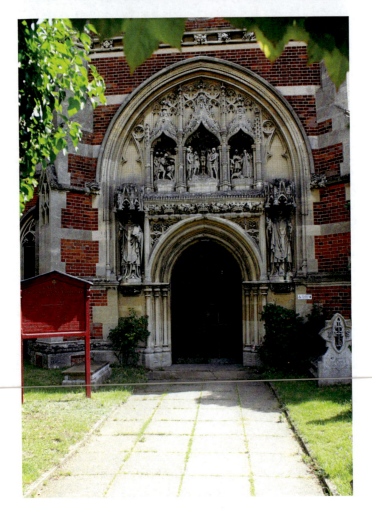

At some point between 1757 and 1761 the monks moved to a purpose-built cottage, the 'Priest's House' close to Flixton parish church.[45] The Priest's House at Flixton was the closest thing in Suffolk to a monastery since the dissolution – a place where more than one monk could live together in a building dedicated to the purpose (although there was often only a single monk at Flixton).

In the 1820s two Bungay merchants, John Cuddon and Richard Wood, entered negotiations with the 12th duke of Norfolk to move the Benedictine mission to a new site in the town of Bungay. The site chosen was, fittingly, on part of the ancient monastic precincts of Bungay Priory, the town's medieval house of Benedictine nuns. A chapel dedicated to St Edmund was opened on 18 June 1823 with great fanfare – remarkable given Bungay's small Catholic population and the fact that Catholic Emancipation was still six years off.[46] The church in Bungay struggled, however, and in the late 1870s the president of the English Benedictine Congregation wrote to the local bishop, Francis Amherst, offering to hand over the Benedictine mission to the diocese of Northampton. Bishop Amherst replied by welcoming the monks to establish 'a regular monastic establishment' at Bungay, and lamented the possibility of losing 'the slender thread that unites us [i.e. eastern England] with the [Benedictine] Order'.[47]

Men from Suffolk continued to join the Benedictine order in the nineteenth century, which was by far the most popular religious order in this regard, perhaps because a few novices were recruited through the Bungay mission. Eight men became Benedictines before 1901; one of them, Henry Palmer Chapman (1865–1933), even became abbot of Downside Abbey in Somerset. Chapman was the son of the archdeacon of Sudbury and converted to Catholicism in 1890, joining a German Benedictine congregation before he switched to the English Benedictines in 1919. He was elected abbot of Downside in 1929.[48]

Bungay remained a Benedictine parish, and was staffed by monks of Downside Abbey (although Downside received abbey status only in 1899) from 1883. In 1885 Ephrem Guy, a monk enthused with the nineteenth-century spirit of monastic revival, became the chaplain at Bungay and set about enlarging St Edmund's church for more elaborate liturgical celebrations. The new chancel was completed in 1889 and a nave in 1891, while a presbytery linked by a cloister to the church was completed in 1894 – a nod to the church's monastic links.[49]

Meanwhile, attempts were made in the late nineteenth century to establish another Benedictine parish in Beccles. Edmund Ford was appointed to Beccles in 1889.[50] Work began on a large Neo-Romanesque church known as St Bene't's Minster in 1898, and it was consecrated in 1908; although Downside Abbey had originally intended to found a dependent priory at Beccles, this never came to pass and the minster remains, like Bungay,

45   Crouzet (2007), pp. 38–40.
46   Crouzet (2007), pp. 49–56.
47   Crouzet (2007), p. 60.
8   D. D. Rees, 'Chapman, Henry Palmer [name in religion John]', *ODNB*, doi.org/10.1093/ref:odnb/65085, accessed 5 August 2019.
49   Crouzet (2007), pp. 66–73.
50   Crouzet (2007), p. 69.

Table 4 Suffolk-born male religious in the nineteenth century

Name	Order	Dates
Campbell, Richard (Osmund)	OSB	1873–1962
Chapman, Henry (John)	OSB	1865–1933 (Abbot of Downside)
Clarkson, John (Athanasius)	OSB	1819–64
Feraud, Charles (Ambrose)	OSB	1786–1847
Griffin, Benedict (Placid)	OSB	1873–1960
Gurdon, Arthur (Edmund)	O.Cart.	1864–1940
Mackey, Hugh (Walter)	OSB	1873–1942
Morgan, Joseph (Romuald)	OSB	1843–1904
Stutter, Edward (John)	OSB	1842–1922

a parish church served by Benedictine monks.[51] The Benedictine mission in north-east Suffolk was not confined to Bungay and Beccles alone; during the Second World War, the monks provided mass for US airmen at Brockdish, Metfield, Harleston, Thorpe Abbotts, Pulham, Flixton and Seething. A mass centre was established at Brockdish in 1946 but it closed in 1951, and a new chapel was founded in a former Primitive Methodist chapel at Wortwell. The chapel endured until 2001.[52]

Bungay and Beccles remain, at the time of writing, Benedictine parishes. They are sometimes viewed as remote outposts of Downside Abbey, but of course the history of these missions long pre-dates Downside and is itself overlaid on a much older monastic history. As we have seen, early monastic foundations clustered particularly in the north-eastern corner of Suffolk, and the later Benedictine mission depended on a family (the Tasburghs) enriched by the dissolution of Flixton Priory and, in the nineteenth century, relocated to a site within the precincts of Bungay Priory. St Edmund's church, Bungay, is the oldest living monastic institution in Suffolk, with a continuous history stretching back to the mid-seventeenth century.

Suffolk also witnessed the earliest revival of Benedictine monasticism in the Church of England. The Oxford Movement and the rise of Anglo-Catholicism made it inevitable, perhaps, that some Catholic-minded Anglicans would begin to look favourably on the idea of reviving the monastic life. Joseph Leycester Lyne (1837–1908) was the curate of St George-in-the-East, London, when he assumed a Benedictine habit and started calling himself Fr Ignatius of Jesus (although he was only in deacon's orders). Lyne resigned his curacy and moved to Claydon, near Ipswich, where the rector, George Drury, hosted the world's first Anglican Benedictine community in Claydon Rectory. The community began on 17 February 1863, observing a punishing schedule of monastic offices which involved rising at 2 o'clock in the morning. However, Lyne refused to engage with practicalities of funding and was refused a licence to preach by the bishop of Norwich. On 30 January

---

51   'A brief history', saintbenetsbeccles.org/our-parish-and-our-services/a-brief-history, accessed 26 May 2019.
52   Crouzet (2007), pp. 84–9.

1864 the community relocated to Elm Hill in Norwich, eventually settling at Capel-y-Ffin in Wales in 1870, where Lyne attempted to re-found Llanthony Abbey.[53]

The Franciscan friars

Medieval Suffolk's Franciscan friaries belonged to the oldest branch of the Franciscan Order, the Friars Minor Conventual, whose English province came to an end at the dissolution. However, Mary I re-founded a house of Observant Friars at Greenwich in 1555, and on their dissolution by Elizabeth the English Observants reorganised in exile. However, the Fransciscans were never significantly involved in the Catholic mission to Suffolk. Arthur Bell (1591–1643) was brought up at Acton Place, the home of the Daniel family, and entered the friars at Segovia in Spain in 1618. In 1634 Bell returned to England as a missionary, where he served as chaplain to Mary Darcy, Countess Rivers. Lady Rivers was the owner of Hengrave Hall (inherited from her father Thomas Kytson), although it is unclear whether Bell ministered there as well as at her house in Colchester. In 1643 he was arrested at Stevenage, found guilty of being a Catholic priest and executed. He was beatified in 1987.[54]

No Suffolk men became Franciscan friars in the post-Reformation period, and only one is known to have ministered in the county. Anthony Tyldesley (1686–1718) was probably born in Lancashire and trained at St Bonaventure's Friary in Douai before returning to England in 1714. He was chaplain to the Mannock family for a time at Giffords Hall, Stoke-by-Nayland, but was buried in St Mary's churchyard in Bury St Edmunds in 1718. We know nothing of his time in Bury, but a branch of the Catholic Tyldesley family settled at Fornham St Genevieve in the late seventeenth century when John Tyldesley married Catherine Stafford, the daughter of Bury's Catholic mayor in the reign of James II.[55] The Franciscans did not return to Suffolk until the twentieth century, when Old Hall in East Bergholt (the former home of the Benedictine nuns of St Mary's Abbey) became the novitiate and house of studies for the Observant Friars Minor in 1946. East Bergholt remained a friary until 1973 when Old Hall passed into the ownership of a secular community.[56]

The Dominican friars

After the Benedictines, Dominicans were the most numerous missionary priests belonging to a monastic order in post-Reformation Suffolk. Five Suffolk men became Dominican friars in the eighteenth century, with the Martin family of Long Melford and the Short family of Bury St Edmunds each providing two friars (see Appendix 2). The Martins and Shorts were also the principal patrons of the Dominicans in the county. On 21 March

---

53 Tricker (2014), pp. 145–6; R. Kollar, 'Lyne, Joseph Leycester', *ODNB*, doi.org/10.1093/ref:odnb/34647, accessed 28 May 2019.
54 T. Cooper (rev. M. E. Williams), 'Bell, Arthur [name in religion Francis]', *ODNB*, doi.org/10.1093/ref:odnb/2000, accessed 6 August 2019.
55 Young (2015), p. 95.
56 J. R. H. Moorman, *The Franciscans in England* (London: Mowbrays, 1974), p. 106.

1709 Sir Roger Martin (1639–1712), first Baronet of Melford Place, Long Melford, created an endowment for a priest to say mass for the souls of his ancestors, stipulating the priest was to be a Dominican friar appointed by the Prior Provincial of the English Dominicans.[57] The Dominican friar John Martin served as chaplain at Melford Place to his own family, including his father, brother and nephew, from 1705 until his death in 1761.[58] The chapel of Melford Place can still be seen on the west side of the B1064 at the southern edge of Long Melford, and is now part of a private house. This domestic chapel replaced the proprietary chapel of St James, which once stood opposite Melford Place and was the Martin family's private chapel before the Reformation.

It was not uncommon for priests from Catholic recusant families to return to minister to their own family. In 1758 the Dominican friar James Ambrose Gage (1723–96), a grandson of Sir Edward Gage of Hengrave, returned to Bury St Edmunds as chaplain to the Short family. Gage held the title of titular prior of Sudbury; a titular prior of Ipswich was also sometimes appointed.[59] In 1761 he moved from Bury to Coulsey Wood House to take over from the Benedictine Maurus Rigmaiden, but had left by 1765, leaving Coulsey Wood without a priest.[60] The Dominicans prioritised learning, education and preaching, and John Jordan Short (1685–1754), who was born in Bury St Edmunds into a family of physicians, never returned to England as a missionary priest but spent the rest of his life teaching at the University of Louvain.[61] Another member of the Short family rose to high office in the Dominican order; William Benedict Short (1723–1800) was elected Prior Provincial of the English Dominicans in 1766.

The Augustinian canonesses

During the 1790s hundreds of priests and religious fled France and other territories invaded by the French Revolutionary Army. Although many of these clerical exiles were French, many were also English Catholic exiles, ironically seeking a home in the land from which they had originally been exiled by their Catholic faith. As a result of the war with France, English attitudes to Catholics (and particularly Catholic exiles) shifted significantly, and the exiles were generally treated with sympathy rather than hostility. Between 1794 and 1802 Hengrave Hall, the home of the Gage family, played host to the Augustinian canonesses of the Priory of Nazareth, otherwise known as the 'English Convent', an important house of English religious women founded in Bruges in 1629. The English Convent had strong East Anglian connections, and 11 women from Suffolk joined the convent during the seventeenth and eighteenth centuries (see Appendix 2), including one member of the Gage family, Penelope Stanislaus Gage (d. 1772). However, the French Revolutionary

---

57   S. Tymms, 'Melford Place', *PSIA* 2 (1859), pp. 84–8, at p. 86.
58   W. Gumbley, 'The English Dominicans from 1555 to 1950', *Dominican Studies* 5 (1952), pp. 103–26, at p. 121.
59   Gumbley (1952), p. 122.
60   Young (2015), pp. 142–4.
61   F. Young, 'The Shorts of Bury St Edmunds: medicine, Catholicism and politics in the 17th century', *Journal of Medical Biography* 16 (2008b), pp. 188–94, at p. 194; Young (2015), p. 143.

Figure 35 The English Convent, Bruges

Army's invasion of the Low Countries made it impossible for the canonesses to remain in Bruges, although they made strenuous efforts to stay and hold on to their beloved convent.

Led by their prioress, Mary More, the canonesses finally abandoned the Bruges convent on 12 June 1794, finally arriving at Hengrave Hall on 16 August. At the time of the canonesses' arrival in England Hengrave Hall was empty, since Sir Thomas Rookwood Gage of Coldham Hall had inherited the Hengrave baronetcy in 1767 and preferred to live at Coldham. It was his son, Sir Thomas Gage, sixth baronet, who invited the Bruges canonesses to Hengrave, remembering that his great aunt Penelope Stanislaus had been a canoness at Bruges. Although at first the local people feared the canonesses were 'French Men in disguise', the community soon received a warm welcome.[62]

On 28 August the community resumed its conventual life at Hengrave, although the canonesses did not dare wear their habits. By 1795 even the habit had been resumed, after Lady Gage consulted the archbishop of Canterbury and two MPs, although the habited canonesses attracted more attention than they would have wished for.[63] The convent school re-opened

62   T. J. Moutray, *Refugee Nuns, the French Revolution, and British Literature and Culture* (London: Routledge, 2016), p. 145.

63   Moutray (2016), p. 146.

Figure 36
Hengrave Hall.
Engraving from
John Gage, *The
History and
Antiquities of
Hengrave* (1822).

Figure 37 Memorial
inscription to Mary
More at the English
Convent, Bruges

as early as September 1794. On 23 December 1795 a new chapel was completed at Hengrave, located in a first-floor room in the east wing of the house later known as the Oakley Chamber. The first new novice was professed in 1796. However, the re-establishment of relations between the Napoleonic regime and the Catholic church after the Peace of Amiens in 1802 led the canonesses to return to Bruges;[64] the community

Figure 38 The author with two canonesses from the English Convent, Bruges, who visited Hengrave Hall in 2002 to celebrate the return of the canonesses to Bruges

was also concerned about a bill passing through Parliament to regulate religious houses, and wondered how secure their future in England was likely to be.[65]

The English Convent remains in Bruges to this day, the sole surviving English religious house on the Continent. However, the canonesses' eight-year sojourn in Suffolk was profoundly important for trans-forming local attitudes to Catholicism, and Mary More succeeded in establishing the first fully functional monastic community in Suffolk since the dissolution. In 2002 representatives of the English Convent visited the Religious of the Assumption at Hengrave Hall in order to celebrate the bicentenary of the canonesses' return to Bruges.

The Benedictine nuns

During the course of the seventeenth and eighteenth centuries 25 Suffolk-born women became Benedictine nuns in the exiled religious houses at Ghent, Brussels, Dunkirk, Cambrai and Pontoise (see Appendix 2). One of them, Ethelrede Mannock (d. 1773), a daughter of Sir Francis Mannock of Giffords Hall, rose to become abbess of the Monastery of the Glorious Assumption of Our Blessed Lady Brussels in 1762.[66] This was the oldest female English Benedictine community, having been established in Brussels in 1598.

---

64   F. Young, 'Mother Mary More and the exile of the Augustinian canonesses of Bruges in
     England, 1794–1802', *Recusant History* 27:1 (2004), pp. 86–102, at pp. 89–94.

65   Moutray (2016), p. 152.

66   *Miscellanea IX*, Catholic Record Society 14 (London: Catholic Record Society, 1914), p. 194.

Figure 39 Dame Aloysia Brenan, first abbess of East Bergholt (1800–1870). Reproduced by kind permission of Downside Abbey (Haslemere Collection).

The Brussels community was one of many that fled the Low Countries in the 1790s, settling in Winchester. However, in 1856, led by Abbess Aloysia Brenan, the community purchased Old Hall in East Bergholt and prepared to move to Suffolk. The nuns ensured that a chapel was fitted out for them on their arrival at East Bergholt in 1857, so they could begin singing the divine office at once.[67] Old Hall became known as St Mary's Abbey, and the community underwent 24 episcopal visitations during the 88 years it was in Suffolk.[68]

The community at East Bergholt found itself at the centre of a controversy in 1911 when a former novice, Margaret Mary Moult, published an exposé of her 'escape' from St Mary's Abbey. Moult came from Beccles, where her vocation was fostered by the Benedictine monks of St Bene't's Minster. On arrival at East Bergholt, Moult was surprised to find that the older nuns had no knowledge of Latin, and were barely able to sing the office, although the abbess, Mary Gertrude Lescher, ensured new entrants knew the language.[69] Moult also complained about the quality of the food in the convent, claiming that rancid meat was often served,[70] and claimed that the nuns' bedding was only washed every 25 years.[71] In spite of feeling she had no vocation to be a nun, Moult became a novice and was professed in 1907,[72]

67   A. Bellenger, 'The Brussels nuns at Winchester, 1794–1857', unpublished conference paper, English Benedictine Congregation History Commission Symposium (1999), monlib.org.uk/papers/ebch/1999bellenger.pdf, accessed 7 August 2019.

68   R. Anderson, 'The visitation records of the English Benedictine monastery of the Glorious Assumption of Our Blessed Lady', unpublished conference paper, Gender, Power and Materiality in Early Modern Europe, 1500–1800, University of Plymouth, Plymouth, 7–9 April 2016, researchspace.bathspa.ac.uk/7859/1/7859.pdf, accessed 7 August 2019.

69   M. M. Moult, *The Escaped Nun: The Story of Her Life* (London: Cassell & Co., 1911), pp. 23–4.

70   Moult (1911), pp. 34–8.

but was unimpressed with the conduct of the nuns and began to doubt the Catholic faith itself.[73] Eventually, in 1909, Moult 'escaped' the abbey and was pursued by lay sisters to Manningtree Station, who attempted in vain to persuade her to return and even (so Moult claimed) tried to physically recapture her.[74]

Given Moult's subsequent abandonment of Catholicism and a prevalent trend for denouncing the monastic life and spreading rumours about convents, Moult's account cannot be taken as entirely factual. However, Moult really was a nun at East Bergholt and her account reveals some of the pressures on a community bound by strict traditions yet attempting to recruit women from an increasingly modern world. The case gained a great deal of attention, and in April 1909 the MP for Belfast South, Thomas Sloan tabled a question in Parliament to the Home Secretary, Herbert Gladstone, about whether the government should inspect convents (something that Moult advocated at the end of her book[75]). Gladstone assured Sloan that the Chief Constable of East Suffolk had found no evidence that force was used in an attempt to bring Moult back to St Mary's Abbey, and added that 'the reports of this case published in the Press were of a garbled and sensational nature'.[76] During the Second World War Old Hall was taken over by the War Office as a transit camp, and on their return at the end of the War the nuns found it so poorly maintained that they sold Old Hall to the Franciscan friars in 1946 and moved to Frensham Hall, Haslemere, Surrey.[77] The community was finally dissolved in 1975, with the surviving nuns moving to other monasteries.

The Augustinian friars

On the death in 1945 of Helena Barker, the last private owner of Clare Priory, the priory passed to her daughters. The daughters sold Clare Priory on 26 April 1953 (the feast of Our Lady of Good Counsel) to the English and Scottish province of the Augustinian friars, who made Clare into their novitiate.[78] Since the English Augustinian friars died out after the dissolution, the province was re-founded by friars from Ireland. However, the Irish Augustinian friars were, in a sense, descended from the friars of Clare in the first place. At some point between 1259 and 1282 friars from Clare founded the mother-house of the Augustinian friars in Ireland, the Priory of the Holy Trinity in Dublin.[79] The

71 Moult (1911), p. 41.
72 Moult (1911), pp. 130–9.
73 Moult (1911), pp. 184–201.
74 Moult (1911), pp. 230–64.
75 Moult (1911), p. 295.
76 Historic Hansard, House of Commons Debates, 6 April 1909, api.parliament.uk/historic-hansard/commons/1909/apr/06/st-marys-roman-catholic-convent-east, accessed 7 August 2019.
77 P. F. Anson, *The Religious Orders and Congregations of Great Britain and Ireland* (Worcester: Stanbrook Abbey Press, 1949), p. 169.
78 F. X. Roth, *The English Austin Friars, 1249–1538* (Villanova, Pa.: Augustinian Historical Institute, 1966), p. 263; Barnardiston (1962), p. 50.

Figure 40 Clare Priory

Irish Augustinian friars initially remained part of the English province, but in 1424 they adopted an observant reform that never caught on in England.[80] The Irish friars' return to a more primitive observance of the Augustinian Rule seems to have been what gave them the dynamic energy to survive the Reformation in Ireland.

Today Clare Priory is the mother house of the English Augustinian friars, as the oldest Augustinian friary in England, as well as the home of a lay community that helps to run a retreat centre and a parish church for the surrounding area.[81] The former monastic infirmary initially served as the church but a new church was built to extend this at a cost of £1.2 million and consecrated in 2015.[82] Clare Priory is today the sole medieval monastic house in Suffolk to have been restored to its original use, albeit the medieval friars of Clare might struggle to recognise their friary in its present form. Central to the contemporary friary is a shrine to Our Lady, Mother of Good Counsel.

79   D. Kelly, 'The Augustinians in Dublin', *Dublin Historical Record* 58:2 (2005), pp. 166–75, at pp. 169–70.
80   Harper-Bill (1991), p. 11.
81   'Clare Priory', clarepriory.org.uk, accessed 7 August 2019.
82   'Bishop consecrates new £1.2m Suffolk church', Roman Catholic Diocese of East Anglia, 7 October 2015, rcdea.org.uk/bishop-consecrates-new-1-2m-suffolk-church, accessed 7 August 2015.

Figure 41 Shrine of Our Lady, Mother of Good Counsel at Clare Priory

Other religious communities

In addition to the medieval religious orders who made a return to Suffolk at various points after the dissolution, the county has also seen the arrival of several newer congregations of religious, as well as some interesting monastic experiments. In the nineteenth century a large number of congregations of religious women, mostly dedicated to education, sprang up in France and around the world. Roman Catholic 'convent schools' soon made an appearance in Suffolk, beginning with the Sisters of Jesus and Mary. The Sisters of Jesus and Mary arrived in Ipswich in 1860 and established a convent on Woodbridge Road, which survives to the present day (although the site of the former convent school is now a housing development).[83] In 1912 the Sisters of Jesus and Mary founded the Convent of Jesus Mary close to St Mary's parish church in Felixstowe.[84] The Sisters of Jesus and Mary arrived in Bury St Edmunds and established a convent in Westgate Street in September 1917;[85] the order also opened a convent and school in Woodbridge in 1923.[86]

One teaching order that made an important contribution to west Suffolk was the St

83   'It all started somewhere in France…', stmarysipswich.co.uk/history.htm, accessed 1 June 2019.

84   Religious of Jesus and Mary, *The Life and Work of Mother Mary St Ignatius (Claudine Thévenet), 1774–1837, Foundress of the Congregation of Jesus and Mary, with an account of the development of the congregation* (Dublin: Clonmore & Reynold, 1953), pp. 302–3.

85   *The Present from Our Past: The History of the Church of St Edmund King and Martyr Bury St Edmunds* (Bury St Edmunds: St Edmund's History Group, 2012), p. 19.

86   B. Pratt, *A History of the Catholic Church of Saint Thomas of Canterbury, Woodbridge* (Woodbridge: privately printed, 1989), online at wfrcp.org.uk/parish-history/woodbridge, accessed 1 June 2019.

Louis Sisters. Four St Louis Sisters from Monaghan, Ireland arrived in Bury St Edmunds in January 1924 to take charge of the town's Roman Catholic school.[87] Later, the Sisters of St Louis founded a Roman Catholic school in Newmarket in 1937.[88] Other teaching orders included the Ursuline Sisters, who established a school at Aldeburgh in 1904,[89] and the Sisters of Mercy, who opened a convent and school at Eaton House, Aldeburgh in 1927.[90] The Benedictine Sisters of Grace and Compassion are not a teaching order and focus instead on healthcare. The sisters have run the Montana care home for the elderly at Great Barton since March 1969, when Cynthia Oakes donated her bungalow to the sisters for use as a care home.[91] Although the Grace and Compassion Benedictines are religious sisters rather than nuns, they nevertheless follow the Rule of St Benedict.

By the late twentieth century many of the teaching orders were struggling to recruit new vocations and several withdrew from direct involvement in education. One teaching order diversified into a very different form of religious life. The Religious of the Assumption purchased Hengrave Hall in 1952 and converted it into a private school for girls. As early as 1967, influenced by the Second Vatican Council, the mother superior of the Convent of the Assumption was feeling uneasy that the sisters were educating those who were already privileged, and felt the sisters were called to a more ecumenical mission.[92] Accordingly, in 1974 the sisters closed the school and began an ecumenical community at Hengrave, inviting families from Catholic, Orthodox, Anglican, Methodist, Quaker and other backgrounds to take up residence and help run a retreat and conference centre.[93] The community later moved away from its focus on families, inviting either long-term or short-term commitment from individuals and drawing many of its members from Eastern Europe long before the end of the Cold War. At the heart of the ecumenical community, the Religious of the Assumption maintained their own conventual life. The Community of Reconciliation came to an end in 2005 and the Assumptionists left Hengrave in 2006, bringing to an end almost 500 years in which Hengrave Hall had been at the centre of Catholic life (in one way or another) in the Bury St Edmunds area.[94]

Not all of Suffolk's nineteenth and twentieth-century communities of religious sisters were Roman Catholic; in fact, the first such community came into being at Shipmeadow

---

87   St Edmund's History Group (2012), p. 21.

88   'About School: St Louis Academy', stlouisacademy.co.uk/about-school, accessed 1 June 2019.

89   '1925: The new church at Aldeburgh', aldeburgh.oneplacestudy.org/news/1925-the-new-church-at-aldeburgh, accessed 1 June 2019.

90   J. E. Pike, *Aldeburgh: The Official Guide of the Aldeburgh Corporation* (Croydon: Home Publishing, 1952), p. 15.

91   G. Beattie (ed.), *Gregory's Angels: A History of the Abbeys, Priories, Parishes and Schools of the Monks and Nuns following the Rule of St Benedict in Great Britain, Ireland, and their Overseas Foundation* (Leominster: Gracewing, 1997), pp. 200–1.

92   Brown (1981), p. 248.

93   On the Hengrave Community see D. Clark, *Basic Communities: Towards an Alternative Society* (London: SPCK, 1977), pp. 25–6, 52–4, 131–2; G. Cashmore and J. Puls, 'Thirsty in a thirsty land', *Ecumenical Review* 46:2 (1994), pp. 204–13, at pp. 210–11.

94   'Mounting debts force Hengrave Hall to close', *Bury Free Press*, 20 May 2005, buryfreepress.co.uk/news/mounting-debts-force-hengrave-hall.1032452.jp, accessed 7 August 2019.

in 1855 when the staff of a 'house of mercy' for 'fallen women' founded in 1854 decided to take religious vows and became the Community of All Hallows. This was at a time when vowed religious life and the deaconess movement were popular in the Church of England, which was becoming aware of the lack of opportunities in the church for unmarried women. The Community of All Hallows moved to Ditchingham, Norfolk in 1859, but retained its connection to Suffolk by opening two hostels for 'fallen women' in Ipswich in 1889 and 1892.[95]

In 1857 the Anglo-Catholic pioneer John Mason Neale sent a group of religious sisters from the convent he had founded in East Grinstead to the parish of St Matthew in Ipswich, where Charles Gaye was rector. The sisters established the Sisterhood of St Mary the Virgin and worked among the poor of Ipswich. However, the sisters encountered hostility from parishioners who perceived them as too 'Romish'; Gaye was exasperated with those who held 'the childish fallacy that a thing is wrong, merely because it was adopted by the Church of Rome'. Yet Gaye also had his own disagreements with the sisters, and asked them to leave in 1858.[96]

In 1866, not long after Joseph Lyne's experiment with Benedictine monasticism at Claydon, George Drury established a community of Anglican Benedictine nuns at Claydon, who set up a school for local children. In 1882, however, Drury fell out with the superior, Mary Ware, claiming that the convent was not being run according to his original wishes. Drury reached an agreement that Ware should have the building provided it was not used as a convent or for religious services, and the monastery disbanded, with the sisters going to other Anglican religious communities.[97] A daughter house of the Clapham house of the Sisterhood of the Holy Childhood at Kettlebaston was a little more successful. The Kettlebaston house was founded in the 1880s and the sisters cared for a small group of children until the departure of the community in around 1930.[98]

From 1902 Woolverstone, just outside Ipswich, played host to St Peter's Home of Rest, which was not a separate religious community in its own right but rather a place where Anglican religious sisters of any community could retire or recuperate. The building housing the Home of Rest was converted into a hospital during the First World War and subsequently became a private house.[99] In 1907 religious sisters from the Community of St Michael and All Angels, Hammersmith (founded in 1895) established St Michael's College, a private girls' boarding school, in the Old Grammar School in Northgate Street. The sisters also assisted in the Anglo-Catholic parish of St John. The school closed in 1945 after the death of the superior, Mother Ethel Mary,[100] marking the end of experiments in Anglican religious life in Suffolk.

---

95   Tricker (2014), pp. 148–9.
96   Tricker (2014), pp. 146–8.
97   Tricker (2014), p. 146.
98   Tricker (2014), p. 149.
99   Tricker (2014), p. 149.
100 Tricker (2014), pp. 149–50.

Figure 42 The Old Grammar School in Northgate Street, Bury St Edmunds, an Anglican convent school until 1945

Conclusion

Monasticism in modern Suffolk took a great variety of forms, from the labours of individual missionary monks and friars in the seventeenth and eighteenth centuries to the establishment of the county's first functioning monastery at Hengrave Hall in the late eighteenth century. The Augustinian canonesses of Bruges who took refuge at Hengrave anticipated the numerous new religious orders which, in the nineteenth century, provided education and other ministries. While some of these communities remain, monastic life in Suffolk has also taken new directions. Clare Priory, Suffolk's most ancient monastic house, is now a lay as well as clerical community, as is the St Thomas Pilgrim Community, a new religious community founded in February 2016 by Jutta Brueck, priest-in-charge of St Thomas' church, Ipswich. Members of the St Thomas Community commit for at least a year to participation in the life of the community, either as non-resident members or

---

101 'St Thomas Pilgrim Community', cofesuffolk.org/fresh-expressions/st-thomass-pilgrim-community, accessed 27 May 2019.

as residents living in a community house.[101] A similar model of mixed clerical, monastic and lay involvement in a religious community can be found at Mettingham, where the Orthodox Collegiate Church of the Ikon of the Mother of God Joy of All Who Sorrow was founded in 2008.[102]

With their mixed clerical and lay composition and interconnectedness with parish ministry, contemporary monastic communities like Clare Priory, the St Thomas Community in Ipswich and the Orthodox College at Mettingham are closer in character to the minsters of Anglo-Saxon Suffolk than to the highly structured post-Norman religious communities that set the pattern for what most people perceive as monasticism. It seems likely that the desire for a more thoroughgoing community life than ordinary parish life provides will continue to produce religious communities for a long time to come, although we should not expect them to take stereotyped monastic forms. Rather than a lifelong commitment to monasticism, people are more likely to commit to community life for a shorter period of time, or to observe a rule of life while participating in rather than living full time in a community. Issues of hierarchy, governance and observance may take second place to the question of how a religious community can serve the wider church and society, while the potential for communities to bridge divides such as denominational differences may take on an important role. Whatever the future may hold, the history of monasticism in Suffolk is far from over.

---

102 'Welcome to our church', joyofallwhosorrow.org.uk/index.php/about/info/welcome_to_the_
    church, accessed 8 August 2019.

Appendix 1

A gazetteer of Suffolk monasteries

This appendix provides a complete list of all religious communities known to have existed in Suffolk from the earliest times (excluding secular colleges and hospitals) to the present day. The list includes both Roman Catholic and Anglican communities as well as churches, chapels and hospitals served by members of monastic orders, but not churches that were simply owned or governed by a monastery. Monasteries are listed under the modern civil parish in which they or their remains are now located. Only a handful of these monastic sites are open to the public. Of the medieval sites, three (Bury St Edmunds, Herringfleet and Leiston) are in the care of English Heritage; nine former monastic churches (Bungay, Creeting St Mary, Great Bricett, Letheringham, Redlingfield, Rumburgh, Stoke-by-Clare, Wangford and Wickham Skeith) are Anglican parish churches, and one site (Clare Priory) is a functioning modern monastery open to pilgrims.

Aldeburgh

Ursuline convent (OSU, religious sisters)

The Ursuline Sisters established a convent and school at Aldeburgh in 1904. They left before 1925.[1]

Convent of Our Lady of Perpetual Succour (RSM, religious sisters)

The Sisters of Mercy opened a convent and school at Eaton House, Aldeburgh in 1927.[2]

Battisford

Preceptory of the Knights Hospitaller of St John of Jerusalem

Battisford Preceptory was founded in around 1154, with Henry II as one of the benefactors. In 1338 the preceptory was led by a preceptor with only a single brother-knight, one corrodiary, a chaplain and eight servants. The preceptory was valued at £53 in 1535.[3] The site of the preceptory is now occupied by the moated St John's House, built in the 1570s or 1580s, perhaps reusing some of the materials of the original building; a terracotta head of St John the Baptist of sixteenth-century date is built into the fireplace. Battisford Preceptory had two subordinate members at Coddenham and Mellis.[4]

---

1   '1925: The new church at Aldeburgh', aldeburgh.oneplacestudy.org/news/1925-the-new-church-at-aldeburgh, accessed 1 June 2019.
2   Pike (1952), p. 15.
3   Taylor (1821), p. 102; *VCH Suffolk*, pp. 120–1; Messent (1934), p. 107; Knowles and Hadcock (1971), pp. 300, 301.
4   Birch (2004), p. 33.

Beccles

Church of St Bene't (OSB, monks)

Known as St Bene't's Minster, the Neo-Romanesque church of St Bene't was built between 1898 and 1908 and was supposed to be a dependent priory of Downside Abbey, although this never came to pass and the minster became instead a parish church served by Benedictine monks from Downside (as it remains to this day).[5]

Bentley

Priory of St Mary the Virgin (OSA, canons)

Dodnash Priory in the parish of Bentley was originally founded on a site in East Bergholt before 1188 by Wimer the chaplain, on land donated by Baldwin de Toeni and his mother Alda (who have been mistakenly given as the founders).[6] The foundation was probably for no more than five canons. The priory had five canons in 1381. It was suppressed in 1525 in order to endow Cardinal Wolsey's colleges.[7] Some building materials from the priory are incorporated into a farmhouse in the parish and a nearby pond may be the remains of monastic fishponds.[8]

Blythburgh

Anglo-Saxon minster

Although no documentary record survives of a minster at Blythburgh, it is possible that a minster was founded in the seventh century close to the site of the Battle of Bulcamp between Anna, king of the East Angles and Penda of Mercia in 654. Anna's body and that of his son Hiurmine (Jurmin) were still being venerated at Blythburgh in the twelfth century, and cult sites of this kind were usually cared for by a religious community. The endowments of Blythburgh church, together with the discovery of an eighth-century whalebone plaque that may once have decorated a book, all suggest that a minster once existed.[9]

Priory of the Blessed Virgin Mary (OSA, canons)

Blythburgh Priory was founded by and remained a dependency of St Osyth's Priory in Essex in the reign of Henry I (perhaps around 1130). The house was a small one, founded originally for four canons, although this may later have increased to six. In 1291 the priory's income was over £59. The priory declined as a result of the encroachment of the sea on its possessions in the fifteenth century. At the dissolution in 1535 the priory's

---

5   'A brief history', saintbenetsbeccles.org/our-parish-and-our-services/a-brief-history, accessed 26 May 2019.
6   Harper-Bill (1998), pp. 1–5.
7   Tanner (1693), p. 214; Taylor (1821), pp. 95–6; VCH Suffolk, pp. 99–100; Messent (1934), p. 108; Knowles and Hadcock (1971), pp. 140, 156; Midmer (1979), pp. 128–9.
8   Birch (2004), p. 40.
9   Pestell (2004), pp. 91–2.

income was assessed at £57.[10] Some meagre architectural remains survive in the garden of a house called The Priory close to Blythburgh parish church. The site was excavated in the mid-nineteenth century.[11]

Dominican Priory (OP, friars)

The Dominicans of Dunwich instigated a move to a new site at Blythburgh in 1384 when the Dunwich friary was threatened by coastal erosion.[12] It is unclear whether this move actually took place, however. The remains of a building known as Holy Rood Chapel, recorded in 1760, may have been connected to this putative foundation.[13]

Brandon

Anglo-Saxon minster

In the 1980s an apparent minster site was excavated on what was once a sand and gravel island in the middle of the River Little Ouse. Discoveries included styli (writing instruments) and a gold plaque bearing the symbol of St John the Evangelist which may have come from a book cover. The site was abandoned around 850.[14]

Bruisyard

Abbey of the Annunciation of the Blessed Virgin Mary (OSC, nuns)

Bruisyard Abbey (sometimes known as Rokehall Abbey) was founded in the period 1364–7 as a daughter house of Denny Abbey in Cambridgeshire when Lionel, duke of Clarence introduced Poor Clare nuns to replace the canons of a secular college, which was surrendered on 4 October 1366. Bruisyard may have been exempted from episcopal visitations. The abbey was valued at £56 2s 1d in 1535. It survived the dissolution of the smaller religious houses in 1536–7 by paying a fine of £60, and Abbess Maria Page finally surrendered to the crown on 17 February 1539.[15] Bruisyard Hall, built in 1610, incorporates some remnants of the monastic buildings.[16]

Bungay

Priory of St Mary and the Holy Cross (OSB, nuns)

Bungay Priory was founded either in around 1160 or in 1183 by Roger de Granville and his wife Countess Gundreda. In 1287 there were 16 nuns, ten in 1493, nine in 1520

10 Dugdale (1693), p. 211; Tanner (1693), p. 211; Taylor (1821), pp. 92–3; VCH Suffolk, pp. 91–4; Messent (1934), p. 108; Knowles and Hadcock (1971), pp. 138, 148; Midmer (1979), p. 71; Wilton (1980), pp. 56–7.
11 Birch (2004), p. 43.
12 Knowles and Hadcock (1971), p. 220; Birch (2004), p. 43.
13 Messent (1934), p. 108.
14 Blair (2005), pp. 206–11.
15 Dugdale (1693), pp. 314–15; Tanner (1693), p. 216; Taylor (1821), p. 105; VCH Suffolk, pp. 131–2; Messent (1934), p. 111; Knowles and Hadcock (1971), p. 286; Midmer (1979), p. 84.
16 Birch (2004), p. 59.

and eight in 1532. The priory was valued at £61 in 1535. The nuns may have left the monastery before surrendering it to the crown in 1536. The nave of the priory church, which was always the parish church of St Mary, survives intact, with the nuns' choir in ruins to the east. The conventual buildings were destroyed in the great fire of Bungay in 1688.[17]

Church of St Edmund, King and Martyr (OSB, monks)

In 1823 the long-established Benedictine mission at Flixton moved to a new chapel dedicated to St Edmund, king and martyr, next to St Mary's church in Bungay.[18] The mission was served by monks from St Gregory's Abbey, Downside. Work on a new Roman Catholic parish church began in 1888 and was completed in 1891.[19] The monks of Downside also served a small chapel at Wortwell (dedicated to St Mary) between 1959 and 2001, and since 2001, the chapel of St Thomas More in Harleston.

Bury St Edmunds

Anglo-Saxon minster (633–1020?)

According to the twelfth-century *Liber Eliensis* the monastery founded by King Sigebert of East Anglia in around 633, which is mentioned but not named by Bede, was located at *Beodericsworth* (the ancient name for Bury St Edmunds). The existence of a pre-Viking monastic site at Bury has not yet been confirmed by archaeology. According to Abbo of Fleury, writing in around 985, there was a wooden church of St Mary at *Beodericsworth* when the body of St Edmund was brought there in the late ninth or early tenth century, and this may have been either the original minster church founded by Sigebert or a later revival of a minster church destroyed in 869 by the Vikings.[20] Following the translation of St Edmund's body to *Beodericsworth* (which may have taken place as early as 889) a community of priests cared for the shrine until their replacement by (or assimilation into) a community of Benedictine monks in around 1020.

Abbey of Christ, the Blessed Virgin Mary and St Edmund (OSB, monks)

According to tradition, Suffolk's greatest medieval monastery, which was one of the largest in England (and indeed Europe) was founded by King Cnut in 1020; monks from St Bene't's Abbey at Holme in Norfolk and Ely Abbey replaced (or assimilated) a group of priests who had been looking after the body of St Edmund in St Mary's church since its translation to *Beodericsworth* in the late ninth or early tenth century. In reality the abbey's true origins are much more murky, but the Benedictine rule had certainly been imposed

17   Dugdale (1693), p. 63; Tanner (1693), pp. 213–14; Taylor (1821), p. 87; *VCH Suffolk*, pp. 81–3; Messent (1934), p. 111; Knowles and Hadcock (1971), pp. 253, 256; Midmer (1979), pp. 86, 88; Wilton (1980), pp. 52–4; Birch (2004), pp. 61–2.
18   Crouzet (2007), p. 51.
19   Crouzet (2007), pp. 70–2.
20   For a discussion of Sigebert's monastery and its possible location at Bury St Edmunds see Young (2016a), pp. 22–4.

on the community by 1032.[21] The documentary evidence for St Edmunds Abbey is some of the richest for any English monastic house, and the historical literature on the abbey is correspondingly vast. St Edmunds was valued at over £1,656 in 1535.[22] St Edmunds was the last monastic house in Suffolk to surrender to the crown, on 4 November 1539. Most of the monastic ruins are in the care of West Suffolk District Council and are open to the public.

Priory of St Francis (OFM Conv., friars)

In 1263 a permanent Franciscan friary was finally established at Babwell on the northern edge of the *banleuca* of Bury St Edmunds (the abbot's immediate jurisdiction) after a prolonged dispute between the monks and friars which saw papal interventions and at least one friary built and then subsequently torn down. The warden surrendered the friary to the crown in December 1538.[23] Midmer gives the dedication of the friary as St Francis, and notes that the friary comprised the largest area of any English Franciscan house.[24] Much of the boundary wall still stands and parts of the friary are incorporated into the present-day Priory Hotel near the Tollgate roundabout.[25]

Benedictine mission (OSB, monks)

Between 1741 and 1755 two Benedictine monks, Francis Howard and Alexius Jones, ran a Roman Catholic mission in Bury St Edmunds (assisted by a third monk, Maurus Heatly, between 1753 and 1755). The mission was centred on the private chapel of the Bond family in Eastgate Street, but the monks also said mass in the Angel Inn (today's Angel Hotel) and the Greyhound Inn (later the Suffolk Hotel).[26]

Dominican mission (OP, friars)

Between 1758 and 1761 the Dominican friar Ambrose Gage led a mission from the home of the Roman Catholic Short family in Risbygate Street.[27]

Community of St Michael and All Angels (Anglican religious sisters)

In 1907 religious sisters from the Community of St Michael and All Angels, Hammersmith founded St Michael's College, a boarding school, in the Old Grammar School in

---

21 For the debate surrounding the foundation of St Edmunds Abbey see Young (2016a), pp. 27–9.
22 Knowles and Hadcock (1971), p. 53.
23 Taylor (1821), p. 104; *VCH Suffolk*, pp. 124–5; Messent (1934), p. 115; Knowles and Hadcock (1971), p. 224; Wilton (1980), p. 68; J. R. H. Moorman, (ed.), *Medieval Franciscan Houses* (St Bonaventure, N.Y.: St Bonaventure University, 1983), p. 47.
24 Midmer (1979), p. 90.
25 Birch (2004), p. 134.
26 Young (2015), pp. 109–25, 137–41.
27 Young (2015), pp. 142–4.

Northgate Street. The sisters also assisted in the Anglo-Catholic parish of St John. The school closed in 1945 following the death of the superior, Mother Ethel Mary.[28]

Sisters of Jesus and Mary (RJM, religious sisters)

The Sisters of Jesus and Mary arrived in Bury St Edmunds and established a convent in Westgate Street in September 1917.[29] The sisters left at Christmas 1923.[30]

Sisters of St Louis (SSL, religious sisters)

Four St Louis Sisters from Monaghan, Ireland arrived in Bury St Edmunds in January 1924 to take charge of the town's Roman Catholic school.[31] In 1929 the St Louis Sisters relocated the school to St Andrew's Castle on St Andrew's Street. The school became St Louis Middle School in 1971 and closed in July 2016 when middle schools were abolished in Suffolk. The school buildings remain the property of the Sisters of St Louis but no sisters are resident there.[32]

Butley

Anglo-Saxon minster

Excavations at Burrow Hill, Butley in 1978–81 revealed telltale signs of the presence of an Anglo-Saxon minster enclosure, although the interpretation of the site continues to be debated and no textual evidence survives of a minster in this place.[33]

Priory of the Blessed Virgin Mary (OSA, canons)

Butley Priory was founded in 1171 by Sir Ranulph de Glanville, who became justiciar of England in 1180. Originally endowed for 26 canons, the priory had 36 in around 1200. In 1291 the house's income was over £195. The prior of Butley was sometimes (though not consistently) referred to as an abbot, and the prior was granted the privilege of wearing a mitre in 1398. Butley Priory had a school attached to it. The number of canons had declined to 12 by the dissolution. The priory was valued at £318 17s 2d in 1535 and surrendered to the crown, after initial resistance, on 1 March 1538.[34] The moat

---

28   Tricker (2014), pp. 149–50.
29   St Edmund's History Group (2012), p. 19.
30   St Edmund's History Group (2012), p. 21.
31   St Edmund's History Group (2012), p. 21.
32   B. McCauley, 'St Louis Middle School, Bury St Edmunds, closes its doors', *Musings: Newsletter of the St Louis Family* 56 (September 2016), sistersofstlouis.newsweaver.com/Newsletter/1xwn e5jjo1x?a=2&p=50859775&t=19890255, accessed 27 May 2019.
33   Blair (2005), p. 210; V. Fenwick, 'Insula de Burgh: excavations at Burrow Hill, Butley, Suffolk, 1978–81', *Anglo-Saxon Studies in Archaeology and History* 3 (1984), pp. 35–54.
34   Dugdale (1693), p. 157; Tanner (1693), p. 213; Taylor (1821), pp. 93–5; *VCH Suffolk*, pp. 95–9; Messent (1934), p. 120; Knowles and Hadcock (1971), pp. 141, 151; Midmer (1979), pp. 90, 92; Wilton (1980), pp. 61–2.

surrounding the priory survives along with the striking gatehouse, decorated with flint flushwork and 35 coats of arms. A single arch of the priory church survives.[35]

Campsey Ash

Priory of the Blessed Virgin Mary (OSA, canonesses)

Founded in around 1195 by Theobald de Valognes (whose sister Joan became the first prioress), Campsey Ash Priory was Suffolk's foremost house of female religious and was endowed for 21 canonesses. In 1291 the house's income exceeded £107. The priory was worth £182 9s 5d in 1535 and was suppressed the following year.[36] The house known as Ash Abbey incorporates part of the monastic buildings, while part of the west range is preserved in a barn.[37]

Cavenham

Preceptory of Knights Templar

A document of 1311 records that the preceptor of 'Caveham' was responsible for a reprise of 5s 11d to Stoke Priory for mills in 'Caveham' and 'Twygrynd'. The preceptory was valued at around £6 (a very low figure) in the period 1308–38, and it was presumably dissolved in 1308–12 along with the other Templar houses. The date of foundation of the preceptory is unknown and, unlike some other Templar houses, it does not seem to have passed to the Knights Hospitaller of St John of Jerusalem after the suppression of the Templars.[38] The place-name Temple Bridge, in the northern part of the parish of Cavenham, may be connected with the preceptory.[39]

Clare

Priory of St John the Baptist (OSB, monks)

The community attached to the church of St John the Baptist in Clare was founded in around 1045, either as a college of priests or as a dependent cell of St Edmunds Abbey under the Benedictine rule. Either way, the priory was re-founded in 1090 as a dependent cell of the Abbey of Bec-Hellouin in Normandy. In 1124 the monks moved to a new site at Stoke-by-Clare (see below).[40]

Priory of Our Lady, St Peter, St Paul and St Augustine (OESA, friars)

Clare Priory is the mother house of the Augustinian friars in England, having been founded in 1248–9 by Richard de Clare, earl of Gloucester. By 1296–7 the priory had

---

35   Birch (2004), p. 71.
36   Dugdale (1693), p. 58; Tanner (1693), p. 214; Taylor (1821), pp. 99–100; *VCH Suffolk*, pp. 112–15; Knowles and Hadcock (1971), pp. 278–9; Midmer (1979), p. 96.
37   Birch (2004), p. 73.
38   Knowles and Hadcock (1971), pp. 292–3.
39   Birch (2004), p. 78.
40   Knowles and Hadcock (1971), pp. 71, 87, 470.

29 friars, and the burial there of Edward I's daughter Joan of Acre brought fame to the priory.[41] The priory surrendered to the crown in November 1538, but after centuries as a private house, the surviving buildings were restored to the Augustinian friars in 1953. Clare Priory remains the sole medieval monastic house in Suffolk to have been restored. A new priory church, attached to the old monastic dormitory which had been in use since 1953, was consecrated on 6 October 2015.[42]

Claydon

Benedictine monastery (Anglican OSB, monks)

Joseph Leycester Lyne (1837–1908) was the curate of St George-in-the-East, London, when he assumed a Benedictine habit and started calling himself Fr Ignatius of Jesus. Lyne resigned his curacy and moved to Claydon, near Ipswich, where the rector, George Drury, hosted the world's first Anglican Benedictine community in Claydon Rectory. The community began on 17 February 1863. Lyne was refused a licence to preach by the bishop of Norwich and on 30 January 1864 the community relocated to Elm Hill in Norwich.[43]

Benedictine monastery (Anglican OSB, nuns)

In 1866 George Drury established a community of Anglican Benedictine nuns at Claydon, who set up a school for local children. In 1882 Drury fell out with the superior, Mary Ware, and the convent was discontinued.[44]

Coddenham

Priory of St Mary (OSA, canons)

In the reign of Henry II Eustace de Merch intended to found a house of Cistercian nuns at Coddenham but the church was granted to Royston Priory before 1184. There is disagreement about whether the Cistercian nuns ever took up residence. The Augustinian canons of Royston subsequently established a cell at Coddenham.[45] A piece of woodland named Priory Grove may be the only reminder of the priory, which was probably so small that the canons had no church of their own.[46]

---

41   Taylor (1821), p. 106; *VCH Suffolk*, pp. 127–9; Messent (1934), p. 123; Knowles and Hadcock (1971), pp. 240–1; Midmer (1979), p. 111; Wilton (1980), pp. 68–70; Birch (2004), pp. 83–4.
42   'Bishop consecrates new £1.2m Suffolk church', Diocese of East Anglia, rcdea.org.uk/bishop-consecrates-new-1-2m-suffolk-church, accessed 29 May 2019.
43   Tricker (2014), pp. 145–6; R. Kollar, 'Lyne, Joseph Leycester', *ODNB*, doi.org/10.1093/ref:odnb/34647, accessed 28 May 2019.
44   Tricker (2014), p. 146.
45   Dugdale (1693), p. 108; Messent (1934), p. 123; Knowles and Hadcock (1971), pp. 154–5; Midmer (1979), pp. 114–15.
46   Birch (2004), p. 88.

Preceptory or chapel (Knights Hospitaller of St John of Jerusalem)

A subordinate preceptory of Battisford (or more likely, merely a chapel served by a chaplain of the order) existed at Coddenham, close to the parish boundary with Hemingstone.[47]

Creeting St Mary

Priory of St Mary (OSB, monks)

A cell of the French Abbey of Bernay was founded at Creeting St Mary before 1156. The priory's income was £12 6s 10d in 1291. From 1327 Creeting Priory was administered by a single prior along with another dependent house of Bernay, Everdon Priory in North-amptonshire; thenceforward Creeting's income was listed along with that of Everdon. Creeting Priory was suppressed in 1414 and its income granted to Eton College in 1462.[48] The site of the priory is unknown, but the monks probably used the parish church.[49]

Priory of St Olave (OSB, monks)

A cell of the French Abbey of Grestein was founded at Creeting St Olave (a parish now united with Creeting St Mary) by Robert, earl of Cornwall before 1087. The cell did not have its own prior and was administered by the prior of Wilmington in Sussex; it was valued at just over £18 in 1291. The priory ceased to be a dependency of Grestein in 1347, and patronage passed to Tydeman de Lymburgh and then to Sir Edmund de la Pole in 1359.[50] St Olave's Priory was located a mile north-west of the parish church of Creeting St Mary; nothing now remains, although reports exist of ploughmen turning up masonry and human remains.[51]

Dunwich

Anglo-Saxon minster(?)

Dunwich was traditionally accepted as the site of *Dommoc*, where according to Bede, St Felix of Burgundy established a see for the Kingdom of East Anglia in around 630 and an accompanying minster.[52] However, scholars are divided on whether *Dommoc* was actually Dunwich, with some identifying the site as the now-submerged Roman shore fort of Walton Castle.

Dunwich Priory (OSB, monks)

A cell of Eye Priory (itself a dependent priory of Bernay) was established at Dunwich late in the reign of William I. In 1331 the prior of Eye complained to the bishop of Norwich

---

47 Knowles and Hadcock (1971), p. 308; Birch (2004), p. 88.
48 Messent (1934), p. 123; *VCH Suffolk*, p. 153; Knowles and Hadcock (1971), pp. 83, 87.
49 Birch (2004), pp. 95–6.
50 Taylor (1821), pp. 81–2; *VCH Suffolk*, pp. 153–4; Messent (1934), pp. 123–4; Knowles and Hadcock (1971), pp. 83, 87. Tanner (1693), p. 211 confuses the two Creeting priories.
51 Birch (2004), pp. 95–6.
52 Knowles and Hadcock (1971), p. 472.

that large parts of the monastic endowment of Dunwich had been lost to the sea, and the priory may have been abandoned soon after. The site is now under the sea.[53]

Dunwich Blackfriars (OP, friars)

Dunwich's priory of Dominican friars was founded before 1256 by Sir Roger de Holish. There were 27 friars by 1277. In 1384 the friars received permission to move their priory inland to Blythburgh on account of coastal erosion, but the move never took place and the friars remained in Dunwich until the dissolution in 1538.[54]

Greyfriars (OFM Conv., friars)

The Franciscan priory at Dunwich was founded by Richard FitzJohn and his wife Alice before 1277, when there were 20 friars. The friars moved to a site farther from the sea in 1289–90. The priory surrendered to the crown in November 1538.[55] It is the only one of Dunwich's monastic houses whose ruins still survive on land.

Preceptory of the Blessed Virgin Mary and St John (Knights Templar, then Knights Hospitaller of St John of Jerusalem)

King John confirmed a preceptory at Dunwich to the Knights Templar in 1199. The preceptory was dissolved in the period 1308–12 and granted to the Knights Hospitaller.[56] However, the Knights Hospitaller did not maintain the preceptory and merely appointed a chaplain to serve the chapel. The chapel was suppressed in 1540.[57]

East Bergholt

Priory of St Mary the Virgin (OSA, canons)

The priory that later became Dodnash Priory (in the parish of Bentley) was originally founded just over the parish boundary in East Bergholt, when it was known as the Priory of St Mary de Alneto ('of the alder grove').[58] On the basis of metal detecting finds and landscape analysis, Nicky Moxey has identified Nortons Barn in East Bergholt as the likely original site of the priory, before it moved across the stream to Dodnash in around 1096.[59]

53   VCH Suffolk, p. 76; Messent (1934), p. 124; Knowles and Hadcock (1971), p. 87.
54   Taylor (1821), p. 103; VCH Suffolk, pp. 121–2; Messent (1934), p. 127; Knowles and Hadcock (1971), p. 216; Midmer (1979), p. 133.
55   Taylor (1821), p. 104; VCH Suffolk, pp. 125–6; Messent (1934), p. 127; Knowles and Hadcock (1971), p. 225; Midmer (1979), p. 133; Moorman (1983), p. 168; Birch (2004), p. 110.
56   Knowles and Hadcock (1971), p. 293.
57   Taylor (1821), pp. 101–2; VCH Suffolk, p. 120; Messent (1934), pp. 124, 127; Knowles and Hadcock (1971), p. 303; Wilton (1980), p. 59; Birch (2004), pp. 110–11.
58   Harper-Bill (1998), pp. 3–5.
59   Nicky Moxey, pers. comm. 13 June 2019.

Abbey of the Glorious Assumption of Our Blessed Lady (OSB, nuns)

The first religious house for women founded by the exiled English Catholic community on the Continent was the Monastery of the Glorious Assumption of Our Blessed Lady in Brussels in 1598. The Benedictine nuns of Brussels fled to England in 1794 during the French Revolutionary Wars and settled at Winchester. The nuns purchased Old Hall in East Bergholt in 1856 and, in 1857, the community relocated to East Bergholt. The nuns departed after the Second World War.[60]

Franciscan house of studies (OFM, friars)

After the departure of the Benedictine nuns from East Bergholt, the Old Hall became a house of studies and novitiate for the Observant Franciscan friars between 1946 and 1973. Old Hall is now occupied by a secular community.[61]

Edwardstone

Priory of the Blessed Virgin Mary (OSB, monks)

In around 1114 Hubert de Monchesney granted the church of Edwardstone to Abingdon Abbey, which established a small cell of two monks there. In around 1160 Abbot Walkelin of Abingdon moved the monks to Earls Colne.[62] Priory Farm may be built on the former site of the priory, while the gatehouse of Edwardstone Hall may incorporate some reused materials.[63]

Eye

Anglo-Saxon minster

Clive Paine and Edward Martin have argued, on the basis of Eye church's large endowment with glebe land in the Domesday Survey and the elliptical shape of Eye churchyard, that the church of St Peter and St Paul was once an Anglo-Saxon minster.[64]

Priory of St Peter (OSB, monks)

Originally founded as a cell of the French abbey of Bernay by Robert Malet before 1087, Eye Priory became independent in 1385. There were nine monks in 1275 but this had dwindled to five by 1381. The priory's income was £161 in 1535. Dunwich Priory was a cell of Eye.[65] A farm called The Priory or Abbey Farm stands on the site of the priory, to the

---

60 Young (2016b), p. 269.
61 Moorman (1974), p. 106.
62 Dugdale (1693), p. 52; Tanner (1693), pp. 211–12; Taylor (1821), p. 82; *VCH Suffolk*, p. 76; Messent (1934), pp. 127–8; Knowles and Hadcock (1971), pp. 53, 64; Midmer (1979), p. 136.
63 Birch (2004), p. 116.
64 Paine and Martin (2013), p. 127.
65 Dugdale (1693), p. 37; Tanner (1693), p. 210; Taylor (1821), p. 83; *VCH Suffolk*, pp. 72–6; Messent (1934), p. 128; Knowles and Hadcock (1971), pp. 54, 65; Midmer (1979), p. 141.

east of the town of Eye, and some masonry of the west wall of the priory church is incorporated into the farmhouse. Part of the south transept is still standing and a sixteenth-century building to the north-west may be a rare survival of a monastic brewhouse.[66]

Felixstowe

Priory of St Felix (OSB, monks)

Walton Priory was founded a cell of Rochester Cathedral Priory in around 1105 by Roger Bigod. The priory was valued at over £6 in 1291. There were three monks in 1381, and a prior and two monks when the priory was suppressed in 1528 in order to endow Cardinal College, Ipswich. The house's income at the time of its dissolution was £40.[67]

Sisters of Jesus and Mary (RJM, religious sisters)

In 1912 the Sisters of Jesus and Mary, an order of missionary teaching religious sisters, founded the Convent of Jesus Mary close to St Mary's parish church.[68] The sisters ran a school which has since closed down, although the sisters continue to live in Felixstowe.

Flixton

Priory of the Blessed Virgin Mary and St Katharine (OSA, canonesses)

Flixton Priory was founded in 1258 by Margery de Crek, widow of Bartholomew de Crek, for a prioress and 18 canonesses. The priory's income was £44 in 1291. The priory was badly affected by the Black Death, and the number of canonesses had declined to eight by 1527. Although the priory was earmarked for suppression to fund Cardinal Wolsey's colleges, Wolsey's fall gave the house a reprieve until its dissolution in 1537, when it was valued at around £23.[69] One wall survives as part of Abbey Farm, together with an archway.[70] Flint flushwork from Flixton Priory was also incorporated by the Tasburgh family into St Peter's Hall in South Elmham St Peter, now a brewery.[71]

Benedictine mission (OSB, monks)

The Roman Catholic Tasburgh family of Flixton Hall had a number of Benedictine chaplains between 1657 and 1734. In that year a fund was established for a Benedictine mission independent of the family's patronage, which was focused on a cottage close to Flixton parish church known as Priests' House.[72] The Benedictine mission remained at Flixton until the monks moved to Bungay in 1823 (see Bungay).

---

66   Birch (2004), p. 125.
67   Tanner (1693), p. 216; *VCH Suffolk*, pp. 80–1; Messent (1934), p. 128; Knowles and Hadcock (1971), pp. 54, 65; Midmer (1979), p. 142.
68   Religious of Jesus and Mary (1953), pp. 302–3.
69   Tanner (1693), p. 215; Taylor (1821), p. 100; *VCH Suffolk*, pp. 115–17; Messent (1934), pp. 128, 131; Knowles and Hadcock (1971), pp. 278, 280; Midmer (1979), pp. 144–5; Wilton (1980), p. 54.
70   Birch (2004), p. 132.
71   Birch (2004), p. 345.
72   Young (2012), pp. 455–70.

Gislingham

Preceptory (Knights Templar, then Knights Hospitaller of St John of Jerusalem)

The earliest reference to a preceptory of Knights Templar at Gislingham is in the period 1222–26. The preceptory was dissolved in 1308 and granted to the Knights Hospitaller, but the site was ruinous in 1338.[73] There is disagreement about where in the parish the preceptory was located: a set of earthworks sometimes called 'Stoland Abbey' is one candidate, as are two different moated sites near Lady Margaret Farm where a number of field names contain the word 'Temple'.[74]

Great Barton

Benedictine Sisters of Grace and Compassion (OSB, religious sisters)

Since 1969 the Benedictine Sisters of Grace and Compassion have run the Montana care home for the elderly at Great Barton. The community was opened on 11 March 1969 after Cynthia Oakes donated her bungalow to the sisters for use as a care home.[75]

Great Blakenham

Blakenham Priory (OSB, monks)

Founded in around 1092 in the reign of William II, Blakenham Priory was a cell of the French abbey of Bec-Hellouin founded by Walter Giffard, earl of Buckingham. The priory soon came to be governed from a larger dependency of Bec-Hellouin, Ogbourne Priory in Wiltshire, and might not have had its own prior. The priory was valued at over £13 in 1291. The revenues of the priory were granted to Eton College in 1460, although it might have been suppressed earlier, in 1414.[76] No remains of the priory appear to survive.

Great Bricett

Priory of St Leonard (OSA, canons)

Bricett Priory was founded by Ralph FitzBrien and his wife Emma in the period 1114–19 as a cell of the Abbey of Saint-Léonard de Noblat in the diocese of Limoges. The priory's income was over £21 in 1291, suggesting there were up to six canons. There was some uncertainty about the priory's dependency but it was confirmed to Saint-Léonard de Noblat in 1310. At the suppression of the alien priories in 1414 Bricett was acquired by the crown, but the monastery was allowed to continue until 1444 when it was granted to Eton College. The monastery burned down in 1416.[77] Much of the priory church

---

73 Taylor (1821), p. 102; Messent (1934), p. 131; Knowles and Hadcock (1971), p. 294.

74 Birch (2004), p. 157.

75 Beattie (1997), pp. 200–1.

76 Dugdale (1693), p. 73; Tanner (1693), p. 210; Taylor (1821), p. 77; *VCH Suffolk*, pp. 152–3; Messent (1934), p. 108; Knowles and Hadcock (1971), pp. 83, 88.

77 Dugdale (1693), pp. 138–9; Tanner (1693), p. 211; Taylor (1821), p. 93; *VCH Suffolk*, pp. 94–5; Messent (1934), p. 108; Knowles and Hadcock (1971), p. 181.

survives as the parish church of St Mary and St Lawrence (where there are even surviving fragments of medieval glass), while a farmhouse opposite the church incorporates most of the priory's west range. A defensive system of moats also survives, and the earthwork known as Nunnery Mount might mark the site of the priory's domestic buildings.[78] Bricett Priory is perhaps the best preserved of Suffolk's smaller religious houses.

Great Whelnetham or Little Whelnetham

Priory of the Holy Cross (Crutched Friars)

There is uncertainty about whether Whelnetham Priory was located in Great or Little Whelnetham. A community of Crutched Friars was established by a member of the De Bures family before 1274 in the chapel of St Thomas the Martyr, dependent on the main London priory of the order, where it remained until its dissolution in 1538. Barham Priory in Cambridgeshire, founded in around 1293, was founded as an offshoot of Whelnetham Priory.[79] Midmer identifies Chapel Hill Farm, Little Whelnetham as incorporating some remains of the friars' house.[80] However, Great Whelnetham church is dedicated to St Thomas the Martyr.[81] Birch places the priory in Little Whelnetham.[82]

Hadleigh

Anglo-Saxon minster

The will of Æthelflaed (962–91) appears to contain a reference to a monastery at Hadleigh.[83] There is a Priory Farm in the parish which may offer a clue as to the location of the site.[84]

Hengrave

Benedictine mission (OSB, monks)

From around 1720 the chaplain to the Gage family at Hengrave Hall was the Benedictine monk Francis Howard, who left to lead a Benedictine mission in Bury St Edmunds in 1741.[85]

Priory of Nazareth (OSA, canonesses)

The Priory of Nazareth, known as the English Convent, was founded in Bruges for English Canonesses Regular of St John Lateran in 1629. In 1794, fleeing the French Revolutionary Wars, the canonesses sought refuge at Hengrave Hall where they re-established

---

78   Birch (2004), p. 165.
79   Knowles and Hadcock (1971), pp. 210–11.
80   Midmer (1979), p. 323.
81   Messent (1934), p. 148.
82   Birch (2004), p. 255.
83   Knowles and Hadcock (1971), p. 474.
84   Birch (2004), p. 176.
85   Young (2015), pp. 109–14.

community life and their school. The canonesses returned to Bruges in 1802 after the Peace of Amiens. Today, the English Convent in Bruges remains the sole survivor of the many English religious houses established in Continental Europe.[86]

Convent of the Assumption and Community of Reconciliation (RA, religious sisters)

Hengrave Hall was purchased by the Religious of the Assumption in 1952, who ran a convent school there until 1974. The Assumptionist Sisters then established an ecumenical religious community consisting of long-term and short-term members who ran Hengrave Hall as a retreat and conference centre. The Community of Reconciliation came to an end in 2005 and the Assumptionists departed in 2006, when Hengrave Hall passed into private ownership.[87]

Herringfleet

Priory of St Mary and St Olave, King and Martyr (OSA, canons)

St Olave's Priory was founded in around 1216 by Richard FitzOsbert for ten canons. Some sources, perhaps incorrectly, give St Edmund as an additional dedicatee. The priory's income was over £27 in 1291. By 1532 there was a prior and five canons. The priory was valued at £49 11s 7d in 1535 and dissolved in 1537.[88] Although much of the priory was demolished in 1784, substantial remains still survive and are in the care of English Heritage and open to the public.[89]

Hintlesham

Benedictine mission (OSB, monks)

The first Benedictine monk to minister in Suffolk after the dissolution was William Palmer (1575–1655), who became chaplain to the Roman Catholic Timperley family of Hintlesham Hall in 1622. Palmer was a monk of the Cassinese congregation; it is not known how long he stayed at Hintlesham but he was at Longwood, Hampshire by the time of his death.[90]

Hoxne

Anglo-Saxon minster

In his will made in the period 942–51 Bishop Theodred of London made land grants to a minster at Hoxne.[91] In the Domesday Survey of 1086 Hoxne was recorded as the episcopal

86 Young (2004), pp. 86–102.
87 Clark (1977), pp. 25–6, 52–4, 131–2; Brown (1981), p. 248; Cashmore and Puls (1994), pp. 210–11.
88 Tanner (1693), p. 215; Taylor (1821), pp. 95–6; VCH Suffolk, pp. 100–1; Messent (1934), p. 132; Knowles and Hadcock (1971), pp. 143, 173; Midmer (1979), p. 275; Wilton (1980), pp. 50–1.
89 Birch (2004), p. 192.
90 MIM, community.dur.ac.uk/monksinmotion/nsearch.php?mid=911, accessed 29 May 2019.
91 VCH Suffolk, pp. 76–7; Knowles and Hadcock (1971), p. 475.

seat for Suffolk, and it has even been suggested that Hoxne could be the site of *Dommoc*, where St Felix established Suffolk's first see.[92]

Priory of St Edmund, King and Martyr (OSB, monks)

Hoxne Priory was founded in 1130 when Maurice of Windsor and his wife endowed a cell of Benedictine monks of Norwich Cathedral Priory attached to the chapel of St Edmund (supposedly located on the site of St Edmund's martyrdom), although the Norwich monks had been in possession of the chapel since 1101. The priory usually had seven or eight monks and ran a school. The priory was valued at only around 14s in 1291 and at just over £18 in 1535. It was dissolved in 1538.[93] Nothing remains of the priory, whose site is occupied by the farmhouse called Hoxne Abbey.[94]

Iken

Anglo-Saxon minster

While several locations have been suggested for St Botolph's monastery of *Icanho*, the scholarly consensus has generally settled on Iken in Suffolk. The monastery was founded in around 653 but does not seem to have survived the Viking invasions of 865–9.[95]

Ipswich

Priory of the Holy Trinity (OSA, canons)

Holy Trinity is first mentioned in a charter of Henry I of about 1133. After a fire the priory was rebuilt by the bishop of Norwich in 1194 for seven canons, later increased to 20. In 1291 the priory had a large endowment of over £47 and over £88 from temporalities. By 1534 there were six canons and the priory was valued at over £88.[96] The priory stood on the site of today's Christchurch Mansion, and only part of its precinct wall now survives.[97]

Priory of St Peter and St Paul (OSA, canons)

Founded before 1189 by ancestors of Thomas Lacy and his wife Alice, the Augustinian Priory of St Peter and St Paul was valued at over £82 in 1291 and was probably endowed for 13 canons or more. The priory was dissolved in May 1528 and its site was supposed to become Cardinal Wolsey's Ipswich college, which never fully came to fruition before Wolsey's disgrace and death.[98] Nothing now remains of the priory buildings.[99]

---

92 Pestell (2004), p. 94 n.155.
93 Taylor (1821), p. 84; *VCH Suffolk*, pp. 76–7; Messent (1934), p. 132; Knowles and Hadcock (1971), pp. 54, 68; Midmer (1979), p. 171; Wilton (1980), p. 50.
94 Birch (2004), pp. 204–5.
95 Knowles and Hadcock (1971), p. 475.
96 Dugdale (1693), p. 164; Tanner (1693), p. 213; Taylor (1821), p. 96; *VCH Suffolk*, pp. 103–5; Messent (1934), p. 135; Knowles and Hadcock (1971), pp. 151, 161; Midmer (1979), p. 174.
97 Birch (2004), pp. 218–19.
98 Tanner (1693), p. 214; Taylor (1821), p. 96; *VCH Suffolk*, pp. 102–3; Messent (1934), p. 135; Knowles and Hadcock (1971), pp. 151, 161; Midmer (1979), p. 175.
99 Birch (2004), p. 219.

Priory of St Francis (OFM Conv., friars)

First recorded in 1236, Ipswich Greyfriars was the first friary in the town and was founded by Sir Robert Tiptot (d. 1298) and Una his wife. The friary was in a state of poverty when it was dissolved in 1538. All that remains of the priory are two window arches and a section of wall in the garden of a house in Friars' Road.[100]

Blackfriars (OP, friars)

Founded in 1263, Ipswich's Dominican friary had 22 friars by 1277, and over 50 by 1296 (making it the largest religious house in Suffolk after St Edmunds Abbey). The priory was dissolved in 1538. The remaining buildings were demolished in around 1852 but seven surviving stone arches in School Street were part of the east wall of the refectory.[101]

Whitefriars (O.Carm., friars)

Founded before 1271, Ipswich's Carmelite friary had 36 friars in 1297. The priory was enlarged in 1321 and 1333. John Bale, the future Reformation controversialist and bishop of Ossory, was prior between 1533 and 1536. The priory was dissolved in 1538.[102] No traces of the priory remain; the Buttermarket Shopping Centre occupies the site.[103]

Institute of Recluses

An institute of female recluses developed in Ipswich in the fifteenth century, connected with the Carmelite friary. The recluses sought to follow as closely as possible the Carmelite rule of life.[104]

Sisterhood of St Mary the Virgin (Anglican religious sisters)

In 1857 John Mason Neale sent a group of religious sisters from the convent he had founded in East Grinstead to the parish of St Matthew in Ipswich. The sisters established the Sisterhood of St Mary the Virgin and worked among the poor of Ipswich, but local opposition to Anglo-Catholic practices led the sisters to leave again in 1858.[105]

Convent of Jesus and Mary (RJM, religious sisters)

The Sisters of Jesus and Mary arrived in Ipswich in 1860 and established a convent on

---

100 Taylor (1821), p. 104; *VCH Suffolk*, pp. 126–7; Messent (1934), p. 136; Knowles and Hadcock (1971), p. 225; Midmer (1979), p. 175; Moorman (1983), p. 231.
101 Taylor (1821), p. 103; *VCH Suffolk*, pp. 122–3; Messent (1934), p. 135; Knowles and Hadcock (1971), pp. 214, 216; Midmer (1979), p. 175.
102 Taylor (1821), p. 105; *VCH Suffolk*, pp. 130–1; Messent (1934), p. 136; Knowles and Hadcock (1971), p. 235; Midmer (1979), p. 175.
103 Birch (2004), p. 219.
104 Zimmerman (1899), p. 198; Gilchrist and Oliva (1993), p. 95.
105 Tricker (2014), pp. 146–8.

Woodbridge Road, which survives to the present day (although the site of the former convent school is now a housing development).[106]

St Thomas Pilgrim Community (Anglican new monastic community)

The St Thomas Pilgrim Community, founded in February 2016 by Jutta Brueck, priest-in-charge of St Thomas's church, is an experiment in 'new monasticism'. Members of the community commit for at least a year to participation in the life of the community, either as non-resident members of as residents living in a community house.[107]

Ixworth

Priory of St Mary (OSA, canons)

Ixworth Priory was founded in 1170 by Gilbert le Blond, probably for 13 canons at first. In 1291 the priory was worth almost £82. The priory was valued at over £160 in 1535. There were 18 canons when the priory was dissolved in 1537. The Prior's House (whose undercroft survives complete) is embedded in Ixworth Abbey, an eighteenth-century house which also incorporates the eastern claustral range. Other remains can be seen in the grounds of the house.[108]

Kersey

Priory of St Mary the Virgin and St Anthony (OSA, canons)

Kersey Priory was founded by Thomas de Burgh in around 1213, initially as a hospital but it was soon converted into a priory by Thomas's widow Nesta de Cockfield. The priory's income was over £33 in 1291, indicating that the house probably supported nine or ten canons. By 1347, however, the priory was struggling to support its canons. In 1443 the priory was suppressed and its revenues applied the following year to King's College, Cambridge. The south chancel chapel still survives, the west wall of the church has been incorporated into a garden wall, and the west claustral range is now part of a farmhouse.[109]

Kettlebaston

Sisterhood of the Holy Childhood (Anglican religious sisters)

The Sisterhood of the Holy Childhood was founded at Clapham in 1881 and established

---

106 'It all started somewhere in France...', stmarysipswich.co.uk/history.htm, accessed 1 June 2019.

107 'St Thomas Pilgrim Community', cofesuffolk.org/fresh-expressions/st-thomass-pilgrim-community, accessed 27 May 2019.

108 Dugdale (1693), p. 150; Tanner (1693), p. 211; Taylor (1821), p. 97; *VCH Suffolk*, pp. 105–7; Messent (1934), p. 139; Knowles and Hadcock (1971), pp. 141, 161; Midmer (1979), p. 176; Birch (2004), p. 223.

109 Dugdale (1693), p. 66; Tanner (1693), p. 215; Taylor (1821), p. 97; *VCH Suffolk*, pp. 107–8; Messent (1934), p. 139; Knowles and Hadcock (1971), pp. 141, 161; Midmer (1979), p. 179; Birch (2004), p. 228.

a daughter house at Kettlebaston where a small group of children were cared for by the sisters. The community departed in around 1930.[110]

Community of St Mary and St Scholastica (Anglican OSB, nuns)

In 1913 a remnant of Anglican Benedictine nuns from St Bride's Abbey, Milford Haven who did not wish to follow the rest of their community into union with the Roman Catholic church settled in various places, before arriving at Kettlebaston in 1920.[111]

Leiston

Abbey of the Blessed Virgin Mary (O.Praem., canons)

Leiston Abbey was initially founded in 1183 by Ranulph de Glanville, who also founded Butley Priory, on an unsuitable site in what is now the Minsmere nature reserve. The abbey was founded for 26 Premonstratensian canons and a colony was sent from Leiston to found Langdon Abbey in 1189. In 1291 the abbey's income was over £130. As a result of the Black Death and flooding, the abbey's original site became unsuitable and in 1365 the canons obtained papal permission to move the abbey to a new site. The original abbey buildings remained a cell of Leiston. The new abbey burned down in 1380 but was rebuilt. In 1381 there were 11 canons and in the fifteenth century the canons were serving five churches. The abbey was valued at over £181 17s 1d in 1535. At the time of the dissolution, in 1537, there were 14 or 15 canons. The remains of Sizewell Chapel, on the site of the first abbey, were used to house a defensive pillbox in the Second World War, while the ruins of the second Leiston Abbey are the best-preserved monastic remains in Suffolk. The site is owned by the Pro Corda Trust and open to the public under the guardianship of English Heritage. The Lady Chapel was re-roofed and restored for worship in 1918.[112]

Letheringham

Priory of the Blessed Virgin Mary (OSA, canons)

Letheringham Priory (also called Trew Priory) was founded before 1200 by William de Bovile as a cell of the Priory of St Peter and St Paul in Ipswich, for three or four canons. The priory was valued at over £12 in 1291 and over £26 18s 5d in 1535. It was dissolved in 1537.[113] The present Letheringham parish church, which was reconstructed in 1789 and incorporates two Norman bays, may have been the original priory church, while

---

110 Tricker (2014), p. 149.

111 Tricker (2014), p. 149.

112 Dugdale (1693), p 212; Tanner (1693), p. 213; Taylor (1821), pp. 100–1; *VCH Suffolk*, pp. 117–19; Messent (1934), pp. 139–40; Knowles and Hadcock (1971), pp. 184, 190; Midmer (1979), pp. 194–5; Wilton (1980), pp. 59–61; Birch (2004), p. 242.

113 Tanner (1693), pp. 215, 216 mistakenly gives Trew and Letheringham as two separate houses; Taylor (1821), p. 98; *VCH Suffolk*, p. 108; Messent (1934), p. 140; Knowles and Hadcock (1971), p. 141, 164; Midmer (1979), p. 197.

the old parish church was lost in the seventeenth century. The fifteenth-century brick
gatehouse and part of the precinct wall also survive.[114]

Long Melford

Dominican mission (OP, friars)

On 21 March 1709 Sir Roger Martin (1639–1712), first baronet of Melford Place, Long
Melford, created an endowment for a priest to say masses for the souls of his ancestors.
The priest was to be a Dominican friar appointed by the Prior Provincial of the English
Dominicans.[115] The last Dominican to serve at Melford Place was John Martin (1677–
1761).[116] The chapel of Melford Place can still be seen on the west side of the B1064 at the
southern edge of Long Melford, and is now part of a private house.

Mellis

Preceptory or chapel (Knights Templar, then Knights Hospitaller of St John of Jerusalem)

Mellis was a subordinate member of Battisford Preceptory, but unlike Battisford and
Coddenham, it originally belonged to the Knights Templar and was transferred to the
Knights Hospitaller in 1308–12; it is likely there was only ever a chapel served by a chaplain
of the order. The name Chapel Farm, close to the parish boundary with Thornham Parva,
may offer a clue as to the chapel's location.[117]

Mendham

Anglo-Saxon minster

The will of Bishop Theodred of London (c. 942–51) makes bequests to a minster at
Myndham, which might be Mendham.[118] Pestell suggests some connection between this
tenth-century foundation and the later Cluniac priory, although it is unclear what this
could have been.[119]

Priory of the Blessed Virgin Mary (Cluniac monks)

Mendham Priory was endowed by William de Huntingfield before 1155 as a dependent
priory of Castle Acre Priory. Mendham originally had only a prior and two monks but this
was increased to eight monks by the founder's son, Roger de Huntingfield. The priory was
valued at over £11 in 1291. Mendham became a non-alien house along with its mother
house of Castle Acre at some point in the period 1351–74. At the dissolution the priory
had 11 monks.[120] Some ruins remained but were demolished in 1943. Some arcading was

114 Birch (2004), p. 243.
115 Tymms (1859), p. 86.
116 Young (2016b), p. 273.
117 Birch (2004), p. 263.
118 Knowles and Hadcock (1971), p. 478; Birch (2004), p. 264.
119 Pestell (2004), p. 207.

removed and installed in Mendham Place, but most of the stone was used for building cottages in Metfield.[121]

Nacton

Priory of the Blessed Virgin Mary (OSA, canons)

Alnesbourn Priory in the parish of Nacton was probably founded by Alberte de Neville in around 1200. In 1291 the priory's income was over £71, which may indicate that there were around 12 canons in residence. Alnesbourn was appropriated to Woodbridge Priory in 1458 but was in ruins by 1514. The priory's notional income (by this time received by Woodbridge) was valued at £13 6s 8d in 1535.[122] The present-day Priory Farm in Nacton stands on the site of the priory church; some septaria walling is incorporated into a barn, while the farmhouse occupies the site of the conventual buildings and incorporates some medieval material.[123]

Newmarket

Sisters of St Louis (SSL, religious sisters)

The Sisters of St Louis based in Bury St Edmunds founded a Roman Catholic school in Newmarket in 1937, which is now St Louis Catholic Academy.[124] The Sisters of St Louis left the Newmarket convent in late 2016, renting it to private tenants.[125]

Orford

Austin Friars (OESA, friars)

Robert Hewell granted land in Orford to the Augustinian friars of London, who founded a house in 1299. The friary was destroyed by lightning in 1363 and rebuilt. It was dissolved in December 1538.[126] Part of the precinct walls remains on Quay Street and Bridge Street.[127]

---

120 Dugdale (1693), p. 81 (incorrectly given as being in Norfolk); Taylor (1821), p. 90; *VCH Suffolk*, pp. 86–7; Messent (1934), p. 140; Knowles and Hadcock (1971), pp. 97, 100; Midmer (1979), pp. 217–18.

121 Birch (2004), p. 264.

122 Taylor (1821), p. 92; *VCH Suffolk*, p. 91; Messent (1934), p. 143; Knowles and Hadcock (1971), pp. 137, 145; Midmer (1979), p. 49.

123 Birch (2004), p. 277.

124 'About school: St Louis Academy', stlouisacademy.co.uk/about-school, accessed 1 June 2019.

125 R. Hannaway, 'Changing times for the English Mission', *Musings: Newsletter of the St Louis Family* 61 (February 2017), sistersofstlouis.newsweaver.com/Newsletter/lgm36cauge9?a=2&p=515513863&t=19890255, accessed 1 June 2019.

126 Taylor (1821), p. 107; *VCH Suffolk*, p. 130; Messent (1934), p. 143; Knowles and Hadcock (1971), p. 242; Midmer (1979), p. 247.

127 Birch (2004), p. 290. There seems to be no support for Birch's assertion that a house of Benedictine nuns also existed at Orford.

Poslingford-cum-Chipley

Priory of the Blessed Virgin Mary (OSA, canons)

Chipley Priory was founded before 1235 with a tiny endowment; its income was £5 in 1291, suggesting there were no more than three or four canons. By 1455 the priory was in a ruinous state and it was annexed to the college at Stoke-by-Clare in 1468.[128] A farmhouse called Chipley Abbey incorporates part of the priory's west range, although most of the ruins (including the remains of the priory church) were pulled down in 1818.[129]

Redlingfield

Priory of the Blessed Virgin Mary and St Andrew (OSB, nuns)

Redlingfield Priory was founded by Manasses, count of Guisnes and his wife Emma, the daughter of William de Arras, lord of Redlingfield in 1120. The house received several endowments in the fourteenth century. There were ten nuns in 1532. A small school was attached to the monastery. The priory was valued at £81 2s 5d in 1535 and dissolved on 10 February 1537. There was no separate conventual church and the nuns made use of the parish church of Redlingfield.[130] Redlingfield Hall incorporates some building remains and might stand on the site of the refectory; a fourteenth-century barn of two storeys might have been a guesthouse or infirmary.[131]

Rumburgh

Priory of St Michael and St Felix (OSB, monks)

Rumburgh Priory (also called Wanburn Priory) was founded in the period 1047–64 by Æthelmær, bishop of Elmham and Abbot Thurstan of St Bene't at Holme. The priory at *Wisseta* (as Rumburgh was then known) had 12 monks at the time of the Domesday Survey. The priory may have become a dependency of St Mélaine, Rennes after the Norman Conquest. In 1135 Stephen, earl of Brittany gave the priory to St Mary's Abbey in York, which thereafter appointed the priors. In 1525 the priory was valued at just over £30;[132] it was reported at the time that 'Seynt Bory' (St Bee) was venerated in the priory church, especially around Michaelmas.[133] The priory was dissolved in 1528 for the benefit

128 Taylor (1821), p. 95; *VCH Suffolk*, p. 99; Messent (1934), p. 143; Knowles and Hadcock (1971), pp. 139, 154; Midmer (1979), pp. 108–9.
129 Birch (2004), p. 301.
130 Tanner (1693), p. 212; Taylor (1821), p. 88; *VCH Suffolk*, pp. 83–5; Messent (1934), p. 143; Knowles and Hadcock (1971), pp. 254, 264; Midmer (1979), p. 262; Wilton (1980), p. 52.
131 Birch (2004), p. 316.
132 Dugdale (1693), p. 43 (who mistakenly locates Rumburgh in Cambridgeshire); Tanner (1693), p. 212; *VCH Suffolk*, pp. 77–9; Messent (1934), pp. 143–4; Knowles and Hadcock (1971), pp. 56, 74, 481; Midmer (1979), pp. 270–1.
133 *VCH Suffolk*, p. 78.

of Cardinal Wolsey's colleges. The priory church survives as Rumburgh parish church; no other monastic buildings remain.[134]

Rushmere

Convent of the Magnificat (OCD, nuns)

Rushmere was briefly home to the Carmelite nuns of the Convent of the Magnificat (established at Woodbridge in 1920) from 9 November 1938 until their departure for Quidenham, Norfolk (where the nuns remain to this day) in 1948.[135]

Shipmeadow

Community of All Hallows (Anglican religious sisters)

The foundation of the Community of All Hallows came about in 1855 when the staff of a 'house of mercy' for 'fallen women' founded in 1854 decided to take religious vows. The community moved to Ditchingham, Norfolk in 1859, but opened two hostels for 'fallen women' in Ipswich in 1889 and 1892.[136]

Sibton

Abbey of the Blessed Virgin Mary (O.Cist., monks)

Sibton Abbey, Suffolk's sole Cistercian house, was founded by William de Cayneto in 1150 and colonised by an abbot and 12 monks from Warden Abbey in Bedfordshire. The abbey received many rich endowments and its income in 1291 was over £154. In 1536, even though Sibton's income was £250 15s 7d and therefore above the £200 required to exempt it from dissolution, the abbot and seven monks sold the property to the duke of Norfolk. A Hospital of St Nicholas under the control of the abbey was located close to the abbey's gatehouse.[137] The ruins of the abbey, on the north bank of the River Yox, can be seen in the distance from the A1120. The south wall of the aisle north of the cloister survives, along with part of the refectory which contains a large Norman arch.[138] Stabilisation work on the ruins took place in 2019.

Snape

Priory of St Mary (OSB, monks)

Snape Priory was founded in 1155 by William Martel and his wife and son as a dependent priory of Colchester Abbey. The priory sought independence from Colchester in the late

---

134 Birch (2004), p. 325.
135 Pratt (1989), online at wfrcp.org.uk/parish-history/woodbridge, accessed 1 June 2019.
136 Tricker (2014), pp. 148–9.
137 Dugdale (1693), pp. 102–3; Tanner (1693), p. 212; Taylor (1821), pp. 88–9; VCH Suffolk, pp. 89–91; Messent (1934), p. 144; Knowles and Hadcock (1971), pp. 114, 125; Midmer (1979), p. 287; Wilton (1980), p. 58.
138 Birch (2004), p. 336.

fourteenth century because it was struggling to maintain its numbers, and obtained a papal decree in 1400, but this was disputed by Henry IV and the priory remained a cell of Colchester. Henry VII granted Snape Priory to Butley Priory in 1508 but Butley renounced its claim the following year. The priory was dissolved in order to endow Wolsey's Oxford foundation in 1525, when it was valued at £99 1s 11d.[139] A farmhouse called The Abbey occupies the site and a thirteenth-century barn survives.[140]

South Elmham St Cross

Anglo-Saxon minster

A moated site in the parish of South Elmham St Cross contains what are apparently the ruins of an apsidal late Anglo-Saxon minster church. The bishops of Norwich maintained a palace at South Elmham St Cross as late as the end of the fourteenth century, leading some scholars to believe these ruins are those of the pre-Conquest cathedral of the diocese of Helmham created for Norfolk at the Council of Hertford in 676. However, there is no agreement on this, and other scholars propose the minster ruins at North Elmham in Norfolk as the site of the cathedral.[141] Either way, South Elmham St Cross was an important ecclesiastical centre of some kind in the late Anglo-Saxon period.

Stoke Ash

Benedictine mission (OSB, monks)

Coulsey Wood House, a property owned by the Roman Catholic Bedingfield family, was the site of a mission led by the Benedictine monk Maurus Rigmaiden between 1715 and 1759.[142]

Stoke-by-Clare

Priory of St John the Baptist (OSB, monks)

In 1124 the Priory of St John the Baptist, founded in Clare Castle to replace an Anglo-Saxon college of priests, was moved to Stoke-by-Clare by Richard de Clare, the son of the founder. Like its predecessor, the priory was a dependency of Bec-Hellouin. The priory's income was over £300 in 1294, but there seem never to have been more than eight monks. The priory became an English denizen independent of its mother house in 1395, but was converted into a secular college in 1415. St Sepulchre's Hospital in Sudbury was a dependency of Stoke Priory.[143] The priory's successor, Stoke College, survived until 1548 when

---

139 Dugdale (1693), p. 237; Tanner (1693), p. 213; Taylor (1821), p. 85; *VCH Suffolk*, pp. 79–80; Messent (1934), p. 144; Knowles and Hadcock (1971), pp. 57, 76–7; Midmer (1979), p. 288.
140 Birch (2004), p. 338.
141 Knowles and Hadcock (1971), p. 472; Birch (2004), p. 343.
142 Young (2015), p. 144.
143 Dugdale (1693), p. 323; Tanner (1693), p. 209; Taylor (1821), p. 86; *VCH Suffolk*, pp. 154–5; Messent (1934), p. 144; Knowles and Hadcock (1971), pp. 85, 92.

it was suppressed under an act of Parliament outlawing chantries.[144] The parish church of St John the Baptist was the church of Stoke College, and before that the priory church.[145]

Stoke-by-Nayland

Anglo-Saxon minster

The will of Ælfgar (c. 946–51) left a bequest to a community at Stoke-by-Nayland.[146] A house named Stoke Priory, located a mile to the north of the parish church, is reputedly on the site of this early monastic site.[147]

Sudbury

Anglo-Saxon minster

St Gregory's, Sudbury, received bequests of land in the wills of Æthelric in 961–5 and Ælfflæd in 1000–2 alongside other minsters, suggesting some sort of community existed in Sudbury at this period.[148]

Priory of St Bartholomew (OSB, monks)

St Bartholomew's Priory in Sudbury was founded in around 1115 as a cell of Westminster Abbey by Wulfric the mintmaster. Sudbury was a very small house, probably with no more than two monks for much of its existence. In 1535 the priory was valued at only £9; it was dissolved in 1538.[149] The priory buildings in St Bartholomew's Lane were pulled down in 1779 but the chapel (which remained in use for occasional services until 1830) still stands.[150]

Priory of St Saviour (OP, friars)

Sudbury's Dominican friary (Blackfriars) was founded before 1248, apparently by Baldwin de Shimpling and his wife. There were 30 friars in 1296. A royal grant of a spring for the construction of an aqueduct from Ballingdon Hall in 1380 produced much local opposition. The priory was dissolved in 1538.[151] The priory on Friars' Street was largely pulled down in 1821, leaving behind only a half-timbered archway and doorway, probably from the gatehouse.[152]

---

144 Knowles and Hadcock (1971), p. 440.
145 Birch (2004), p. 353.
146 Knowles and Hadcock (1971), p. 483.
147 Birch (2004), p. 354.
148 Knowles and Hadcock (1971), p. 483.
149 Dugdale (1693), p. 39; Tanner (1693), p. 217; Taylor (1821), p. 86; Messent (1934), p. 147; Knowles and Hadcock (1971), pp. 57, 77; Midmer (1979), p. 298.
150 Birch (2004), p. 368.
151 VCH Suffolk, pp. 123–4; Messent (1934), p. 147; Knowles and Hadcock (1971), pp. 214, 219; Midmer (1979), p. 298.
152 Birch (2004), p. 367.

Knights of St Thomas of Canterbury at Acre (?)

According to Taylor, the 'Brothers of St Thomas the Martyr' (probably the small military order the Knights of St Thomas of Canterbury at Acre) had a chapel just outside Sudbury at a place called 'Siddolves Mere' on the road to London. Birch, on the other hand, places a preceptory of Knights Hospitaller at or near this site.[153]

Wangford

Priory of St Mary, St Peter and St Paul (Cluniac monks)

Wangford Priory (sometimes known as Reydon Priory) was a dependent cell of Thetford Priory and was founded (perhaps by 'Ansered of France' or Duodo d'Asini) before 1159. Wangford was denizenised between 1376 and 1393 after paying a fine of £100 to Richard II. The number of monks was fixed at four or five in 1405. The priory's income was £48 8s 10d in 1535. The priory was ruinous and the community was recalled to Thetford in 1537, although Wangford was not formally dissolved until 1540.[154] The monks made use of the chancel of St Peter's church, Wangford.[155]

Wherstead

Wherstead Priory (OSA, canons?)

It is uncertain whether a monastery actually existed at Wherstead; a monastery of Wervestede is mentioned in an undated deed (written before 1225) that unites the monastery to the Priory of St Peter and St Paul, Ipswich.[156]

Wickham Skeith

Wickham Skeith Priory (OSB, monks)

This very short-lived monastery was founded by John (or Robert) de Sakeville, who later became a monk at St John's Abbey in Colchester, in the reign of Stephen; in around 1164, however, his son Jordan de Sakeville agreed that the four monks at Wickham Skeith should be transferred to St John's, Colchester and the priory came to an end. The monks made use of St Andrew's parish church.[157] An Abbey Farm in the parish might indicate the site of the monastery.[158]

---

153 Taylor (1821), p. 116; Birch (2004), p. 368.

154 Tanner (1693), p. 215; Taylor (1821), p. 91; *VCH Suffolk*, pp. 88–9; Messent (1934), p. 148; Knowles and Hadcock (1971), pp. 98, 103; Midmer (1979), p. 318.

155 Birch (2004), p. 397.

156 Knowles and Hadcock (1971), p. 462; Birch (2004), p. 413.

157 Taylor (1821), p. 87; Messent (1934), p. 151; Knowles and Hadcock (1971), pp. 58, 80; Midmer (1979), p. 328.

158 Birch (2004), p. 418.

Woodbridge

Priory of St Mary (OSA, canons)

Woodbridge Priory was founded by Ernaldus Rufus in around 1193 for five or six canons. The priory's income was over £23 in 1291. Alnesbourn Priory was appropriated to Woodbridge in 1458. The priory was valued at over £50 in 1535, and it was dissolved in 1537 when there was a prior and six canons.[159] The priory was located to the south of St Mary's church on the site now occupied by a house called The Abbey.[160]

Convent of the Magnificat (OCD, nuns)

In 1920 a community of Carmelite nuns from Notting Hill, London moved to Woodbridge. On 8 September 1920 Cardinal Bourne named the house the Convent of the Magnificat. As Woodbridge expanded the nuns sought a more secluded place to live, and they moved to Rushmere in 1938.[161]

Sisters of Mercy (RSM, religious sisters)

The Sisters of Mercy ran a convent and school in Woodbridge between 1923 and 1943.[162]

Woolverstone

St Peter's Home of Rest (Anglican religious sisters)

St Peter's Home of Rest was founded in 1902 for the retirement and recuperation of Anglican religious sisters (of any community). The building was converted into a hospital during the First World War and subsequently became a private house.[163]

---

159 Taylor (1821), p. 98; *VCH Suffolk*, pp. 111–12; Messent (1934), p. 151; Knowles and Hadcock (1971), pp. 144, 180; Midmer (1979), pp. 334–5.
160 Birch (2004), p. 426.
161 Pratt (1989).
162 Pratt (1989).
163 Tricker (2014), p. 149.

Appendix 2

Suffolk-born religious men and women, 1558–1800

Religious men

	Name	Dates	Order	House	MIM
1	Danvers, William (Romuald)	d. 1634	OSB	Douai	439
2	Everard, Dunstan	d. 1650	OSB	Douai	449
3	Gage, James (Ambrose)	1723–96	OP	Louvain	–
4	Godfrey, Arthur (Michael)	d. after 1626	OSB	Cassinese	905
5	Golding, Edward	1599–1666	OFM Cap.	–	–
6	Mannock, John (Anselm)	1681–1764	OSB	Douai	535
7	Martin, Edward	1673–1753	OP	Louvain	–
8	Martin, John	1677–1761	OP	Louvain	–
9	Normanton, Thomas (Leander)	1615–65	OSB	Douai	551
10	Nuttal, Edward (Constantius)	d. 1659	OSB	Dieulouard	301
11	Roe, Bartholomew (Alban)	1583–1642	OSB	Dieulouard	321
12	Roe, James (Maurus)	d. 1657	OSB	Dieulouard	322
13	Rookwood, Francis	1660–1750	OSB	Douai	584
14	Sayer, Robert (Gregory)	1560–1602	OSB	Cassinese	914
15	Short, John (Jordan)	1685–1754	OP	Louvain	–
16	Short, William (Benedict)	1723–1800	OP	Louvain	–
17	Sulyard, Francis (Augustine)	1686–1768	OSB	Dieulouard	338
18	Tasburgh, Richard (Felix)	1660–1731	OSB	Paris	168
19	Timperley, Henry (Gregory)	1631–1709	OSB	Douai	170

Religious women

	Name	Dates	Order	House	WWTN
1	Baldwin, Catherine (Catherine Theresa de Sancta Birgitta)	d. 1756	OSsS	Rouen/ Lisbon	LB007
2.	Bedingfield, Agnes (Agnes Genoveva)	d. 1725	OSA	Bruges	BA016
3.	Bedingfield, Ann (Ann Bonaventure)	1623–97	OSC	Gravelines	GP026

Name	Dates	Order	House	WWTN
4 Bedingfield, Anne (Augustine of St Anne)	1623–57/8	OCD	Antwerp	AC010
5 Bedingfield, Dorothy	1657–1734	CJ	Hammersmith/ York	W015
6 Bedingfield, Frances	1616–1704	CJ	Munich	MW017
7 Bedingfield, Grace	d. 1679	OSA	Louvain	LA024
8 Bedingfield, Helen (Augustina)	1604–61	OSA	Louvain	LA023
9 Bedingfield, Jane (Teresa of Jesus Mary)	d. 1625	OCD	Antwerp	AC011
10 Bedingfield, Katherine (Lucy of St Ignatius)	1614–50	OCD	Antwerp	AC012
11 Bedingfield, Magdalen (Magdalen of St Joseph)	1620–83	OCD	Antwerp	AC013
12 Bedingfield, Margaret (Margaret Ignatia)	d. 1670	OSC	Gravelines	GP027
13 Bedingfield, Margarita (Eugenia)	1619–37	OSB	Ghent	GB016
14 Bedingfield, Maria	–	CJ	Flanders	MW018
15 Bedingfield, Mary	d. 1671	OSA	Louvain	LA025
16 Bedingfield, Mary	1630–93	OSA	Bruges	BA019
17 Bedingfield, Mary	d. 1712	OSA	Bruges	BA018
18 Bedingfield, Philippa (Tecla)	1609–36	OSB	Ghent	GB015
19 Bedingfield, Winefrid	1610–66	CJ	Munich	MW019
20 Bond, Mary Charlotte (Teresa Joseph of the Sacred Heart)	1690–1735	OCD	Antwerp	AC015
21 Burton, Catherine (Mary Xaveria of the Angels)	1668–1714	OCD	Antwerp	AC020
22 Burton, Margaret (Agnes Frances of the Holy Cross)	d. 1742	OCD	Hoogstraten	HC014
23 Burton, Mary (Mary Alexia)	d. 1727	OSA	Bruges	BA040
24 Chenery, Sara (Marie Peter)	d. 1640	OSB	Brussels	BF043
25 Cockes, Judith (Judith Tecla)	1648–85	CRSS	Liege	LS047
26 Cockes, Mary (Marie Anna)	1648–1714	CRSS	Liege	LS046
27 Daniell, Dorothy	1633–1719	CRSS	Liege	LS058
28 Daniell, Elizabeth (Flavia of St Joseph)	1635–69	CRSS	Liege	LS057
29 Downes, Margaret (Frances of St Ignatius)	d. 1650	OCD	Antwerp	AC040
30 Forster, Anna (Anne)	d. 1717	OSB	Brussels	BB076
31 Forster, Elisabeth (Teresa of St Augustine)	d. 1672	OCD	Lierre	LC031
32 Forster, Etheldreda (Placida)	d. 1714	OSB	Brussels	BB077

	Name	Dates	Order	House	WWTN
33	Forster, Frances Teresa (Francis of St Teresa)	d. 1654	OCD	Lierre	LC032
34	Forster, Margaret Monica (Catherine of St Austin)	1620–1711	CRSS	Liege	LS077
35	Forster, Mary (Mary Anne of Jesus)	1600–79	OCD	Lierre	AC049
36	Forster, Mary (Mary Anne)	1623–57	CRSS	Liege	LS076
37	Gage, Dorothy	d. 1700	OSB	Dunkirk	DB067
38	Gage, Penelope (Stanislaus)	d. 1772	OSA	Bruges	BA085
39	Hamilton, Catherine	1628–85	CJ	Munich	MW078
40	Hamilton, Elizabeth (Augustina)	d. 1683	OSA	Bruges	BA094
41	Lomax, Mary (Augustine of Jesus Maria)	d. 1713	OCD	Hoogstraten	HC042
42	Mannock, Anne (Anne Cecily)	d. 1780	OSB	Brussels	BB118
43	Mannock, Dorothy (Angela)	d. 1691	OSA	Bruges	BA134
44	Mannock, Elizabeth (Dorothea)	d. 1635	OSB	Brussels	BB122
45	Mannock, Ethelrede	d. 1773	OSB	Brussels	BB119
46	Mannock, Faith (Ursula)	d. 1732	OSB	Brussels	BB120
47	Mannock, Margaret (Constantia)	d. 1730	OIC	Paris	PC073
48	Mannock, Mary (Mary Agnes)	d. 1774	OSB	Brussels	BB120
49	Mannock, Teresa (Augustina)	d. 1698	OSA	Bruges	BA135
50	Mannock, Teresa (Elizabeth)	1639–1711	OSB	Ghent	GB138
51	Mannock, Ursula (Anastasia)	d. 1746	OSB	Brussels	BB117
52	Martin, Anne	d. 1629	OSsS	Rouen/ Lisbon	LB117
53	Morgan, Frances (Aloysia Francisca of Jesus)	1634–72	OCD	Lierre	LC061
54	Rookwood, Anna (Anna Maria)	1662–1743	OSC	Dunkirk	DP117
55	Rookwood, Dorothy	d. 1624	CJ	Flanders	MW134
56	Rookwood, Dorothy (Dorothy Maria Joseph)	1639–1704	OSC	Dunkirk	DP115
57	Rookwood, Elizabeth	d. 1621	OSB	Brussels	BB151
58	Rookwood, Frances (Apollonia)	d. 1717	OSA	Bruges	BA164
59	Rookwood, Frances (Clare Frances)	1625–92	OSC	Gravelines/ Dunkirk	GP240
60	Rookwood, Margaret	1663–1743	OSC	Dunkirk	DP118

Name	Dates	Order	House	WWTN
61 Rookwood, Mary (Mary Collett)	1623–76	OSC	Gravelines/ Dunkirk	GP241
62 Rookwood, Mary (Mary Francis)	1654–99	OSC	Dunkirk	DP116
63. Rookwood, Susannah	1583–1624	CJ	St Omer/ Naples	MW135
64 Short, Margarit (Mary Agnes)	d. 1780	OSB	Brussels	BD061
65 Short, Mary (Mary Ursula)	d. 1741	OSB	Brussels	BD062
66 Short, Ursula (Ursula Mary of St Joseph)	d. 1755	OCD	Antwerp	AC110
67 Simmions, Anne (Anne Josephine of Jesus)	1630–70	CRSS	Liege	LS200
68 Simmions, Mary (Mary of the Holy Ghost)	1626–84	CRSS	Liege	LS201
69 Smith, Ann (Mary Anne of Jesus)	d. 1629	OCD	Antwerp	AC111
70 Stafford, Alix (Francis of St Xaverius)	d. 1684	CRSS	Liege	LS207
71 Sulyard, Margaret (Alexia)	d. 1699	OSA	Bruges	BA187
72 Sulyard, Penelope Charlotte (Frances Xaveria of the Holy Ghost)	d. 1719	OCD	Antwerp	AC117
73 Tasburgh, Agnes	d. 1657	OSA	Louvain	LA256
74 Tasburgh, Anne (Anne Francis)	d. 1732	OFS	Bruges	BF234
75 Tasburgh, Catherine (Cecilia)	d. before 1696	OSB	Ghent	GB215
76 Timperley, Anne (Scholastica)	d. 1640	OSB	Cambrai	CB188
77 Timperley, Elinor (Teresa)	1606–71	OSB	Cambrai	CB189
78 Timperley, Frances (Francis Anthony)	d. 1661	OSB/OIC	Cambrai/Paris	PC117
79 Timperley, Justina (Margaret)	1638–84	OSB	Pontoise	OB129
80 Warner, Catherine (Agnes)	1660–96	OSB	Dunkirk	DB180
81 Warner, Elizabeth (Mary Clare)	1641–81	CRSS	Liege	GP302
82 Warner, Susan (Ignatia)	1662–1711	OSB	Dunkirk	DB179
83 Woolmer, Ann (Anna Mary of St Xaverius)	1662–1740	OCD	Antwerp	AC139
84 Yaxley, Dorothy (Ursula of St Bernard)	d. 1653	OSC	Gravelines	GP301
85 Yaxley, Margaret (Placida)	1593–1666	OSB	Cambrai	CB211
86 Yaxley, Mary (Viviana)	1603–54	OSB	Brussels	BB201

Bibliography

Allen, D. 2006. 'A newly discovered survival from the muniments of Maud of Lancaster's Chantry College at Bruisyard', *PSIAH* 41:2, pp. 151–74.

—— (ed.). 2018. *The Cartulary and Charters of the Priory of Saints Peter and Paul, Ipswich: Part I: The Cartulary*, SRS 20C (Woodbridge: Suffolk Records Society).

—— (ed.). 2019. *The Cartulary and Charters of the Priory of Saints Peter and Paul, Ipswich: Part II: Charters*, SRS 21C (Woodbridge: Suffolk Records Society).

Anson, P. F. 1949. *The Religious Orders and Congregations of Great Britain and Ireland* (Worcester: Stanbrook Abbey Press).

Arnold, T. (ed.) 1890–96. *Memorials of St Edmund's Abbey*, 3 vols (London: Her Majesty's Stationery Office).

Arnott, J. 1897. 'The Church and Priory of St Mary, Woodbridge', *PSIAH* 9:3, pp. 338–46.

Ashdown-Hill, J. 2009. *Mediaeval Colchester's Lost Landmarks* (Derby: Breedon).

Banham, D. 2014. 'Medicine at Bury in the time of Abbot Baldwin' in T. Licence (ed.), *Bury St Edmunds and the Norman Conquest* (Woodbridge: Boydell Press), pp. 226–46.

Barnardiston, K. W. 1962. *Clare Priory: Seven Centuries of a Suffolk House*, ed. N. Scarfe (Cambridge: Heffer).

Baskerville, G. 1933. 'Married clergy and pensioned religious in Norwich Diocese, 1555 (continued)', *English Historical Review* 48:190 (April), pp. 199–228.

Bately, J. M. (ed.). 1986. *The Anglo-Saxon Chronicle*, vol. 3 (Cambridge: D. S. Brewer).

Bates, D. 2014. 'The Abbey and the Norman Conquest: an unusual case?' in T. Licence (ed.), *Bury St Edmunds and the Norman Conquest* (Woodbridge: Boydell Press), pp. 5–21.

Beattie, G. (ed.). 1997. *Gregory's Angels: A History of the Abbeys, Priories, Parishes and Schools of the Monks and Nuns Following the Rule of St Benedict in Great Britain, Ireland, and their Overseas Foundation* (Leominster: Gracewing).

Beck, E. 1913. 'The Order of the Holy Cross (Crutched Friars) in England', *Transactions of the Royal Historical Society* 7 (December), pp. 191–208.

Bede. 1990. *Ecclesiastical History of the English People*, 4th edn, trans. L. Sherley-Price (London: Penguin).

Bernard, C. W. 2005. *The King's Reformation: Henry VIII and the Remaking of the English Church* (New Haven, Conn.: Yale University Press).

Birch, M. 2004. *Suffolk's Ancient Sites – Historic Places* (Mendlesham: Castell).

Birt, N. 1913. *Obit Book of the English Benedictines 1600–1912* (Edinburgh: Mercat Press).

Blackwood, B. G. 2001. *Tudor and Stuart Suffolk* (Lancaster: Carnegie).

Blair, J. 1999. 'Parochial organisation', in M. Lapidge, J. Blair, S. Keynes and D. Scragg (eds), *The Blackwell Encyclopaedia of Anglo-Saxon England* (Oxford: Blackwell), pp. 356–8.

——. 2005. *The Church in Anglo-Saxon Society* (Oxford: Oxford University Press).

Blake, E. O. (ed.) 1962. *Liber Eliensis*, Camden 3rd Series 92 (London: Camden Society).

Blanton, V. 2007. *Signs of Devotion: The Cult of St Æthelthryth in Medieval England, 695–1615* (University Park, Pa.: Pennsylvania State University Press).

Brodman, J. W. 2001. 'Rule and identity: the case of the military orders', *Catholic Historical Review* 88:3, pp. 383–400.

Brown, L. 1981. *Three Worlds, One Word: Account of a Mission* (London: Collings).

Brown, P. (ed.). 1985. *Sibton Abbey Cartularies and Charters: Part One*, SRS 7C (Ipswich: Boydell Press for Suffolk Records Society).

—— (ed.). 1986. *Sibton Abbey Cartularies and Charters: Part Two*, SRS 8C (Ipswich: Boydell Press for the Suffolk Records Society).

—— (ed.). 1987. *Sibton Abbey Cartularies and Charters: Part Three*, SRS 9C (Ipswich: Boydell Press for Suffolk Records Society).

—— (ed.). 1988. *Sibton Abbey Cartularies and Charters: Part Four*, SRS 10C (Ipswich: Boydell Press for Suffolk Records Society).

Brown, V. (ed.). 1992. *Eye Priory Cartulary and Charters: Part One*, SRS 12C (Ipswich: Boydell Press for Suffolk Records Society).

—— (ed.). 1994. *Eye Priory Cartulary and Charters: Part Two*, SRS 13C (Ipswich: Boydell Press for Suffolk Records Society).

Burton, J. 1998. 'The Cistercian adventure' in D. Robinson (ed.), *The Cistercian Abbeys of Britain: Far from the Concourse of Men* (London: Batsford), pp. 1–33.

——. 1999. *The Monastic Order in Yorkshire, 1069–1215* (Cambridge: Cambridge University Press).

Burton, J. and Stöber, K. 2011. 'Introduction' in J. Burton and K. Stöber (eds), *The Regular Canons in the Medieval British Isles* (Turnhout: Brepols), pp. 1–18.

Camden, W. 1610. *Britain,* trans. P. Holland (London).

Cane, L. B. 1935. 'Rumburgh Priory church', *PSIAH* 22:2, pp. 155–69.

Canon, C. 1999. 'Monastic productions' in D. Wallace (ed.), *The Cambridge History of Medieval English Literature* (Cambridge: Cambridge University Press), pp. 316–48.

Carey Evans, M. 1987. 'The contribution of Hoxne to the cult of St Edmund king and martyr in the Middle Ages and later', *PSIAH* 36:3, pp. 182–95.

Cashmore, G. and Puls, J. 1994. 'Thirsty in a thirsty land', *Ecumenical Review* 46:2, pp. 204–13.

Catholic Record Society. 1914. *Miscellanea IX*, Catholic Record Society 14 (London: Catholic Record Society).

Cheney, C. R. 1932. 'A visitation of St Peter's Priory, Ipswich', *English Historical Review* 47:186 (April), pp. 268–72.

Chettle, H. F. 1949. 'The Friars of the Holy Cross in England', *History*, New Series 34:122 (October), pp. 204–20.

Clark, D. 1977. *Basic Communities: Towards an Alternative Society* (London: SPCK).

Colk, J. 2005. 'Twelfth-century East Anglian canons: a monastic life' in C. Harper-Bill (ed.), *Medieval East Anglia* (Woodbridge: Boydell & Brewer), pp. 209–24.

Cox, J. C. 1907. 'Ecclesiastical history' in W. Page (ed.), *The Victoria History of the County of Suffolk, Vol. 2* (London: Archibald Constable), pp. 1–156.

Cramp, R. J. 1984. 'The Iken cross shaft', *PSIAH* 35:4, pp. 291–301.

Crouzet, E. 2007. *Slender Thread: Origins and History of the Benedictine Mission in Bungay, 1657–2007* (Downside: Downside Abbey).

Davis, K. R. 1975. *St Olave's Priory, Herringfleet, Suffolk* (London: Her Majesty's Stationery Office).

Davison, K. 1974. 'History of Walton Priory', *PSIAH* 33:2 (1), pp. 141–9.

Denney, A. H. (ed.). 1960. *The Sibton Abbey Estates: Select Documents, 1325–1509*, SRS 2 (Ipswich: Suffolk Records Society).

Dickens, A. G. 1951. *The Register or Chronicle of Butley Priory, Suffolk, 1510–1535* (Winchester: Warren).

Duffy, E. 2012. *Saints, Sacrilege and Sedition: Religion and Conflict in the Tudor Reformations* (London: Bloomsbury).

Dugdale, W. 1693. *Monasticon Anglicanum*, 3 vols (London).

Dymond, D. 1988. 'Vicarages and appropriated church livings' in D. Dymond and P. Northeast (eds), *An Historical Atlas of Suffolk* (Ipswich: Suffolk County Council/ Suffolk Institute of Archaeology and History), pp. 56–7.

'Edwardstone: its church and priory'. 1914. *PSIAH*, pp. 87–99.

Elton, G. R. 1972. *Policy and Police: The Enforcement of the Reformation in the Age of Thomas Cromwell* (Cambridge: Cambridge University Press).

Emden, A. B. (ed.). 1967. *A Survey of Dominicans in England based on the Ordination Lists in Episcopal Registers, 1268–1538* (Rome: S. Sabina).

Fairclough, J. 2003. 'The bounds of Stoke and the hamlets of Ipswich', *PSIAH* 40:3, pp. 262–77.

Fairclough, J. and Plunkett, S. J. 2000. 'Drawings of Walton Castle and other monuments in Walton and Felixstowe', *PSIAH* 39:4, pp. 415–59.

Fairweather, F. H. 1927a. 'Excavations on the site of the priory church and monastery of St Peter, Eye, Suffolk', *Antiquaries Journal* 7:3, pp. 299–312.

——. 1927b. 'Excavations on the site of the Augustinian alien priory of Great Bricett, Suffolk', *PSIAH* 19:2, pp. 99–109.

——. 1934. 'Excavations in the ruined choir of the church of St Bartholomew, Orford, Suffolk', *Antiquaries Journal* 14:2, pp. 170–6.

Farrer, E. 1928. 'Letheringham Abbey', *PSIAH* 20:1, pp. 7–11.

Fenwick, V. 1984. 'Insula de Burgh: excavations at Burrow Hill, Butley, Suffolk, 1978–81', *Anglo-Saxon Studies in Archaeology and History* 3, pp. 35–54.

Field, P. J. C. 1977. 'Sir Robert Malory, prior of the Hospital of St. John of Jerusalem in England (1432–1439/40)', *Journal of Ecclesiastical History* 28:3, pp. 249–64.

Filmer-Sankey, W. 1983. 'The dissolution survey of Snape Priory', *PSIAH* 35:3, pp. 213–21.

Finlay, A. 2009. 'Chronology, genealogy and conversion: the afterlife of St Edmund in the North' in A. Bale (ed.), *St Edmund, King and Martyr: Changing Images of a Medieval Saint* (York: York Medieval Press), pp. 45–62.

Fisher, M. 2009. '"A thing without rights, a mere chattel of their lord": the escape from villeinage of a Suffolk family', *PSIAH* 42:1, pp. 32–7.

Foot, S. 2006. *Monastic Life in Anglo-Saxon England, c. 600–900* (Cambridge: Cambridge University Press).

——. 2014 .'Households of St Edmund', *Studies in Church History* 50, pp. 47–58.

Galban, C. 2019. 'The regular canons in Early Modern Ireland' in M. Browne and C. Ó. Clabaigh (eds), *Households of God: The Regular Canons and Canonesses of St Augustine and of Prémontré in Medieval Ireland* (Dublin: Four Courts), pp. 266–74.

Gilchrist, R. and Oliva, M. 1993. *Religious Women in Medieval East Anglia: History and Archaeology c. 1100–1540* (Norwich: Centre of East Anglian Studies).

Gillow, J. 1885–1902. *A Literary and Biographical History, or Biographical Dictionary of the English Catholics*, 4 vols (London: Burns & Oates).

Gilyard-Beer, R. 1974. 'The buildings of Walton Priory', *PSIAH* 33:2, pp. 138–41.

——. 1977. 'Ipswich Blackfriars', *PSIAH* 34:1, pp. 15–23.

Gorman, S. 2011. 'Anglo-Norman hagiography as institutional historiography: saints' lives in late medieval Campsey Ash Priory', *Journal of Medieval Religious Cultures* 37:2, pp. 110–28.

Gransden, A. 1981. 'Baldwin, abbot of Bury St Edmunds, 1065–1097', *Proceedings of the Battle Conference on Anglo-Norman Studies* 4, pp. 65–76.

——. 1985. 'The legends and traditions concerning the origins of the Abbey of St Edmund',

English Historical Review 100, pp. 1–24.

——. 2004. 'The cult of St Mary at Beodericsworth and then in Bury St Edmunds Abbey to c. 1150', *Journal of Ecclesiastical History* 55, pp. 627–53.

——. 2009. *A History of the Abbey of Bury St Edmunds 1182–1256* (Woodbridge: Boydell).

——. 2015. *A History of the Abbey of Bury St Edmunds 1257–1301* (Woodbridge: Boydell).

[Greene, M. K.] 1861.*The Secret Disclosed: A Legend of St Edmund's Abbey* (Bury St Edmunds: Samuel Gross).

Grey, W. B. 1902. 'Kersey. The priory', *PSIAH* 11:2, pp. 216–19.

Gribbin, J. A. 2001. *The Premonstratensian Order in Late Medieval England* (Woodbridge: Boydell & Brewer).

Grimsey, B. P. 1897. 'The Grey-friars Monastery, Ipswich', *PSIAH* 9:3, pp. 372–8.

Grimwood, C. G. and Kay, S. A. 1952. *History of Sudbury, Suffolk* (Sudbury: privately published).

Gumbley, W. 1952. 'The English Dominicans from 1555 to 1950', *Dominican Studies* 5, pp. 103–26.

Haigh, C. 1969. *The Last Days of the Lancashire Monasteries and the Pilgrimage of Grace* (Manchester: Manchester University Press for Chetham Society).

Harper-Bill, C. 1977. 'A late medieval visitation: the diocese of Norwich in 1499', *PSIAH* 34:1, pp. 35–47.

—— (ed.). 1980. *Blythburgh Priory Cartulary: Part One*, SRS 2C (Ipswich: Boydell Press for Suffolk Records Society).

—— (ed.). 1981. *Blythburgh Priory Cartulary: Part Two*, SRS 3C (Ipswich: Boydell Press for Suffolk Records Society).

—— 1983. 'Church and society in twelfth-century Suffolk', *PSIAH* 35:3, pp. 203–12.

—— (ed.). 1991. *The Cartulary of the Augustinian Friars of Clare*, SRS 11C (Ipswich: Boydell Press for the Suffolk Records Society,).

—— (ed.). 1994. *Charters of the Medieval Hospitals of Bury St Edmunds*, SRS 14C (Ipswich: Boydell Press for Suffolk Records Society).

—— (ed.). 1998. *Dodnash Priory Charters*, SRS 16C (Ipswich: Boydell Press for Suffolk Records Society).

Harper-Bill, C. and Mortimer, R. (eds). 1982. *Stoke by Clare Cartulary, BL Cotton Appx. xxi: Part One*, SRS 4C (Ipswich: Boydell Press for Suffolk Records Society).

—— (eds). 1983. *Stoke by Clare Cartulary, BL Cotton Appx. xxi: Part Two*, SRS 5C (Ipswich: Boydell Press for Suffolk Records Society).

—— (eds). 1984. *Stoke by Clare Cartulary, BL Cotton Appx. xxi: Part Three*, SRS 6C (Ipswich: Boydell Press for Suffolk Records Society).

Harris, B. J. 1993. 'A new look at the Reformation: aristocratic women and nunneries, 1450–1540', *Journal of British Studies* 32:2, pp. 89–113.

Harrison, S. M. 2000. *Butley Priory 1171–1538: An East Anglian Monastery* (Woodbridge: B. J. and S. M. Harrison).

Hart, C. and Syme, A. 1987. 'The earliest Suffolk charter', *PSIAH* 36, pp. 165–81.

Haslewood, F. 1892. 'Inventories of monasteries suppressed in 1536', *PSIAH* 8:1, pp. 83–116.

Hayden, J. M. 2000. 'Religious reform and religious orders in England, 1490–1540: the case of the Crutched Friars', *Catholic Historical Review* 86:3, pp. 420–38.

Heale, M. V. 2001. 'Rumburgh Priory in the Later Middle Ages: some new evidence', *PSIAH* 40:1, pp. 8–23.

——. 2004a. *Dependent Priories of Medieval English Monasteries* (Woodbridge: Boydell & Brewer).

——. 2004b. 'Dependent priories and the closure of monasteries in Late Medieval England, 1400–1535', *English Historical Review* 119, pp. 1–26.

——. 2007. 'Training in superstition? Monasteries and popular religion in Late Medieval and Reformation England', *Journal of Ecclesiastical History* 58, pp. 417–39.

Hervey, F. (ed.) 1907. *Corolla Sancti Eadmundi: The Garland of Saint Edmund King and Martyr* (London: John Murray).

Hoggett, R. 2010. *The Archaeology of the East Anglian Conversion* (Woodbridge: Boydell & Brewer).

——. 2014. 'The mystery of the seven Anglo-Saxon *monasteria*', *Norfolk Archaeology* 46, pp. 55–60.

Houlbrooke, R. 2018. *Love and Dishonour in Elizabethan England: Two Families and a Failed Marriage* (Woodbridge: Boydell & Brewer).

Hunt, N. 1971. 'Cluniac monasticism' in N. Hunt (ed.), *Cluniac Monasticism in the Central Middle Ages* (Basingstoke: Palgrave Macmillan), pp. 1–10.

Irvine, S. (ed.). 2004. *The Anglo-Saxon Chronicle*, vol. 7 (Cambridge: D. S. Brewer).

James, M. R., 1930. *Suffolk and Norfolk* (London: J. M. Dent & Sons).

Keen, L. 1970. 'Medieval floor-tiles from Campsea Ash Priory', *PSIAH* 32:1, pp. 140–51.

Kelly, D. 2005. 'The Augustinians in Dublin', *Dublin Historical Record* 58:2, pp. 166–75.

Knowles, D. 1940. *The Monastic Order in England: A History of its Development from the Times of St Dunstan to the Fourth Lateran Council, 940–1216* (Cambridge: Cambridge University Press).

Knowles, D. and Hadcock, R. N. (eds). 1971. *Medieval Religious Houses: England and Wales*, 2nd edn (London: Longman).

Layard, N. F. 1899a. 'Recent discoveries on the site of the Carmelite Convent of Ipswich, and the old river quay', *PSIAH* 10:2, pp. 183–8.

——. 1899b. 'Remarks on Wolsey's College and the Priory of St Peter and St Paul, Ipswich', *Archaeological Journal* 56:1, pp. 211–15.

——. 1899c. 'Original researches on the sites of religious houses of Ipswich', *Archaeological Journal* 56:1, pp. 232–8.

Licence, T. (ed.), *Bury St Edmunds and the Norman Conquest* (Woodbridge: Boydell Press).

Lunn, D. 1980. *The English Benedictines 1540–1688* (London: Burns & Oates).

Luxford, J. M. 2003. 'A Leiston document from Glastonbury', *PSIAH* 40:3, pp. 278–88.

MacCulloch, D. 1986. *Suffolk and the Tudors: Politics and Religion in an English County 1500–1600* (Oxford: Clarendon Press).

Martin, E., Pendleton, C. and Plouviez, J. (eds). 1989 .'Archaeology in Suffolk 1988', *PSIAH* 37:1, pp. 59–77.

Martin, E., Plouviez, J. and Feldman, H. (eds). 1985. 'Archaeology in Suffolk 1984', *PSIAH* 36:1, pp. 43–57.

—— (eds). 1991. 'Archaeology in Suffolk in 1990', *PSIAH* 37:3, pp. 255–79.

—— (eds). 2009. 'Archaeology in Suffolk in 2008', *PSIAH* 42:1, pp. 61–88.

Martin, E., Plouviez, J. and Wreathall, D. (eds). 2013. 'Archaeology in Suffolk in 2012', *PSIAH* 43:1, pp. 87–116.

Mays, S. A. 1991. *The Medieval Burials from the Blackfriars Friary, School Street, Ipswich, Suffolk (excavated 1983–85)* (London: Historic Buildings and Monuments Commission for England).

McCann, J. and Connolly H. (eds). 1933. *Memorials of Father Augustine Baker and Other Documents Relating to the English Benedictines*, Catholic Record Society 33 (London: Catholic Record Society).

Meeres, F. 2001. *Not of This World: Norfolk's Monastic Houses* (Norwich: privately published).

Messent, C. J. W. 1934. *The Monastic Remains of Norfolk and Suffolk* (Norwich: H. W. Hunt).

Middleton-Stewart, J. 1994. 'The provision of books for church use in the deanery of Dunwich, 1370–1547', *PSIAH* 38:2, pp. 149–66.

Midmer, R. (ed.). 1979. *English Medieval Monasteries 1066–1540* (London: Heinemann).

Milner, J. B. 2013. *Six Hospitals and a Chapel: The Story of the Medieval Hospitals of Bury St Edmunds, Suffolk* (Bury St Edmunds: St Nicholas Hospice/Suffolk Institute of Archaeology and History).

Moorman, J. R. H. 1974. *The Franciscans in England* (London: Mowbrays).

—— (ed.). 1983. *Medieval Franciscan Houses* (St Bonaventure, N.Y.: St Bonaventure University).

Moreira, I. 2000. *Dreams, Visions, and Spiritual Authority in Merovingian Gaul* (Ithaca, N.Y.: Cornell University Press).

Morgan, M. M. 1941. 'Historical revision no. XCIX: the suppression of the alien priories', *History*, New Series 26:103 (December), pp. 204–12.

Mortimer, R. (ed.) 1979. *Leiston Abbey Cartulary and Butley Priory Charters*, SRS 1C (Ipswich: Boydell Press for Suffolk Records Society).

—— (ed.). 1996. *Charters of St Bartholomew's Priory, Sudbury*, SRS 15C (Ipswich: Boydell Press for Suffolk Records Society).

Moult, M. M. 1911. *The Escaped Nun: The Story of Her Life* (London: Cassell).

Moutray, T. J. 2016. *Refugee Nuns, the French Revolution, and British Literature and Culture* (London: Routledge).

Mulder-Bakker, A. B. 2005. *Lives of the Anchoresses: The Rise of the Urban Recluse in Medieval Europe* (Philadelphia, Pa.: University of Philadelphia Press).

Murdie, A. 2006. *Haunted Bury St Edmunds* (Stroud: Tempus).

Myres, J. N. L. 1933. 'Butley Priory, Suffolk', *Archaeological Journal* 90:1, pp. 177–281.

Newton, S. 2016. 'The forgotten history of St Botolph (Botwulf)', *PSIAH* 43:4, pp. 521–50.

Norris, N. E. S. 1936. 'First report on excavations at Grey Friars Monastery, Dunwich, Suffolk', *PSIAH* 22:3, pp. 287–93.

Northeast, P. 1988. 'Religious houses' in D. Dymond and P. Northeast (eds), *An Historical Atlas of Suffolk* (Ipswich: Suffolk County Council/Suffolk Institute of Archaeology and History), pp. 54–5.

Oliva, M. 1995. 'Counting nuns: a prosopography of Late Medieval English nuns in the diocese of Norwich', *Medieval Prosopography* 16:1, pp. 27–55.

——. 1998. *The Convent and the Community in Late Medieval England: Female Monasteries in the Diocese of Norwich, 1350–1540* (Woodbridge: Boydell Press).

Owles, E. and Smedley, N. (eds). 1963. 'Archaeology in Suffolk, 1962', *PSIAH* 29:2, pp. 166–74.

Paine, C. 1996. 'The chapel of Our Lady at Woolpit', *PSIAH* 38:1, pp. 8–12.

Paine, C. and Aitkens, P. 1988. 'Excursions 1987', *PSIAH* 36:4, pp. 323–8.

Paine, C. and Martin, E. 2013. 'Excursions 2012', *PSIAH* 43:1, pp. 127–63.

Palmer, C. F. R. 1886. 'The Friar-Preachers, or Blackfriars, of Dunwich', *The Reliquary* 26 (April), pp. 209–12.

——. 1887. 'The Friar-Preachers, or Blackfriars, of Ipswich', *The Reliquary* 27 (April), pp. 70–8.

Parry, G. 1995. *The Trophies of Time: English Antiquarians of the Seventeenth Century* (Oxford: Oxford University Press).

Pestell, T. 2004. *Landscapes of Monastic Foundation: The Establishment of Religious Houses in East Anglia c. 650–1200* (Woodbridge: Boydell & Brewer).

Pike, J. E. 1952. *Aldeburgh: The Official Guide of the Aldeburgh Corporation* (Croydon: Home Publishing).

Plunkett, S. J. 2005. *Suffolk in Anglo-Saxon Times* (Stroud: Tempus).

Potts, C. 1997. *Monastic Revival and Regional Identity in Early Normandy* (Woodbridge: Boydell Press).

Pratt, B. 1989. *A History of the Catholic Church of Saint Thomas of Canterbury, Woodbridge* (Woodbridge: privately printed).

PSIA. 1853. 'Quarterly meetings: Ixworth, 14 June 1849', *PSIA* 7, pp. 84–8.

Redstone, L. J. 1928. 'Notes on Suffolk manuscript books', *PSIAH* 20:1, pp. 80–92.

Redstone, V. B. 1899. 'The Carmelites of Ipswich', *PSIAH* 10:2, pp. 189–95.

Religious of Jesus and Mary, A. 1953. *The Life and Work of Mother Mary St Ignatius (Claudine Thévenet), 1774–1837, Foundress of the Congregation of Jesus and Mary, with an account of the development of the congregation* (Dublin: Clonmore & Reynold).

Ridyard, J. (ed.). 1985. *Medieval Framlingham: Select Documents 1270–1524*, SRS 27 (Woodbridge: Suffolk Records Society).

Roskell, J. S. 1957. 'Sir Richard de Waldegrave of Bures St. Mary, Speaker in the Parliament of 1381–2', *PSIAH* 27:3, pp. 154–75.

Roth, F. X. 1966. *The English Austin Friars, 1249–1538* (Villanova, Pa.: Augustinian Historical Institute).

Rowe E. A. 2012. *Vikings in the West: The Legend of Ragnarr Loðbrók and his Sons* (Vienna: Faessbender Verlag).

Rowe, J. 1958. 'The medieval hospitals of Bury Sr. Edmunds', *Medical History* 2:4, pp. 253–63.

——. 1965. *Ixworth Abbey, Bury St Edmunds: A Short and Simple Guide*, 2nd edn (Ixworth: Paul & Mathew).

St Edmund's History Group. 2012. *The Present from Our Past: The History of the Church of St Edmund King and Martyr Bury St Edmunds* (Bury St Edmunds: St Edmund's History Group).

[Scarisbrick, E.]. 1691. *The Life of Lady Warner* (St Omer, France).

Scott, G. 1995. 'Three seventeenth-century Benedictine martyrs' in D. H. Farmer (ed.), *Benedict's Disciples*, 2nd edn (Leominster: Gracewing), pp. 266–81.

Sherlock, D. 1971. 'Excavation at Campsea Ash Priory, 1970', *PSIAH* 32:2, pp. 118–39.

Smith, W. A. S. 1914. *St Olave's Priory and Bridge, Herringfleet, Suffolk* (Norwich: Goose).

Spelman, H. 1698. *The History and Fate of Sacrilege, discover'd by examples of scripture, of heathens, and of Christians; from the beginning of the world continually to this day* (London).

Stokes, J. 2012. 'Women and performance in Medieval and Early Modern Suffolk', *Early Theatre* 15:1, pp. 27–43.

Suffolk Records Society. 2017. *The Suffolk Records Society: Celebrating Sixty Years and Sixty Volumes, 1957 to 2017* (Ipswich: Suffolk Records Society).

Swanson, R. N. 2001. 'Fundraising for a medieval monastery: indulgences and Great Bricett Priory', *PSIAH* 40:1, pp. 1–7.

Tanner, J. R. (ed.). 1930. *Tudor Constitutional Documents A.D. 1485–1603 with Historical Commentary* (Cambridge: Cambridge University Press).

Tanner, T. 1693. *Notitia Monastica* (London).

Taylor, R. C. 1821. *Index Monasticus* (London: Richard and Arthur Taylor).

Tricker, R. 2014. *Anglicans on High: The Anglo-Catholic Revival in Suffolk and the Surrounding Area* (Snetterton: Fitzwalter Press).

Tymms, S. 1859. 'Melford Place', *PSIA* 2, pp. 84–8.

Ward, J. C. 1981. 'Fashions in monastic endowment: the foundations of the Clare Family, 1066–1314', *Journal of Ecclesiastical History* 32:4, pp. 427–51.

——. 1983. 'The place of the honour in twelfth-century society: the Honour of Clare 1066–1217', *PSIAH* 35:3, pp. 191–202.

Warner, P. M. 1996. *The Origins of Suffolk* (Manchester: Manchester University Press).

West, S. E. 1974. 'The excavation of Walton Priory', *PSIAH* 33:2, pp. 131–8.

——. 1983. 'A new site for the martyrdom of St Edmund?', *PSIAH* 35:3, pp. 223–5.

Whitelock, D. 1972. 'The pre-Viking age church in East Anglia', *Anglo-Saxon England* 1, pp. 1–22.

Wickham, W. A. 1920. '*Nonarum Inquisitiones* for Suffolk', *PSIAH* 17:2, pp. 97–122.

Wilton, J. W., 1980. *Monastic Life in Norfolk and Suffolk* (Fakenham: Acorn).

Wynne, W. A. S. 1914. *St Olave's Priory and Bridge, Herringfleet, Suffolk* (Norwich: Goose).

Yates, R. 1843. *History and Antiquities of the Abbey of St. Edmund's Bury*, 2nd edn (London: J. B. Nichols & Son).

Young, F. 2004. 'Mother Mary More and the exile of the Augustinian canonesses of Bruges in England, 1794–1802', *Recusant History* 27:1, pp. 86–102.

——. 2006. 'An horrid popish plot': the failure of Catholic aspirations in Bury St Edmunds, 1685–88', *PSIAH* 41:2, pp. 209–25.

——. 2008a. 'John Battely's *Antiquitates S. Edmundi Burgi* and its editors', *PSIAH* 41, pp. 467–79.

——. 2008b. 'The Shorts of Bury St Edmunds: medicine, Catholicism and politics in the 17th century', *Journal of Medical Biography* 16, pp. 188–94.

——. 2011. 'The Tasburghs of Bodney: Catholicism and politics in South Norfolk', *Norfolk Archaeology* 46, pp. 190–8.

——. 2012. 'The Tasburghs of Flixton and Catholicism in North-East Suffolk', *PSIAH* 42:4, pp. 455–70.

——. 2015. *The Gages of Hengrave and Suffolk Catholicism, 1640–1767* (Woodbridge: Boydell & Brewer for Catholic Record Society).

——. 2016a. *The Abbey of Bury St Edmunds: History, Legacy and Discovery* (Norwich: Lasse Press).

——. 2016b. 'Appendix 1: Notable East Anglian Catholics' in F. Young (ed.), *Catholic East Anglia: A History of the Catholic Faith in Norfolk, Suffolk, Cambridgeshire and Peterborough* (Leominster: Gracewing,), pp. 221–66.

——. 2018. *Edmund: In Search of England's Lost King* (London: I. B. Tauris).

——.2019. 'The dissolution of the monasteries and the democratisation of magic in post-Reformation England', *Religions* 10:4, 241, doi.org/10.3390/rel10040241.

Zimmerman, B. 1899. 'The White Friars at Ipswich', *PSIAH* 10:2, pp. 196–204.

Unpublished sources

Anderson, R. 2016. 'The visitation records of the English Benedictine monastery of the Glorious Assumption of Our Blessed Lady', unpublished conference paper, Gender, Power and Materiality in Early Modern Europe, 1500–1800, University of Plymouth, Plymouth, 7–9 April, researchspace.bathspa.ac.uk/7859/1/7859.pdf.

Bellenger, A. 1999. 'The Brussels nuns at Winchester, 1794–1857', unpublished conference paper, English Benedictine Congregation History Commission Symposium, monlib.org.uk/papers/ebch/1999bellenger.pdf.

Hoggett, R. 2018. *The Abbey of St Edmund: Heritage Assessment*, unpublished report, June.

Lyon, H. K. 2018. 'The afterlives of the dissolution of the monasteries, 1536–c. 1700', PhD thesis, University of Cambridge.

Mattich, J. L. W. V. 1995. 'Friars and society in Late Medieval East Anglia: mendicants and their material culture in Suffolk, Norfolk and Cambridgeshire, c. 1225–1538', PhD thesis, University of Cambridge.

Pestell, T. 1999. *An Analysis of Monastic Foundation in East Anglia, c. 650–1200*, PhD thesis, University of East Anglia.

Wessex Archaeology. 2009. *Blythburgh Priory, Blythburgh, Suffolk: Archaeological Evaluation and Assessment of Results*, unpublished report, September.

Online sources

'1925: The new church at Aldeburgh', aldeburgh.oneplacestudy.org/news/1925-the-new-church-at-aldeburgh

'About school: St Louis Academy', stlouisacademy.co.uk/about-school

'A brief history', saintbenetsbeccles.org/our-parish-and-our-services/a-brief-history

'Bishop consecrates new £1.2m Suffolk church', Roman Catholic Diocese of East Anglia, 7 October 2015, rcdea.org.uk/bishop-consecrates-new-1-2m-suffolk-church

Bury Free Press, buryfreepress.co.uk

'Clare Priory', clarepriory.org.uk

Hannaway, R. 'Changing times for the English Mission', *Musings: Newsletter of the St Louis Family* 61 (February 2017), sistersofstlouis.newsweaver.com/Newsletter/lgm36cauge9?a=2&p=51513863&t=19890255

Historic Hansard, House of Commons Debates, 6 April 1909, api.parliament.uk/historic-hansard/commons/1909/apr/06/st-marys-roman-catholic-convent-east

'It all started somewhere in France…', stmarysipswich.co.uk/history.htm

McCauley, B. 'St Louis Middle School, Bury St Edmunds, closes its doors', *Musings: Newsletter of the St Louis Family* 56 (September 2016), sistersofstlouis.newsweaver.com/Newsletter/1xwne5jjo1x?a=2&p=50859775&t=19890255.

'Monks in Motion' project database, community.dur.ac.uk/monksinmotion

'Mounting debts force Hengrave Hall to close', *Bury Free Press*, 20 May 2005, buryfreepress.co.uk/news/mounting-debts-force-hengrave-hall.1032452.jp

Oxford Dictionary of National Biography

'St Thomas Pilgrim Community', cofesuffolk.org/fresh-expressions/st-thomass-pilgrim-community

'Welcome to our church', joyofallwhosorrow.org.uk/index.php/about/info/welcome_to_the_church

'Who were the nuns?' project database, wwtn.history.qmul.ac.uk

Index

Also by Francis Young
and published by the Lasse Press

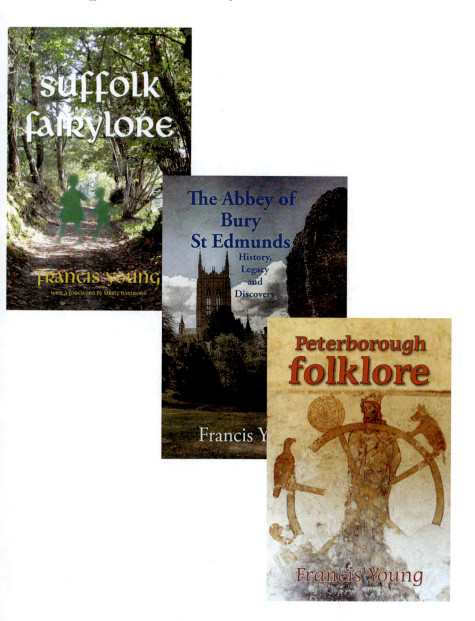

www.lassepress.com

Also published by the Lasse Press

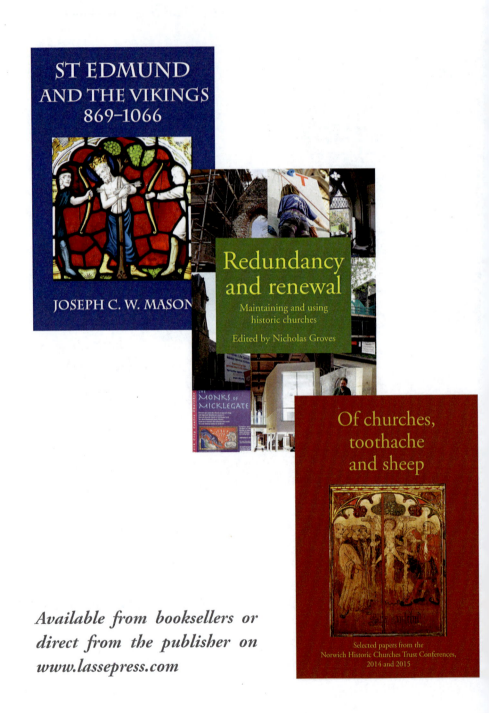

ST EDMUND
AND THE VIKINGS
869–1066

JOSEPH C. W. MASON

Redundancy
and renewal

Maintaining and using
historic churches

Edited by Nicholas Groves

THE MONKS of
MICKLEGATE

Of churches,
toothache
and sheep

Selected papers from the
Norwich Historic Churches Trust Conferences,
2014 and 2015

*Available from booksellers or
direct from the publisher on
www.lassepress.com*